Yiddish in America

Social and Cultural Foundations

Yiddish in America

Social and Cultural Foundations

by

Milton Doroshkin

Fairleigh Dickinson

Rutherford • Madison • Teaneck
FAIRLEIGH DICKINSON UNIVERSITY PRESS

Associated University Presses, Inc.
Cranbury, New Jersey 08512

SBN: 8386 7453 4
Printed in the United States of America

To my children and young grandchildren
and those of our progeny still to come,
this modest work is dedicated,
with a fervent hope that their lives may be fruitfully involved
in a reblossoming of their culture
within a pluralistic brotherhood of man.

Contents

Contents

Preface

It is my fondest hope that this study may contribute toward a fuller understanding, scientifically and historically, of a vital epoch in the social history of the community of American Jews.

If I have succeeded in developing some insight into the world of Yiddish language and culture much credit is due to the circumstance of my birth into a family or "clan" within which an aura of folkistic Yiddish social-consciousness prevailed and influenced my life from the very beginning.

For my scientific training, I am indebted to the sociology faculty of the New School from 1959 to this present day. Dr. Stanley Diamond must be credited, not only for supervising my work, but also for incisively understanding its implications, staunchly supporting my scientific premises and insisting that the book be written. Dr. Peter Berger's warm assistance as a member of the dissertation committee was inspiring and invaluable.

I am indebted to Dr. Arthur J. Vidich, chairman of the sociology department, for his most helpful suggestions for improving the manuscript and for his interest and involvement in assisting me during the difficult days of completion of the work.

Dr. Carl Mayer, Professor Emeritus and former department chairman, is the teacher who encouraged and stimulated my work at an early stage. His unique devotion to knowledge and his meticulous standards of scientific scholarship provided me with continuous incentive for learning. He and Mrs. Mayer, whose empathy with the student during his trials and tribulations was always a comfort, are well remembered at this time.

During a career in the *academe* one is constantly influenced by contemporary colleagues. In my work I have been especially privileged to benefit from associations with two distinguished sociologists: Dean Joseph B. Gittler of the Ferkauf Graduate School, Yeshiva

University, and Professor Milton L. Barron, Director of the doctoral program in sociology at the City University of New York. Their personal and professional help to me is gratefully acknowledged.

I am grateful to Dean Morton Rosenstock, author of *Louis Marshall: Defender of Jewish Rights,* who, after reading a late draft of the manuscript, made several cogent analytical suggestions and enthusiastically encouraged me to publish the work.

The book has benefited from the efforts of Mr. Arnold Schwartz, researcher at the American Jewish Committee, who assisted me in gathering much of the material used in the study, particularly the data comprising the appendixes to chapters 5, 7, and 8.

The project could not have been completed without relief for several years from summer and evening teaching. This was made possible by grants from the Lucius N. Littauer Foundation and the Sol and Lillian Ash Foundation.

Very special appreciation is expressed to Mr. Harry Starr, President of the Littauer Foundation, for unusual generosity; but even more for coupling his generosity with a warm and intelligent understanding of my project and of my personal needs in completing the work and finally preparing it for publication. Similarly, my gratitude is extended to Mr. Sol Ash and Professor Gershon Churgin of the Ash Foundation for giving their support, unquestionably and enthusiastically, when it was needed.

The major research for this study was done within the limits of resources available in New York City. The institutions that were most cooperative and helpful are: The library and archives at YIVO; the New York University Tamiment Library; the Jewish Division, New York Public Library; the library and archives, American Jewish Historical Society; and the library at the New School for Social Research. The intelligent assistance of the staffs at these institutions is hereby acknowledged. The CYCO (Central Yiddish Culture Organization) and the YKUF (Yiddish Kultur Farband) were sources for the purchase of "hard to get" Yiddish volumes.

Finally, a salute to my wife, Osnas, and my 21-year-old daughter, Wendy, for their heroic ability to survive the ordeal of sharing one roof with me during the tense and hectic final months of writing and completion of this study. Without their love and patient endurance this work would not have become a reality.

M. D.
Bronx Community College
The City University of New York

Yiddish in America

Social and Cultural Foundations

1

Introduction

Why This Study Now?

Why should a sociologist indulge in a study of Yiddish at this time?

There is a very apparent contemporary interest in the Yiddish language and culture in America. I observe that the interest falls into two broad categories. The first might be termed socio-emotional; the second, scholarly and scientific.

The initial category would of course also include the artistic, the creative, the cultural. Here the phenomenon would have two elements: the artists, the creators, the performers; and the audiences, the public, the respondents to the artistic stimuli. There is considerable evidence that both are present today.

> Fascination with things Jewish (Yiddish), whether spiritual, sociological or comic has for several years been evident in the arts in America, in books, painting, theater and music.[1]

The author of the above quotation goes on to describe a number of good phonograph record albums featuring Jewish artists that have recently been released. Describing an album by Martha Schlamme he says it includes "17 Yiddish songs guaranteed to whisk anyone who knows about it back, in reverie, to the shtetl, the little Jewish town of East Europe."[2]

Leonard Lyons, in the New York Post, Thursday, December 28th, 1967 wrote: ". . . ABC-TV's 'Directions' will start on January 7th,

---

[1] Richard F. Shepard, "And Now There's Chasidic Rock," *New York Times*, 28 January, 1968.
[2] *Ibid.*

its four-part survey of the Yiddish language, literature, press, and theatre. . . ." About the same time, another newspaper announced: "Channel 13 plans 'special' on Yiddish theatre, January 18th."

In Central Park Sholem Aleichem is Also a Bard. . . . The New York Shakespeare Festival declaimed in Yiddish accents last night, something that would make a delightful habit—at least part time.

The festival presented an evening of Yiddish poetry, readings and folk music in its Central Park arena, the Delacorte Theater, which was as full as a sage's beard. It was an upbeat crowd of about 2,300, all ages and sizes. Nobody came to bury Yiddish, or even mourn it; just to enjoy it.

Under the pale moon hanging over the south part of the park, Yiddish became a natural element of Central Park. Even the English translations of the Yiddish seemed Yiddish. It took everyone back to the days when he or his parents or his grandparents came to a new land and made a niche for a culture they all still love. And then, as the words ran out, it ended.[3]

January 27, Hershl Rosen produced an evening of Yiddish poetry, song and drama at the High School of Fashion Industries Auditorium for an audience of over 1,000 people.[4]

Warsaw Yiddish Troupe Finds its Language is Spoken Here. The Jewish State Theater of Poland may have found in New York an audience that speaks its language. . . . The troupe has come to a place where there are more people who know Yiddish than there are in its home town of Warsaw. . . . Marian Melman, Ida Kaminska's husband: 'Everywhere I met Jews it was the same. . . . The best audience is the East European Jewish Audience.'[5]

Harold Clurman, who reviewed the Kaminska theater, seems to have been more overcome with reminiscence of the past in the Yiddish theater than with the theater he was reviewing. When you read his article in *Midstream* it sometimes becomes difficult to differentiate between Clurman the professional reviewer, and the other Clurman, the devotee and sentimental lover of the best in

---

[3] *New York Times*, 7 July, 1967.
[4] *Ibid.*, 29 January, 1968.
[5] Richard F. Shepard, "Warsaw Yiddish Troupe Finds Its Language is spoken here," *New York Times*, 28 October, 1967.

the old Yiddish theater. The following clipping, however, reveals his accurate conception of the social role of the Yiddish theater:

> The theatre, even more than the lodge or the synagogue, became the meeting place and forum of the Jewish community in America between 1888 and the early 1920's, at which time immigration was curtailed by an act of the U.S. government.
>
> This is a universal theatre pattern. 'Not until actors and spectators are united in a common belief,' Gordon Craig once said, 'can plays become a revelation of the inner life and values.'
>
> Whatever the answer, the many people who attended the Kaminska season came in fond recollection of something which still dwells within them as a yearning, or if they were too young to harbor such feelings, then to spin a cultural tie between themselves and those who did.[6]

And now the second area of interest in Yiddish: the scholarly and scientific.

Instead of paraphrasing, I think that I can do greater justice to the subject by reproducing self-explanatory extracts from Mrs. Dawidowicz's article in *Commentary,* a few years back:

> On hearing that the first volume of an unabridged ten-volume Yiddish dictionary has just been published, people ask, 'Today?' Their skepticism reflects the common knowledge that Yiddish has fewer speakers today than ever before. Why, then, an unabridged dictionary of the Yiddish language now? The editors of the Great Dictionary of the Yiddish Language, Judah A. Joffe and Yudel Mark, linguists and Yiddish scholars, explain in their introduction that they wished to create 'a monument' to the centuries of Ashkenazic creativity. Under the pressure of history, Mark and Joffe see their responsibility as primarily to preserve the Yiddish language for the historical record and secondarily to set standards for and define its usage as a living language. . . .
>
> . . . Yet however melancholy the outlook for Yiddish today, its prestige in America has never been higher. Madison Avenue dictates: 'Dress British, think Yiddish.' Yiddish is taught at many universities; Yiddish writers, in translation, have attained considerable vogue; adult education courses in Yiddish and Yid-

---

[6] Harold Clurman, "Ida Kaminska and the Warsaw Yiddish Theatre," *Midstream*, vol. 14, no. 1, January, 1968.

dish literature have unpredicted popularity. The Yiddish novelist Isaac Bashevis Singer recently commented on this phenomenon, formulating what may be designated as the law of Yiddish status: the fewer its speakers, the greater its prestige.

About three million people—nearly a quarter of all Jews—speak Yiddish today or know it well enough to speak. Perhaps half as many more understand it. Before the Nazi holocaust Yiddish had nearly 7 million speakers, or 40 per cent of all Jews. Back in 1900 over 60 per cent of all Jews spoke Yiddish. Most Yiddish speakers nowadays are bilingual, knowing and speaking also the language of the country they live in, but Yiddish was predominantly once the spoken language of the Jews.

The editors estimate that upon completion the Great Dictionary of the Yiddish Language will contain about 180,000 words. In comparison with Webster's 450,000, Yiddish may seem poor, but not in comparison with other major European languages like French, Russian, Spanish, or Italian, whose total vocabularies are estimated to range from 140,000 to 210,000 words. But though Yiddish is undoubtedly not what the linguists call a 'sociologically complete' language, being deficient in scientific, technical, and military vocabularies, and meager in botanical, zoological, and agricultural terminology, it is nevertheless linguistically abundant in other areas of expression—religion, personal and social relations, morality, ethics, intellect, and feeling.

Yiddish can help give the individual access to his past, the world from which his parents came and whose culture, however attenuated its form, has had some influence on him. . . . Today, the importance—sometimes the crucial importance—of Yiddish for an understanding of the history and culture of Ashkenazic Jewry for the last five hundred years has been generally acknowledged. Neither Hasidism nor the Jewish labor movement, neither Zionism nor the Agudas Israel movement, can be understood without Yiddish. The scholar will need Yiddish for his work and his Yiddish, in time to come, will have to depend greatly upon Mark's and Joffe's Great Dictionary of the Yiddish Language.[7]

More than a year ago a New York Times story announced that the second volume of the *Great Dictionary of the Yiddish Language* has been completed and published. The total entries for the ten

---

[7] Lucy S. Dawidowicz, "Yiddish: Past, Present and Perfect," *Commentary*, vol. 33, no. 5, May, 1962.

volumes has been extended, it seems, to 225,000 words. "By the time it is all done, the dictionary will have cost $1,275,000 . . . completion could take 16 years."[8]

Seven hundred forty-eight Yiddish books have been published from 1961 through 1965. Of that number, 240 were written in the United States.[9]

> . . . There are some 300 Yiddish writers in the United States today . . . 150 in Israel and the same number in Argentina.
> Yiddish is now taught at the New School for Social Research, at City, Brooklyn, and Queens Colleges and at Columbia University in New York City, and at the University of California. Perhaps Yiddish in the United States will find its future in the seats of higher learning.[10]

One of the fascinating areas (and probably the most deeply rooted) of Yiddish usage is found among the Chasidic Jews. Last year a reporter of the *New York Times* paid a visit to the renowned Lubavitcher Rebbe, Dr. Schneerson, at his Brooklyn headquarters, during the festive holiday of *Simchas Torah*. Menachem M. Schneerson is the leader of 250,000 Yiddish-speaking Jews—the world's largest Chasidic group. At the celebration, the rabbi:

> . . . spoke in Yiddish to 1,500 people on subjects ranging from the mystical interpretation of the scriptures as contained in the Cabala to hippies. Rabbi Schneierson stopped speaking from time to time to serve vodka and sponge cake to those around him. . . .
> A visitor, the Rev. William Sloane Coffin, Jr., Chaplain of Yale University, smiled as he watched the celebration. 'Wonderful,' he said, 'wonderful, just wonderful.'[11]

---

[8] Richard F. Shepard, "A New Dictionary Says it in Yiddish," *New York Times*, 30 December, 1966.

[9] Nachman Meisel, ed., *Ykuf Almanach* (Yiddish), New York, 1967 (based on statistics developed by the late Isser Goldberg of CYCO), p. 365.

[10] Hasye Cooperman, "Yiddish Literature in the United States," in Oscar Janowsky, ed., *The American Jew: A Reappraisal* (Philadelphia: Jewish Publication Society, 1964), pp. 208–209.

[11] Sidney E. Zion, "Chasidic Jews Celebrate 3 Days of Simchas Torah," *New York Times*, Monday, 30 October, 1967.

Henry L. Lennard made a study of the attitudes of American Jewish college youth toward Jews and Jewishness. One of the factors in the study was whether the parents of the subjects were, or were not, Yiddish speaking. Of the students coming from Yiddish-speaking homes, 75% believed in the importance of Jewish survival. Of those coming from non-Yiddish speaking homes, half said they saw no necessity for Jewish survival. Dr. Lennard's conclusion was:

> These data show that in those instances where the parents of the subjects speak Yiddish, the subject is three times as likely to have a positive attitude towards Jewish survival as in those instances where the parents do not speak the language. . . . The speaking of Yiddish in the home can thus be assumed to create a favorable climate for a later positive orientation towards one's Jewishness.[12]

Dr. Fishman in his authoritative study of the linguistics of Yiddish in America came to some fascinating conclusions in a little "epilogue" called "Concluding Sentiments." Again, instead of paraphrasing I will reproduce some interesting sections of the chapter:

> . . . Yiddish might be in a sad, sad state indeed. Its imminent demise has been predicted repeatedly for well over a century—by advocates of 'enlightenment' who considered it a deterrent to Westernization; by Hebraists and Zionists who considered it a deterrent to Hebrew and to the 'ingathering of exiles'; by cosmopolitan socialists who considered it a deterrent to the unity of the proletariat; for scholars and sinners alike—Yiddish was always fair game. And yet it survives—although it is hard to say how and why.
>
> The professors and poets are unexpected companions for Yiddish. How does a 'handmaiden' come to have professors and poets among her suitors? And yet it is so—another anomaly to add to a collection of anomalies. From a crude folk vernacular to a language of scholarship and poetic finesse within a single generation!
>
> These devotees believe that it may yet come to pass that the linguistic, literary, and historical-cultural research on Yiddish now conducted by professors at Columbia, Brandeis and elsewhere will

---

[12] Henry L. Lennard, "Jewish Youth Appraising Jews and Jewishness," *Yivo Annual of Jewish Social Sciences*, vols. 2-3, New York, 1948, pp. 262-81.

capture the imagination, interest and devotion of an important segment of the growing Jewish-American college population. If such a 'miracle' were to come to pass it would not surprise the older generation of lovers of Yiddish in the very least.

At another level, languages survive as long as the ideals, aspirations, and creations expressed through them continue to elicit interest. At this level, Yiddish will never die, for Yiddish literature and Yiddish writings on Zionism, Jewish socialism and labor movement, Hasidism and other religious, moralistic and folkistic expressions of Eastern European Jewry, will constantly elicit interest among cognoscenti and scholars. In this sense, very little of what Jews have ever created has ever died, for the Jewish cultural experience has always been that of a constantly growing heritage rather than of a permanently fixed one. Jewish generations vary as to their interest in their own heritage, but in every generation there are a few conscientious keepers of the flame and, among these, Yiddish will always have its share of true scholars and true believers.[13]

Methodology

Our work proceeds on the premise that Sklare was correct when he said that today a reference to American Jews is equivalent to saying, Eastern European Jews.[14] This is supported by the following quotations from Rischin and Glazer:

The Jews of New York are the direct heirs of the Jewish enlightenment and the great migration, the Lower East Side and the great strikes in the needle trades, socialism and the settlements. . . .[15]
There is first of all the fact that the overwhelming majority of American Jews *do* stem from a single culture—the Yiddish-speaking culture of Eastern Europe. . . .[16]
This great migration (from the Russian Empire), which con-

---

[13] Joshua A. Fishman, "Yiddish in America," *International Journal of American Linguistics*, vol. 31, no. 2, April, 1965, pp. 73–76.
[14] Marshall Sklare, *Conservative Judaism* (Gencoe: The Free Press, 1955), p. 21.
[15] Moses Rischin, *The Promised City* (Cambridge: Harvard University Press, 1962), p. 267.
[16] Nathan Glazer and Daniel P. Moynihan, *Beyond The Melting Pot* (Cambridge: Harvard University Press, 1963), p. 141.

tinued, except for the interruption of the First World War, until
it was reduced by law in 1924, has stamped the character of New
York. The city's Jews are descendants of the Yiddish-speaking,
Orthodox and Socialist Jews of Eastern Europe. Despite a half
century of American Life, . . . they retain much that recalls their
origins.[17]

The contemporary American Jewish population is largely of East
European descent. Even most of the rabbis in the Reform movement
are Eastern European Jews, or descendants of such. The old culture
has not died. It has flowed into, and become fused with, the new.
The new community is heir to the old.

But as this work begins to develop we shall cite authoritative
historians and rabbis who seem to belittle the old era by alluding
to it as a period of lack of organization, and a period of disaffiliation in the large population. There is a contemporary view that
only in the last decades have American Jews achieved the status of
an organized community.

We think this is a serious error. But why does a distorted perspective prevail in so many quarters of the Jewish community today?
We attribute this loss of perspective to the sociological phenomenon
of rapid (almost overnight) restratification of the Jewish population
from working class to predominantly middle and upper class. With
new status, new needs, new interests, it became easy to lose perspective regarding the old.

Later on we shall quote Louis Wirth as saying that "It may be
a platitude to say that the Jews are what their history has made
them, but it is a platitude worth reiterating." With that premise
in mind, we devote two chapters to a socio-historical examination
of Jewish migrations to America, and to the characteristics of the
communities resulting from those migrations. Chapter four very
briefly deals with the earlier Sephardic and German periods, and
Chapter five more fully examines the later, the Eastern European
or "Russian" immigration.

In comparing the three migrations, an interesting thing emerges—

---

[17] *Ibid.*, p. 139.

the cultural role of language or mother-tongue in the three societies. The first two (Sephardic and German) maintained religious institutions but as rapidly as possible abandoned their "native" languages and language-cultures in favor of cultural assimilation to American English. On the other hand, the Eastern Europeans not only maintained their Yiddish language, but wove a deep and broad network of secular and religious institutions with the mother-tongue as a cultural tool.

This brings us to the heart of our study, namely, the social and cultural role of Yiddish in the community of "Russian" immigrants. The method adopted here is to analyze the cultural institutions that the Eastern Jews have created and thus reveal the role of the Yiddish language.

In this work I devote Chapters seven and eight to a rather full analysis of the "Social Role of the Press," and "Landsmanshaften and Fraternal Organization," respectively. In the background of both chapters there is a continuous reference to the Jewish labor movement, and some reference to the Yiddish synagogue in Chapter eight. In Chapter five (in the over-all treatment of the community), brief references to the theater are included.

Chapter six is not an analytical section. The purpose here is to acquaint the reader, very briefly, with the origin, and process of development, of the Yiddish language and literature.

The Theses

It is hoped that the reader may find a number of meaningful concepts, views, and facts emerging from the following chapters. Some are obvious, some more subtle, others may be debatable. My goal, however, has been to make two main points, as follows:

1. Sociologically, there was a developed, organized community of Jews in the United States during the period of Eastern European immigration (1880–1924), represented by cultural institu-

tions that reflected the needs of the people, and with which the individual Jew identified and affiliated.

2. Yiddish culture was the vehicle, Yiddish language the tool, with which the people shaped and formed their institutions. This factor differentiated the community of Eastern European Jews from the Sephardic and German communities.

2

Who Are The Jews?

Melville J. Herskovits attempts a definition of: "Who Are The Jews?"[1] He encounters a dilemma:

> Of all human groupings, there is none wherein the problem of definition has proved to be more difficult than for the Jews. Even when all possibilities seem to have been exhausted—race, people, nation, religion, cultural entity, historic group, linguistic unit—we find students casting about for other, more precise, more comprehensive designations.[2]

He turns to several authorities:[3]

> Ripley, in his classic *Races of Europe* [1900] concludes by affirming that 'the Jews are not a race but only a people after all'. . . . Coon [in 1939] [concludes] the ethnic solidarity of the Jews is remarkable for its strength and constancy . . . they are a population . . . not a race. . . .
> Krogman [1945] . . . [A Jew] has a set of behavioral attitudes and responses . . . that . . . are cultural, not biological. He summarizes his position with the statement: 'A Jew belongs not to a race but to a Jewish community.'
> Seltzer [1939]: [Jews] include the individuals of the so-called "White" races of mankind . . . who do practice, or whose ancestors did practice, the religion of Judaism.
> Kennedy [1942]: The issue can be resolved by designating the Jews as a 'religio-national' group.

---

[1] Melville J. Herskovits, "Who Are The Jews?" in Louis Finkelstein, *The Jews: Their History, Culture, and Religion*, pp. 1151-69.

[2] *Ibid.*, p. 1153.

[3] *Ibid.*, p. 1153-55.

25

Professor Herskovits goes through many possibilities, including those by Joseph Jacobs[4] that there may be:

1. Jews both by religion and by birth;

2. Jews by religion, but not by birth; and

3. Jews by birth, but not by religion.

He eventually draws upon a definition that he devised in 1927, which stated, "A Jew is a person who calls himself a Jew or who is called Jewish by others."[5] Here we are not concerned with anthropological definitions or with anthropometric criteria, but rather with sociological observations regarding the cultural phenomenon of Yiddish as a factor in the life of the community of American Jews. Regardless of the shadings of any definition of a Jew, one fact stands out clearly to the informed observer of the American Jewish community, and that is that American Jews put a high value on the phenomenon of *identification* as Jews and *affiliation* with Jewish communal institutions.

Those who are involved in the organized American Jewish community are often led to believe that it represents a new "high" in identification for American Jews following a period of disaffiliation and disorganization in Jewish life. The period of Eastern European immigration to the United States is stamped as the hiatus by many of our "official" historians.

About ten years ago a talented young rabbi[6] was the guest speaker at a fund-raising dinner in a small industrial New England community. He was appealing for financial support of a worthy educational and spiritual organization. During the course of many years we have heard countless orations for similar purposes. Some are better, others worse. The degree of interest generally depends upon the public stature of the speaker and his personality, as expressed

---

[4] Joseph Jacobs, "On The Racial Characters of Modern Jews," *Journal Of The Royal Anthropological Institute*, 15, 1885, London, pp. 24–25.
[5] Herskovits, p. 1158.
[6] Rabbi Saul Teplitz, then of the Laurelton Jewish Center, New York, speaking at Fall River, Mass., on behalf of the Jewish Theological Seminary of America.

in his unique ability to entertain and manipulate the reactions of the listeners.

This speaker made an earnest and rather successful effort at presenting a meaningful talk. He was impressive. His method was to develop a historical concept of the continuity of the Jewish people, relating it to the present high level of religious and communal organization. He showed good understanding of early Jewish history and an adequate knowledge of the early American settlements. But either out of ignorance, or because of a zealous effort to stress the high level of Jewish organization in our current society, he referred to the early decades of this century as the period of disaffiliation, of lack of organization, in the community of American Jews. There was no effort at evaluation, no recognition of what had happened in the vast Jewish community during the four decades of Eastern European immigration.

A startling example of this poor evaluation and misinterpretation of the social forces during the Eastern European immigration is supplied by Dr. Abram L. Sachar.[7] Speaking of the Jews who had just arrived in America "from Pinsk and Kishinev," who could not yet "manage the *W* and the *Th*," he writes:

> These were the vast *unaffiliated* who made up a substantial part of the new immigration, and they were identified with their people only when they felt the pinch of discrimination. They were the *'pogrom'* Jews who felt no obligations to Jewish institutions.

Dr. Sachar seems to believe that the immigrants came here in haste with anxiety to become "Americanized," and in the process lost their identity as Jews, and abandoned their responsibility to the Jewish community. The facts are that the migrants left their old countries because of their personal insecurity as a result of being identifiable members of Jewish communities. They came here not to become assimilated or acculturated to an American culture,

---

[7] Abram Leon Sachar, *A History of the Jews* (New York: Knopf, 1953), pp. 396–97.

but rather to find a sanctuary for religious freedoms, and economic improvement and social progress.

When they arrived their first steps were to attempt to reestablish the religious and social institutions of the old country. They were strangers. Finding fertile soil for the old roots was not always easy. Some did not succeed. For others, it was dreary and sad—life represented a longing for the old world. The sometimes melancholy Yiddish writer Joseph Opatoshu gives the following poetic, if rather macabre description:

> Meantime the hurly-burly of American life, rushing along with giant steps, wound about the necks of these immigrants like a hangman's noose. To protect themselves from this danger, that lurked in the streets and even in their own homes, they began to transplant their 'Cities of God' to the mundane surroundings. Soon in all larger American cities there appeared cultural microcosms simulating their native towns in Poland, Lithuania, the Ukraine, Rumania, and Hungary. All over the Jewish quarter there sprung up signs announcing improvised synagogues for the natives of Zamosc, Lublin, Vilna, Kovno, Jassi, Pressburg, etc.
>
> These organizations were formed not only for religious prayer but also for burial purposes. Jewish cemeteries were divided into sections, and each section was enclosed by an iron fence with a carved gate. The gilt letters on these portals made known that Jews clung to their native towns not only in life but in the hereafter. Here on the cemetery it was obvious that these Jews failed to take root in the United States; that they worked hard, very hard, for the devil, but their souls remained in their native towns. One became fearful at the thought that their yearning did not subside even with death.[8]

They did not forsake members of the old communities from which they had themselves been rescued. It is common knowledge that individually and collectively the immigrants hustled in the sweat-shops, saving their meager dollars to bring to America relatives and "landsleit."

---

[8] Joseph Opatoshu, "Fifty Years of Yiddish Literature in the United States," in *Yivo Annual of Jewish Social Science,* 9 (1954), 74.

It is estimated that more than 80 percent of the over two million Jewish immigrants from Eastern Eprope between the early 1880's and 1915 were brought over to America by relatives who had arrived here earlier.[9]

Another example of distorted perspective: Speaking of the *contemporary* community of American Jews, the respected historian, Professor Marcus writes,

> . . . Jewish cohesiveness, Jewish sympathies, the feeling of intra-Jewish kinship—these are stronger today than they have ever been . . . the Jews of today cluster together around their Jewish institutions. To promote their survival as Jews, they are fashioning a rather compact form of Jewish settlement . . . with a full complement of Jewish institutions . . . all held together by a Jewish community council. This development of an ethno-religious enclave has characterized the direction of Jewish life in America since the 1930's.[10]

He continues:

> There is no lack of togetherness in contemporary American Jewish life. The middle-class American Jews who live in the fluid, wandering expanses of suburbia dwell together, often worship together, commonly receive their Jewish education together, and almost invariably swim and play golf together.[11]

However, to Professor Marcus it seems that:

> In 1920, even though there were over 3,500,000 Jews in the country, one could not speak of a genuine American-Jewish community. *Such a community simply did not exist.* [Emphasis added][12]

---

[9] Abraham Menes, "The Jewish Labor Movement," *The Jewish People: Past and Present* (New York: Jewish Encyclopedic Handbooks (CYCO), Vol. 4, 1955), p. 339.

[10] Jacob Rader Marcus, "Background for the History of American Jewry," in Oscar I. Janowsky, ed., *The American Jew: A Reappraisal* (Philadelphia: Jewish Publication Society of America, 1964), p. 14.

[11] *Ibid.*, p. 15.

[12] *Ibid.*, p. 9.

The position we take in this study is better expressed by Louis Wirth's concept of a community:

> What makes the Jewish community—composed, as it is in our metropolitan centers in America, of so many heterogeneous elements—a community is its ability to act corporately. It has a common set of attitudes and values based upon common traditions, similar experiences, and common problems. . . . The Jewish community is a cultural community. It is as near an approach to communal life as the modern city has to offer.[13]

Is it possible that the historians and rabbis cannot see that before 1920 the Jews did "dwell together, worship together, receive their education together?" If the historian disqualifies the millions of Eastern European Jews from being a community because they did not "invariably swim and play golf together" or because they did not belong to rich country clubs or build multimillion-dollar temples and Jewish Centers, he might be reminded that they did build labor unions (instead of country clubs), landsmanshaft-synagogues (instead of temples), a literature, a theater, a press, a language culture.

The historian who sees no community of Jews in America between 1880 and 1920 may find it interesting to read the following excerpts from a speech delivered by David Blaustein (former Director of the Educational Alliance) at a National Conference of Jewish Charities, on May 24th, 1904:[14]

THE LOWER EAST SIDE
32 Streets South of Houston and East of the Bowery
There are 5,007 tenements, with 64,268 families. Of these I found that 6,499 persons have 84 different occupations . . . ; there are here among 1,069 professional people, 361 teachers or proprietors of Hebrew Schools.

There are in this particular section of the city as many as 306 synagogues. . . .

On May 1, 1903, there were 72 pleasure places, clubs of the people, library and social.

[13] Louis Wirth, *The Ghetto* (Chicago: University of Chicago Press, Phoenix Books, 1928 and 1965), p. 290.
[14] Miriam Blaustein, *Memoirs of David Blaustein, Educator and Communal Worker* (New York: McBride, Nast and Co., 1913), pp. 138–41.

. . . in 306 synagogues, 276 of these are regular, only 30 are special, not counting what is done during the holidays. I find highest seating capacity was 1,500 and the lowest was 76. The total number of seats . . . 71,024. . . .

. . . Only 25 were regular synagogues, the rest while they are regular organized places of worship, yet during the week they are used for different purposes. 37 are used during the week for dancing purposes; 77 are shops and factories, 36 in the rear of saloons; 19 are halls and private places.

. . . With 307 'cheders', there are 8,616 boys and 361 girls. The ages of the pupils vary from 8 years. . . . The total amount paid out in this neighborhood for instruction amounts to $10,000 a month or $120,000 a year. . . . The 'cheders' of this neighborhood are not supported by outsiders, but by the people of the lower East Side.

There are 4 Theaters in this neighborhood. One of them is open on Friday, Saturday and Sunday and the rest of the week it is always open for the performances of the societies of the neighborhoods. Each house brings in at least $1,000 and any society that wants to can have the theater. . . . Now they have 4 afternoons in the week, 16 performances a week in 4 theaters, given by benevolent societies, lodges, unions, synagogues and sometimes private individuals. . . . and in that way I say an average of $1,800 a week is raised from pleasure . . . I think $1,000,000 is being raised by the people of this neighborhood to ameliorate the condition of the people who have not had the advantage of an education.

The immigrants organized their institutional life in a manner to implement their religious, social, and political ideologies and traditions. As will be seen, the Jewish immigrants who arrived during the early decades of the century were drawn into the economy as workers. They lived in concentrated low-class tenement areas described by Louis Wirth and Robert E. Park as Ghetto-like communities.[15]

Nathan Glazer finds that "The Jewish workers violated most of the patterns of lower-class behavior."[16] Studies have revealed that the higher the class, the larger the number of persons enrolled and

[15] Wirth, *The Ghetto.*
[16] Nathan Glazer, "The Attainment of Middle-Class Rank," in Marshall Sklare, *The Jews: Social Patterns of an American Group* (Glencoe: The Free Press, 1958), pp. 144–45.

active in organizations. "But," Glazer observes, "the Jewish *workers* break this pattern—more of them belong to organizations than do Jewish white-collar workers."

Glazer's observations are sustained by the results of several revealing studies. The survey of New York City in 1934–35, reported by Mirra Komarovsky in the American Sociological Review supports this position.[17] The same article by Nathan Glazer quotes a Chicago survey by Herbert Goldhammer, where the author says: "Whereas amongst Protestants and Catholics, working-class persons belong to fewer associations, among Jews the relationship is reversed."[18]

Rabbi Hertzberg in an article on religion concluded that either through direct membership or through the use of sacramental services 4,000,000 of the 5,000,000 American Jews are synagogue-affiliated.[19] Referring to a Washington study, he finds that: "Eighty-seven percent expressed a specific identification with one of the three major (Jewish) denominations. . . ."

This sort of statistic, even when objectively presented, grows into our consciousness, creating the impression of allegedly solid identification with religiosity and Jewishness in our contemporary society.

Much too little reservation of the kind made by Will Herberg[20] is given broad public attention and discussion:

> We are confronted today with the strange paradox of more religiousness and less religion: indeed we are confronted with the possibility that, with the rapid spread of religiousness among American Jews in the form of religious identification and syna-

---

[17] Mirra Komarovsky, "The Voluntary Associations of Urban Dwellers," *American Sociological Review,* 11, 1946, pp. 686–98.
[18] Glazer, p. 145.
[19] *American Jewish Year Book,* vol. 59, 1958, pp. 115–16.
[20] Paper by Will Herberg on the "Integration of the Jew in America," delivered in 1957 at the Second Annual General Assembly of the Synagogue Council of America at Columbia University, March 24th and 25th.

gogue membership, the very meaning of religion in its authentic sense may be lost for increasing numbers.

Marshall Sklare, in his excellent analysis of the process of re-orientation of the Jewish religious scene,[21] refers to a "religious disorganization" that is a by-product of the "conflicts which take place between the first and second generation (of American Jews)."

What must be added to Dr. Sklare's correct analysis is that the Eastern European Orthodoxy that dominated the religious scene during the decades of Russian-Jewish immigration to the United States was not the only factor in the total social scene.

In addition to religious and spiritual tradition, the Jewish immigrants brought qualities of intellectual and artistic dynamism, a radical desire for freedom and progress, and a drive for nationalistic expression and identification.

As we shall show, there certainly was no ethnic dis-identification. On the contrary, the period from 1880 to 1920 represented an epoch of great social organization and personal identification with a Jewish way of life, albeit not the way of life we know today. We shall see that the Eastern European Jewish immigrants formed close affiliations through fraternal groups, landsmanshaften, synagogues, the labor movement, and a dynamic press.

---

[21] Marshall Sklare, *Conservative Judaism* (Glencoe, Illinois: The Free Press, 1955), pp. 31–32.

3

Higher Status: The Restratified Community

A process was started in the decades after 1920 that marked a drastic change in Jewish life. Immigration was ended. A larger percentage of the Jewish population was native-born. Yiddish language institutions were becoming smaller. Press circulation dropped to about half of the 600,000 peak.[1] A social process was under way that tended to change economic and social differences among the Jews.[2]

The Jewish working class was shrinking to a point where after World War II it was almost insignificant. The sweat-shop era was only a memory. Most of those who worked for wages were wearing "white collars." Increasing numbers of Jews turned to the offices, laboratories, schools, and universities for a livelihood.

The number of Jews active in finance did not grow. There was a gravitation toward the center—small business, real estate, the professions. By the middle of the century the patterns and standards took on the characteristics of middle-class life in America.[3]

The Jewish population, which was now largely native born, was less concentrated in the large Eastern cities. There was a considerable shift to the West and the South, with about 300,000 Jews living in Los Angeles alone.[4] Following the general industrial migration Jewish communities were established in sections of the country

---

[1] Oscar Handlin, *Adventure in Freedom* (New York: McGraw Hill, 1954), p. 232.
[2] Louis Wirth, *The Ghetto* (Chicago: University of Chicago Press 1956 [Phoenix Ed.]), pp. 254–61.
[3] Handlin, pp. 250–53.
[4] *Ibid.*, p. 215.

where there were no Jews previously and enlarged in areas that had contained few Jews in the past.

The process of restratification that was started in the 1920s often worked rapidly in changing the "face" of the Jewish communities. As occupations were changing so were the communities, geographically. A vivid example is given by Louis Wirth, illustrating the migration from the predominantly Jewish West Side of Chicago in less than a decade.[5] (See table 1.)

TABLE 1

SCHOOL	Total Pupils		Jewish Pupils		Per Cent Jewish	
	1914	1923	1914	1923	1914	1923
Washburne	1,575	Closed	1,464	Closed	93	Closed
Garfield	1,525	1,351	1,400	1,079	92	30
Foster	2,075	1,360	1,640	775	80	57
Smythe	1,225	1,176	1,078	1,052	88	89
Goodrich	1,200	1,200	736	23	65	2
Dore	1,093	850	329	25	30	3
Medill (grade)	837	Closed	335	Closed	40	Closed
Polk	1,250	Closed	250	Closed	20	Closed

In a study of Jewish middle-class life, Nathan Glazer hypothesizes that "a majority of the younger generation is now composed of business and professional men." He reveals that, "in the 1930's about half of those American Jews who were immigrants were still workers; . . . however the fifteen years of prosperity from the end

---

[5] Wirth, p. 245.

of the thirties to the mid-fifties have wrought great change, and created the Jewish community as we know it today."[6]

During this period the older generation of European Jews, with its large proportion of workers, was further reduced by the natural effects of age. The younger generation has simultaneously risen on the social scale.

Outside of New York the Jewish community is more homogeneous than in the city. Between 1948 and 1953, surveys in fourteen communities revealed: "that the proportion of Jews in the non-manual occupations (that is, of those working in the professions, as proprietors, managers, and officials, and as clerks and salesmen) ranged from 75 to 96 per cent."[7]

While it is only in the large cities that one finds any substantial proportion of Jewish workers, Glazer discovered "that even in New York City two-thirds of the gainfully employed Jews, both immigrants and native-born, are engaged in non-manual work."

Since there is considerable variation of status even in the non-manual group, Glazer finds it significant that the Jews rank "high in the group, which is to say that a large proportion of them are professionals."

It is important that: "This rise in the proportion of professionals has been accompanied by a fall in the number of Jews engaged in the lower levels of white-collar work—as clerks and salesmen."[8]

With Herbert Hyman and S. M. Lipsit, N. Glazer has analyzed public opinion polls conducted by the National Opinion Research Center in 1948 and 1951. They found that, though there were still considerable numbers of foreign-born Jews in the population, about one-sixth of those over eighteen had completed college. In some cities the percentage was even grater. Glazer writes: "Statistics demonstrate that the rise in the social and economic position of the Jews has been extremely rapid, far surpassing that which can be shown for any other immigrant group, and indeed surpassing, for

---

[6] Nathan Glazer, "The American Jew and the Attainment of Middle Class Rank," in Marshall Sklare, *The Jews: Social Patterns of an American Group* (Glencoe, Ill.: The Free Press, 1958), p. 138.

[7] *Ibid.*

[8] *Ibid.*, p. 139.

the same period, changes in the socio-economic position of long-settled groups."[9] His hypotheses are substantiated by a study of American college graduates made in 1947, which showed that more Jews than non-Jews became professionals and that more Jews became proprietors, managers, or officials; fewer Jews became any type of white-collar and manual workers.[10]

An interesting insight into the rapid restratification in the Jewish community may be gained when we realize that fewer of the parents of the Jewish students had been professionals, proprietors, managers, and officials than the parents of the non-Jewish students. While there is no survey of Jewish male college students showing the occupation of their parents, the above conclusion was drawn from a survey of five thousand female college graduates.[11] Further interesting evidence is given in the study of Jewish demography made by Ben B. Seligman and Aaron Antonovsky, which reveals that within the professions the Jewish occupations are largely in the high-status groups. The data show that, on the average, one out of each three Jewish professionals is either a physician or a dentist. In some cities, such as Passaic, New Jersey, the percentage is four out of ten. Attorneys and judges number 20 percent of the professionals; and technologists (chemists, engineers, architects) occupy the talents of two to three, out of ten professionals, in some cities.[12]

The shift into the professions by the native-born Jews is illustrated by the researchers: "Where almost a quarter of the *native born* are in professional and semi-professional occupations, we find only 13 per cent of the *foreign born*."[13]

The pattern of restratification is further highlighted by the statistics showing that: "Of Jews (aged) 41 to 50, four out of every ten had some college; of those 61 to 70, only two out of every ten

[9] *Ibid.*, pp. 140–41.
[10] Ernest Havemann and Patricia West, *They Went to College* (New York, 1952), p. 187.
[11] Robert Shosteck, *Five Thousand Women College Graduate Report*, (B'nai B'rith Vocational Service Bureau, 1953), pp. 8–9.
[12] Seligman and Antonovsky, "Some Aspects of Jewish Demography," Sklare, p. 78. See table 10.
[13] *Ibid.*, pp. 79–80.

had attended college."[14] The older group obviously includes many who are either foreign born or are early second-generation Americans.

The following table 2 is adapted from an economic study of gainfully occupied Jews in New York City in 1957 by Nathan Reich.[15]

TABLE 2

Percentage Distribution of Gainfully Employed Jews (1945–46)

Occupations	Communities 61	Communities 4
Manufacturing	12.4	34.8
Trade	47.3	33.3
Professions	11.9	11.3
Clerical	15.7	...
Domestic and personal	6.8	12.4
Public service	2.9	2.6
Transportation and communication	1.9	3.7
Other and unknown	1.1	1.9

When we compare this to a table reflecting the Jewish occupational structure from 1900 to 1925 (see chapter four of this study) prepared by Jacob Lestschinsky, we observe that there has been a sharp increase in trade corresponding to a similar drop in industry. While there is still a considerable level of domestic and personal service, professional service has risen sharply and for the first time exceeds the percentage, in that category, of the general population.

Table 2, which covers the period of 1945–46, shows a dramatic

14 *Ibid.*, p. 86.
15 *The Economic Structure of Modern Jewry*, in Louis Finkelstein, *The Jews: Their History, Culture, and Religion* (Philadelphia: 1949), pp. 1244–45.

increase in trade at the expense of manufacturing. Professions have risen to a new high of almost 12 percent and clerical occupations appear strongly for the first time.

This table divides the communities into two categories. The second column (four communities) represents industrial centers such as New York City; the larger category represents the smaller cities. In the industrial centers industry is now on an equal level with trade, while previously it was much larger.

TABLE 3

Percentage Distribution of Gainful
Jewish Workers in New York City (1937)

	Jewish Gainful Workers (Per Cent)	All Gainful Workers (Per Cent)
Trade	25.7	16.9
Manufacturing Industries	25.4	19.8
Domestic and personal service	10.9	14.2
Professional service	7.4	6.6
Construction industries	5.2	9.9
Transportation industries	2.7	5.7
Finance	2.4	5.4
Amusements	2.4	1.7
Public service	2.2	2.9
Public utilities	0.5	3.6
Other	1.7	2.3
Unemployed	13.5	11.0

The following tabular illustrations are taken from the study by Seligman and Antonovsky, referred to earlier in this section.[16] These figures are not in percentages but in numbers. The totals show the size of the samples.

In table 4 the large number of self-employed stands out strongly, particularly in the trades. Only Passaic (an industrial city) has a significantly larger number of wage-earners.

The second fact that emerges is the tremendous emphasis on trade and professions with a corresponding de-emphasis on manufacturing (even in Passaic). These characteristics combine to form a picture of a typical middle-class group.

Table 5 presents a breakdown of the special groups falling under wholesale and retail trades in table 4. The obvious concentration is in food establishments, apparel and shoes, and furniture, hardware, and lumber.

Another study of New York City (1952) was made by Seligman.[17] The tables shown below shed light on the place of employment and the occupation of the "heads of households" by place of birth. From table 6 we see the following:

1. New York City, the most proletarian urban center, traditionally a center of foreign-born, now has about 50 per cent U.S. born breadwinners in the Jewish population.

2. Even in New York about 3 out of 10 family-heads own their own business.

3. More than 15 per cent of the "heads" are out of the labor force, most of them foreign-born. It is reasonable to assume that the aged and retired are represented in that group. Therefore within a decade (as these are replaced by younger and native-born "heads") New York City will experience an even greater social re-stratification in the Jewish community.

---

[16] Pp. 78–79.
[17] "The Population of New York City: 1952," in Sklare, p. 105.

TABLE 4

Employment Status and Industry

	Passaic		Port Chester		New Orleans	
	Self Employed	Wage Earner	Self Employed	Wage Earner	Self Employed	Wage Earner
Construction	25	15	27	14	31	56
Manufacturing	130	425	38	81	118	153
Transportation-communication	25	50	7	14	10	83
Wholesale-retail trade	970	775	256	123	933	912
Real estate, insurance	70	25	14	14	118	243
Professional and business service	635	630	77	33	465	280
Government	...	165	...	31	34	208
Other	15	25	4	8		
No answer	45	230	22	53	3	3
Total	1,915	2,340	445	371	1,712	1,938

TABLE 5

	Passaic		Port Chester	
Trade	Number	Per Cent	Number	Per Cent
Analysis of Wholesale and Retail Trades				
Food establishments	420	24.3	75	19.9
Eating and drinking places	110	6.4	9	2.3
Liquor	85	4.9	5	2.3
Apparel and shoes	375	21.8	75	19.9
Furniture, hardware, lumber	185	10.7	58	15.3
Auto and related	45	2.6	24	6.3
General merchandise	45	2.6	36	9.5
Other	320	18.6	63	16.6
No answer	140	8.1	30	7.9
	1,725	100.0	379	100.0

Table 7 shows that while the total labor force is about equally divided between native and foreign born, about two-thirds of the categories that include 1) professional and semi-professional; 2) proprietors and managers; and 3) clerical and sales, are born in the U.S., while one-third are European. This is balanced against two-thirds of the craftsman and operatives who are European, while one-third are American born.

These facts and conclusions lucidly illustrate the process of social change in the Jewish community.

A study by David Goldberg and Harry Sharp[18] of socio-economic characteristics of the Detroit area throws interesting light

---

[18] David Goldberg and Harry Sharp," "Some Characteristics of Detroit Area Jewish and Non-Jewish Adults," in Sklare, pp. 107–18.

TABLE 6

Place of Employment of Household Head
by Birthplace (Per Cent) (New York City)

	United States	Other Western Hemisphere	Europe	Other	Unknown	Total
Privately Employed	25.1		22.8	.8	.2	48.9
Government Employment	4.1		.7			4.8
Own or Family Business	15.4	.23	12.4	.1	.2	28.33
Unknown	1.7		.9		.1	2.7
Total	46.3	.23	36.8	.9	.5	84.73
Heads not in Labor Force	2.9	.23	11.9	.27	.2	15.27
Total	49.2	.23	48.7	1.17	.7	100.

N—1161

TABLE 7

Occupation of Head of Household by Place of Birth (Per Cent) (New York City)

	United States	Other Western Hemisphere	Europe	Other	Unknown	Total
Profession & Semi-Prof.	8.7	.1	2.8	.3	.2	12.1
Proprietors & Managers	12.3	.13	8.9	.25		21.58
Clerical & Sales	13.4		6.2	.25	.1	19.95
Craftsmen & Operatives	9.6		17.2	.1		26.9
Service	.5		1.			1.5
Unknown	1.8		.7		.2	2.7
Total	46.3	.23	36.8	.9	.5	84.73
Heads Not in Labor Force	2.9		11.9	.27	.2	15.27
Total	49.2	.23	48.7	1.17	.7	100.

N—1161

on the social nature of the Jewish population, since, in the authors' words: "The occupational composition of the Jewish population of greater Detroit probably represents an intermediate position between the relatively proletarian Jews of New York City and the virtually complete white-collar concentration of Jews in some of the smaller communities of the country."

The survey reveals that 73 percent of the heads of Jewish families hold white-collar jobs. This divides into 42 percent proprietors, managers, and officials; 16 percent professionals; and 15 percent clerical and sales workers. Almost half of those breadwinners in these categories are self-employed. The data presented by the researchers shows that 34 percent of the Jewish family-heads earn more than $10,000 per annum while the white Catholics and Protestants in that bracket number only 4 and 8 percent respectively.

A pertinent aspect of the social restratification of the new generation is revealed in the statistics on the educational level of the Jewish adults. The percentage of all Jewish adults (including those of middle-age and older) who completed the 12th grade is 41; those who had "some college" number 18 percent. However, the figures on the adults under 40 years of age (which virtually excludes the older and foreign-born generation) shows that 59 percent have completed the 12th grade (high school), and 27 percent have had "some college."

All the evidence illustrating the restratification of the Jewish population and the attainment of middle-class rank should not lead us to believe that this tendency in Jewish life ran contrary to the socio-economic trend of the country. On the contrary, between 1910 and 1950, the proportion of the general population engaged in nonmanual work rose from 21 to 38 percent.[19] This "climate" offered great opportunity for the Jews to effect a rapid social transition from working-class to predominantly middle-class status. Glazer sums it up well: "Hence, while America in general became more markedly middle-class in its occupational structure, Jews became even more so." (P. 146)

---

[19] A. J. Jaffe and C. D. Stewart, *Manpower Resources and Utilization* (New York: 1951), p. 190.

New panoramas opened for jobs, professions, and business. By law there was less discrimination, socially more acceptance. The "one-world" concept and the popular principles of "brotherhood" seemed to have offered many an opportunity to draw upon traditional American doctrine to, at least theoretically, and often practically, exercise some of the lessons learned from the recent world upheavals. Judaism was accepted by the government and most communities as the "third official religion." In this social climate Jews were faced, more than ever before, with a sense of permanency on the American scene and a role in the annals of Jewish history. They thus devised new forms of affiliation, reflecting their reaction to recent history and responding to their new social needs. This consolidation seems dramatic and impressive in its current form. It reflects the new position in American society of a socially restratified national and religious minority.

With higher social status and relief from the sharp economic problems of early migration there were, however, often the accompanying psychological and social problems that come with the tempo of middle-class life. Handlin states the case well:

> There were fewer calls upon the welfare agencies for relief of pauperism and more frequent calls for advice on the relief of personality maladjustments.[20]

The organization of the Jewish community around a temple or a Jewish center is interpreted as a "return to religion." An examination of the facts may reveal that it is not entirely so. For instance, the survey conducted by Sklare reveals that one half of the Conservative synagogues offer no facilities for daily prayer.[21] Two thirds of the worshipers either cannot read or cannot understand the Hebrew prayers.[22]

However, the modern synagogue, or temple, or Jewish center serves as more than an edifice for occasional worship. It provides im-

---

[20] P. 253.
[21] P. 100.
[22] *Ibid.*, p. 123.

portant social and educational facilities.[23] It becomes the controlled vehicle for centralizing and channeling the functions that serve the needs of the members of the community. It offers a new way of life but is somehow "hinged" to the past. Perhaps this form of religious affiliation offers to many American Jews some assurance that they have not entirely abandoned the old ways of religious traditionalism and Yiddish culture, that they have not forsaken their heritage.

The new mid-century Jewish community has taken shape. Its economic and social middle-class structure is clearly defined. Religious and community leaders have "made hay while the sun was shining." Jews are today identifiable as such, and at least their nominal affiliation with the religious and communal institutions is undeniably high.

But where did all this spring from? We cannot agree that some unknown hiatus was magically bridged to make the American Jewish community what it is today.

Among American Jews, the impact and consequence of the Hitler attack have opened eyes and minds to social issues. The phenomenon of the new State of Israel has directed many to seek a national identity. There is a serious effort to find meaning in life.

Forty years ago Louis Wirth wrote: "It may be a platitude to say that the Jews are what their history has made them, but it is a platitude worth reiterating."[24]

---

[23] *Ibid.*, pp. 129–58.
[24] P. 288.

4

The Early Immigrants
The Sephardim — The Ashkenazim

The Sephardim

Occasional individual Jews undoubtedly drifted into the New World, each on his own way, passing anonymously, leaving no trace of his venture for the scrutiny of posterity.

Columbus' search for a route to India coincided with the expulsion of Jews from Spain under the Inquisition. There has been repeated speculation that his crew contained a number of Marranos (Jews who publicly converted under the pressure of the Inquisition but privately retained Jewish identity).

However, the first recorded settlement of Jews in the American Colonies goes back to the initial week of September in the year 1654, when the tiny bark, St. Charles, arrived in Nieuw Amsterdam carrying a unique cargo—23 Jews. Four were adult men, the rest were women and children. The group consisted of settlers who had come to the Brazilian town of Recife to live under the relative security of Dutch government. There they enjoyed a quarter-century of prosperity and religious freedom. When the territory was reconquered by the Portuguese in 1654, they fled from the prospect of persecution.[1]

Through the decades that they lived under Dutch sovereignty the group still identified with their Portuguese origin in their tradition and ritual. They represented the last remnant of the Sephardic[2] culture of medieval Spain.

---

[1] Oscar Handlin, *Adventure in Freedom* (New York: McGraw Hill, 1954), pp. 3–5.
[2] Sephardic refers to the Iberian and certain Mediterranean Jews as against

When they arrived in Nieuw Amsterdam they were greeted by Governor Stuyvesant's unpleasant reception. He saw no need for the newcomers and invited them to depart in a friendly way. Those in the group who were unable to pay for their passage were obliged to sit in jail for their indebtedness. Ultimately, the Dutch West India Company, which was influenced by Jewish stockholders, permitted the small band to stay unhampered. By the end of the century they numbered about one hundred.[3]

After 1700 additional Jews migrated to New York. Now Jews other than Sephardic were slowly coming to our shores. By mid-century the Jewish population of New York was three hundred. Other communities were established in Newport, Philadelphia, and Charleston. With sprinklings along the coast from Massachusetts down to Georgia, the total Jewish population in the Colonies by 1776 was over 2,000.[4]

At the middle of the century the Ashkenazic (Yiddish-speaking) Jews were the majority within the group of Jewish colonists. They had come from Germany, Holland, Poland, and England. None of them were wealthy. They were mainly shopkeepers, artisans, and peddlers.

In spite of their superior number this group was historically overshadowed by the smaller Sephardic (Spanish-Portuguese) population. The Sephardic Jews, who had been the earlier arrivals in the colonies, enjoyed superior education and cultural and financial status. Socially, they constituted a Jewish upper class.[5]

> . . . A few hundred Sephardim, at the most, came to these shores, and by 1720 they no longer constituted a majority among American Jews.[6]

---

the classification of Ashkenazic, which applies to the German and Central European Jews. There is a further reference to the distinction in the chapter on Yiddish Language and Literature.

[3] Handlin, pp. 3-7.

[4] *Ibid.*

[5] Nathan Ausubel, *Pictorial History of the Jewish People* (New York: Crown Publishers, 1954), p. 271.

[6] Jacob Rader Marcus, "Background for the History of American Jewry," in *The American Jew: A Reappraisal*, Oscar I. Janowsky, ed. (Philadelphia: Jewish Publications Society of America, 1964), p. 2.

. . . The first Sephardim who came here in the middle 1600's were devoted religionists and with little delay set about re-constituting the European-type religious community to which they were accustomed. . . . Despite Germanic origins which pre-vailed among them, by the 1720's . . . the immigrants were content to join . . . and establish—Spanish-Portuguese congrega-tions, so that the Sephardi rite became typically American and was accepted by all Jews until the early 1800's.

The domination of the Orthodox Sephardim began to wane in the 1820's and 1830's . . . Sephardi Orthodoxy began losing ground even among the older, well established families, whose desire to integrate more closely with the relatively liberal Ameri-can culture led some of them, as early as 1824, to reject Orthodoxy and the authority of the traditional law. . . .[7]

Weinryb sees the members of the early Sephardic community in America as being culturally assimilated in terms of language and social patterns. He claimed that they were "little versed in Jewish Learning."[8]

However, the fact remains that they did establish and (as their social status grew) maintain their characteristic Spanish-Portuguese synagogues. Thus, we can say that they maintained the characteristics of a *community* only in the sense of their *religious* separateness: in most other cultural respects they were assimilated Americans.

Very early the Sephardim seized every opportunity to shift from Spanish to English.

The first local Jewish sermon to be published appeared in English in Newport in 1773; it was preached in Spanish in the Newport Synagogue at Shevouth (Pentecost) by Rabbi Chaim Isaac Karigal.[9]

The following is an example of the strong emphasis on retaining a Jewish religious tradition that is exclusively Sephardic but ex-

---

[7] *Ibid.*, p. 5.

[8] Bernard D. Weinryb, "Jewish Immigration and Accommodation to Amer-ica," in Marshall Sklare, *The Jews: Social Patterns of an American Group* (Glencoe, Ill.: The Free Press, 1958), p. 5.

[9] Morris U. Schappes, *The Jews in the United States* (New York: Ter-centenary Book Committee, 1958), p. 24.

pressed in English. The excerpts are from the Constitution of the Hebrew Congregation of the Dispersed of Judah, established in 1847 at New Orleans. It appeared officially in English:

> Article II—The prayers and ceremonies shall forever be read and performed according to the manner and customs of the Portuguese Jews, according to Minhag Sephardim.
> Article III—No laws or regulations shall be established in this congregation which are incompatible with the code of laws by which the Jewish nation is governed.[10]

Although the Sephardim dominated the Ashkenazim socially, their language was influenced by some of the latter's Yiddishisms. *The Publication of the American Jewish Historical Society,* 1937, p. 72, cites a letter written in 1770 by Abraham Halevy (who evidently had made a journey from Newport to Europe) to his friend Aaron Lopez in Newport, reporting his safe arrival. Referring to the character of this letter, Samuel Niger writes:

> . . . We may conclude that even the Sephardic Jews in the colonies acquired a little Yiddish from their Ashkenazic neighbors. . . . Abraham Halevy's Hebrew letter is interspersed with Yiddish words and almost complete Yiddish sentences.

To further support this point of view, Niger states that:

> Isolated words borrowed from Yiddish, such as *shul, Yohrzeit* and *rebbe* (in the sense of teacher) are found in the minutes of (the Sephardic) Congregation Shearith Israel.[11]

Although the social climate and the spirit of the new world offered unprecedented opportunities of freedom for the Jews, there still were stumbling blocks. There were prejudices to be reckoned with. Peter Stuyvesant, "Hardkoppige Piet," felt that the Jews would

---

[10] Copy of the Constitution is at the American Jewish Historical Society Archives.
[11] Samuel Niger, "Jewish Culture," in *Jewish People: Past and Present*, Vol. 4, CYCO (New York: 1955), p. 267.

be detrimental to Christian business,[12] and Asher Levy had to conduct a fight for the right to stand guard in defense of the colony.[13]

Religious rights, too, had to be won. While the Jews in Holland enjoyed the privilege of worshiping in their own synagogue, in Nieuw Amsterdam they were obliged to bow to the power of the official Dutch Reformed Church, and were restricted to worship in their homes. (Of course, this restriction applied to Catholics, Lutherans, Mennonites, and Puritans, as well.)

However, under English rule, when Nieuw Amsterdam had become New York, the Jews achieved the privilege of public worship and they built their first synagogue in 1695.[14] Even though each Colony had an official religious denomination that was favored and privileged over all other groups, the conditions of colonial life discouraged the strict enforcement of discriminatory laws.

It was not difficult for the small Jewish population to feel at home in the Colonies. Prejudices were overcome and there were many friends. In New England, for example, they were often treated with special privilege as well as friendship. The Puritans respected "the children of the Old Testament" and their Hebrew culture was held in high regard.[15]

At the beginning of the 19th century the Jews had already developed social roots. In their dealings with the gentiles and each other, their identity as Jews was now not limited to their affiliation with the synagogue. Handlin says:

> In religious matters, for instance, the synagogue was no longer coterminous with the community, for it had ceased to be an agency of all Jews and had become a voluntary agency created by some of them.[16]

By the 40's the greater devolpment of social needs continued and there was a definite trend towards secularization of Jewish life. Schappes observes that:

---

[12] Morris U. Schappes, p. 10.
[13] *Ibid.*
[14] *Ibid.*, p. 12.
[15] Handlin, pp. 14–16.
[16] *Ibid.*, p. 32.

More and more the synagogue became one of many institutions in Jewish life, and the many others became increasingly important to more and more Jews.[17]

Dr. Moshe Davis sustains this point of view when he notes that:

. . . slowly the Jews were weaned away from the synagogue as their central communal institution.[18]

This should not lead us to believe that the Jews abandoned the synagogue. Secular and social needs and functions developed as the Jews were enlarging and integrating their lives into a land which was more securely becoming their home. Consequently the synagogue did not stand out alone as the symbol of Jewish life.

However, an examination of some statistics reveals that the per capita seating capacity of the synagogue in 1850 was probably greater than what we have today. In 1850 the Jewish population was about 50,000. The United States census of that year shows that there were 77 congregations, in 40 cities, in 21 of the 31 states. The total seating capacity of all the synagogues was 16,575.[19] This would have averaged 215 seats per congregation, and about one seat for every three Jews, including women and children. There were clearly enough seats to accommodate all the men and many of the women even if the entire Jewish population had desired to attend any one service at any one time.

The current Jewish population is over 5,000,000. The total number of congregations claimed by the three groups. Orthodox, Conservative, and Reform, is about 1,850, with a combined membership estimated at 3,000,000.[20] Checking several sources, I was not successful in finding data on the total seating capacity of the 1,850 congregations. If, however, there was one seat for each three Jews (as there was in 1850), there should now be a total of more than

17 Schappes, p. 71.
18 Moshe Davis, "Jewish Religious Life and Institutions In America," in *The Jews*, Louis Finkelstein, ed. (Philadelphia: 1949, 1), p. 364.
19 Schappes, p. 67.
20 *American Jewish Year Book*, 59: 114–15.

1,600,000 seats in the aggregate of the synagogues, or about 900 seats, on the average, in each of the 1,850 congregations. Common knowledge tells us that this is not the case. Only a small number of the synagogues have enough seats to accommodate all their members. It is necessary to draft ballroom and makeshift facilities on the High Holidays, when large numbers of the population require a place of worship.)

The dynamics of political, economic, and social conditions in Europe was always the determinant in the character of Jewish immigration to America.

During the early part of the 19th century, the economic and industrial changes in Europe brought a shift of Jewish population into the towns and cities. There was an orientation from eastern to western Europe. In the forty or fifty years prior to 1870, Jewish immigration to America was largely from western Europe. The immigration had a German character, since those who came had lived in Germany or under the influence of German rulers. The Jewish population in 1820 was about 5,000. Estimates of the "German" immigration run from two to four hundred thousand in the half-century to 1870. At that time, therefore, we had a Jewish population of several hundred thousand.[21]

Most of the immigrants were poor. They came with no property or capital. But there was no problem of destitution. They arrived at a time when the economy of the country was developing and expanding. There were many opportunities for those with skills and ingenuity.

There were very few Jews in the arts and sciences. Many went into the trades and crafts. Some sought opportunities in commerce, largely peddling and small merchandising. Several succeeded in developing prosperous stores and larger commercial enterprises. They did not restrict themselves to limited areas. There were Jews on all the frontiers of America.

As the character of the new community jelled, its members de-

---

[21] Handlin, pp. 47–49.

veloped an awareness of social needs. A network of secular organizations developed. The immigrants turned to each other to contrive organizations that could serve their particular requirements and strengthen their chances for survival and growth in a strange new world. They could meet their religious, social, and charitable needs by banding together. At the same time opportunities were provided for socializing and relaxing with kindred souls.

The congregations and secular groups were organized on the basis of country of origin. By the time the Civil War had broken out there were in New York, in addition to the old "American" Sephardic group, congregations of Polish, Bohemian, German, Dutch, English, and Russian Jews. A little later the organizations and congregations exhibited even greater differentiation by organizing as "Landsleit,"[22] according to specific towns or regions of origin. It was common to find congregations called the Jassier, the Berditchever the Odesser, the Krakauer, etc.[23]

The social motivaton for the growth of the fraternal organizations may be put into three general divisions. First, there was the obvious need for common company and friendship, especially as a buttress against strangeness. Then there was the fear of economic insecurity, particularly in times of illness, accident, or death. Last, there was the need of the ethnic group for cultural expression through literary, dramatic, and musical groups.

A variety of organizations sprang up to serve these purposes. "Bikur Cholim" societies were organized for visiting the sick. "Gemilath Chasodim" societies engaged in fund raising and making small loans to the needy. The "Mutual Benefit" societies eventually became very important and popular. They engaged in collecting dues from members which were used as insurance benefits for illness and death. But they offered much more than insurance. They offered the feeling of security that comes from solidarity of purpose and largeness of number. During illness there were visitation and friend-

---

[22] "Landsleit" means literally "countrymen." It was, and is still, used to designate Jews who originated not from one country, but rather from a common province, town, or area in the old country. (See Chapter 8 of this work.)

[23] Handlin, p. 60.

ship and in time of death there were mourners and consolation. (See Chapter eight for full development of this subject.)

Some Jews took to joining existing American fraternities such as the Knights of Pythias and the Odd Fellows. In many instances special Jewish chapters were set up within these organizations. This process led subsequently to the organization of national Jewish fraternal bodies such as B'nai B'rith in 1843, and later B'rith Abraham.[24]

During the first decades after mid-century, forces were mustered to provide for larger philanthropic needs. Jewish hospitals were established in Cincinnati (1850), New York (1852), and Chicago (1868). Orphanages were founded in Philadelphia (1855), Cleveland (1868), and New York (1879).[25]

Community activities also included recreational and cultural functions. By the 70s and 80s the larger cities could boast of Jewish literary, dramatic, music, and library societies.

The Jewish communities found themselves literally living in a "new world." True, they fought handicaps. There were strangeness, poverty, hard work, and some prejudice to be contended with. But there were many factors in favor of social development. The social structure was different from what they had known in Europe. Here there was no feudal tradition. On the contrary, in many quarters they were favored by the Puritan attitude toward the Jew.

There was less traditionalism and greater class mobility. The looser stratification system permitted newcomers to earn rank in society more easily.

Former President Eisenhower has been quoted as saying that he did not care what religion Americans had, as long as all Americans had some religion. He was enunciating the concept of latitudinarianism, the idea that, whatever its doctrines, any religion was good if it fostered the good life and inculcated good morals. This was the attitude to religion that the Jews found early in the 19th

---

[24] *Ibid.*, p. 66. See also Chapter 8 of this work.
[25] *Ibid.*, pp. 67–68.

century and it meant that at least theoretically, and so very often practically, they stood on a footing in society equal with that of citizens of other faiths.

But there were problems within the Jewish community. There were the "native" Jews, those of Sephardic (Spanish) background, and the "newcomers," who were Polish, Czech, Hungarian, Dutch and German Jews. The latter group spoke a variety of dialects, mostly Yiddish, and were referred to as the "Germans." These newcomers were not accepted as equals by the Americanized Sephardic community.

By mid-century the Sephardic community was two hundred years old. During the period of their settlement, immigration was slow. They had no serious problems on the American social horizon. They succeeded in retaining their religious identity without being threatened by social pressures. Raising their children to be secure both in the social environment of their country and in the traditions of Judaism was a problem that they largely solved through the many years of slow adjustment from the old to the new.

The Ashkenazim

The immigration of several hundred thousand "German" or Ashkenazic Jews within four or five decades posed an entirely different problem. Everything happened more rapidly to them. They came in vastly larger numbers; the industrialization and urbanization of the country were proceeding at an unprecedented pace; and they were eager to become quickly Americanized.

The Sephardim would not accept them. They had to set new standards for themselves. Some tightened their orthodoxy; others relaxed it. There was considerable disorientation. There is evidence that a rather large number ceased to affiliate with the Jewish community and there was a substantial rate of intermarriage.[26]

The great problem was accommodation to the attitudes and needs of the younger generations. The acculturated Sephardim were sub-

---

[26] *Ibid.*, p. 75.

stantially free from this concern, but for the Ashkenazim it became a life-and-death problem. In their rush for adjustment and Americanization, the "German" Jews were losing their foothold in traditional Judaism and their children were defecting to Christianity or to ethnic nothingness.

Within the three decades following 1855 the Reform creed of Judaism was emerging.[27] Contrary to some popular notions the movement was promulgated in America not as a result of ideological differences in theology but rather as a consequence of demands for change in the externals of worship and ritual.

There was a tremendous desire to conform to the social standards of other Americans. This constituted respectability and status. To accomplish this transformation it was felt necessary to substitute English for the "foreign" languages used both in the synagogue and in the home. Standards of American chivalry seemed to require the abolition of the women's curtained gallery in the synagogue. The inclusion of an organ and mixed choir provided color and upper-class prestige to the service.

This process started with the Reform movement in Germany. Speaking of Berlin's Mendelssohnian German Jews we are told:

> First of all the Berliners disowned the East European Jew. . . . Then they eliminated Yiddish . . . the articulated disparity between Jew and German. . . . The rapid abandonment of Yiddish and then Hebrew, of the belief in the Messiah's coming . . . did not guarantee entry into Christian society. . . .[28]

The Germans in America, at mid-century, fought for official recognition of the German language. The German Jews joined them. In 1845 an elementary school was being established for German Jewish children in New York. The trustees defended the use of German:

> I fail to see why the teacher, a native of Germany, should force himself, or be forced to teach the children the elementary sub-

[27] Ibid., pp. 76-79.
[28] Lucy S. Dawidowicz, The Golden Tradition (New York: Holt, Rinehart and Winston, 1967), p. 16.

jects in English. Why should the German language in general be ignored or thrust aside?[29]

The German Jews clung for awhile to German language and culture, which distinguished them from the Eastern Jews. But they very smoothly made the change to English and thus completed the transition of the cultural process: from Hebrew and Yiddish to German, then to English. Three classical examples of that process follow:

1. Detroit's Congregation Beth-El—a transition in outline:

   a) Congregation established in 1850, by Orthodox German Jews.

   b) 1855—new constitution written in German, containing Reform tenets.

   c) 1860—Orthodox elements challenge the legality of the constitution; reformers prevail.

   d) 1862—New constitution, containing additional reforms.

   e) ENGLISH IS INTRODUCED AS OFFICIAL LANGUAGE.[30]

2. Cincinnati's K. K. Beneh Yeshurun (Issac M. Wise Temple): This famous temple was organized by German Jews as an Orthodox synagogue, 1840. In 1847, the Rev. James K. Gutherin was chosen as their rabbi. At his installation he preached a sermon in English. From his sermon:

   . . . diffident as I feel in my humble capacities, chiefly on account of its being the first time I have the honor to address by word of mouth a congregation of my coreligionists in English.[31]

---

[29] *Allgemeine Zeitung des Yudenthums*, 1845, p. 407.

[30] The Historical Committee, *A History of Congregation Beth-El, Detroit, Michigan, from its organization to its Semi-Centennial 1850–1900*, Detroit, 1900.

[31] Cited by James G. Heller, *As Yesterday When it is Past*, (Cincinnati: 1942) (Printed in the Occident, April, 1864, p. 34.)

3. H. B. Grinstein tells us that:

> In 1873 German Temple Emanu-El in New York turned to Manchester, England, and called Gustav Gottheil to its pulpit to preach Judaism's universal message in impeccable English accents, comprehensible to all New Yorkers.[32]

In conclusion, Jacob R. Marcus notes:

> After two generations of lingering affection for their original German vernacular, the German-Jewish immigrants on these shores began to employ English almost exclusively.[33]

One reform led to another and soon many felt that observing the restrictions of the dietary laws was unwieldy and that attending Saturday services conflicted with business and social obligations.

Another important social change concerned the position and nature of the Jewish clergy. From the beginning, the American synagogues had no rabbis. The services were conducted by chasonim (cantors). The cantors were pious Jews who were familiar with the liturgy, had good singing voices, and could lead the congregations in prayer. At first most of them had additional occupations outside the synagogue. Eventually they took on the character of full-time clergymen, also teaching the children, preparing boys for Bar Mitzvah, officiating at weddings, and so on.

Past the mid-point of the century there developed among the synagogues, reformed or otherwise, a desire to "import" trained rabbis as spiritual leaders. Now most congregations could afford them. Since there were no facilities for training rabbis in America, they were drawn mostly from Germany. Some of the rabbis were still orthodox, some were changing to liberalism, while others brought established Reform principles with them.

The Reform rabbis found fertile ground. Some of the immigrants had had contact with Reform ideology in Germany and many others

---

[32] Quoted by Moses Rischin, *The Promised City* (Cambridge: Harvard University Press, 1962), p. 96.
[33] Marcus, p. 8.

were amenable to change. Reforms of worship, kashruth, Sabbath observance, language, and social attitudes were radically introduced all at once in some congregations, such as Temple Emanu-El in New York and Temple Har-Sinai in Baltimore. Others, such as Rodeph Shalom and Kneseth Israel in Philadelphia, took gradual liberalizing steps.

The reformers effected fundamental changes in social and historical attitudes. They rejected the principles of the nationhood of the Jews. To them Jews were a religious group belonging to the political state under which they happened to be living. They expurgated the nationalistic idiom in religion and dropped holidays such as Purim. The Talmud was no longer a strict guide and the Mosaic law represented primarily a code of ethics.

There are some who expound the view that the Reform movement was a consequence of a sincere desire to stem the tide of assimilation and retain the children within the fold of liberalized Judaism. Oscar Handlin seems to share that opinion when he writes:

> But the immigrants feared a split between the generations and, out of love for their children, attempted to hold them to the synagogue by Americanizing it in one fell swoop.[34]

While the above motivation may have been true and sincere in some quarters, it seems that eventually it was overshadowed by another explanation, that of social and economic expediency. The Reform tenets ultimately became admirably suited to the social status of the German Jews who achieved success and financial attainment in business, finance, and the higher professions.

Speaking about the period when Reform was gaining headway, S. Grayzel writes that the "attainment of economic security was accompanied by a spurt in internal organization . . . with the object of uniting for social, cultural and philanthropic purposes, those Jews who already differed widely in their religious views.[35]

---

[34] Handlin, p. 76.
[35] Solomon Grayzel, *A History of the Jews* (Philadelphia: The Jewish Publication Society of America, 1948), p. 629.

The social aspects of the Reform phenomenon are well set forth by E. Digby Baltzell in his study of the Jewish upper-class of Philadelphia.[36] He writes:

> In Philadelphia and elsewhere most of the upper-class German Jews belonged to Reform synagogues, while the Russian and Polish Jews were Orthodox . . . membership in a fashionable Reform congregation became a symbol of social and economic achievement and acculturation. It was much the same as the Quaker-turned-Episcopal or the Ashkenazi-turned-Sephardi process of an earlier Philadelphia.

---

[36] "The Development of a Jewish Upper Class in Philadelphia," in Sklare, p. 283. In this same paper see also pp. 278–82 and note table 3, p. 282, which shows the movement of the Reform synagogues following the social movement of the upper class in the community.

Eastern European Immigration: The New Community

The period from 1880 to 1920 is regarded as the second era of Jewish mass immigration to America. This was characterized as the "Russian" or "Eastern European" immigration as contrasted to the earlier "German" migration. After 1870 the number of German Jews coming into the U.S. was reduced to a trickle and the Eastern exodus began picking up momentum. In 1881 almost 6,000 Jews came to America, the next year more than 13,000. At the end of a decade (1881 through 1900) almost 200,000 had arrived, mainly from Eastern European countries.[1]

Again the stimulus for Jewish immigration to America was economic disequilibrium and social unrest in Europe. Social change in the semi-feudal eastern countries dragged the large Jewish population into the maelstrom of poverty, war, economic and political dislocations, and persecution.[2]

It was becoming increasingly difficult for the Jewish trader or "middleman" to earn a livelihood from the "liberated" peasant. Changes in economics made it harder for the Jewish artisan to earn a living. The restrictions of the Czarist regime kept the Jew within the pale of settlement, preventing him from living in the larger cities.

---

[1] HIAS Chart of Jewish Immigration, in Morris U. Schappes, *The Jews in the United States* (New York: Tercentenary Book Committee, 1958), p. 119.
[2] For more information on the economic status of European Jewry, see Raphael Mahler, "The Economic Background of Jewish Emigration from Galicia to the U.S.A.," in *Yivo Annual*, No. 7 (New York: Jewish Scientific Institute).

The following description of the characteristics of the Jews who came from Eastern Europe is interesting and authoritative:[3]

> About 50 percent of the Russian-Polish Jews were employed in trade, tavernkeeping, brokerage, makeshift occupations, as rabbis and other religious functionaries; about 25 percent artisans, and the rest were servants and declassed persons, beggars and paupers. This was the general picture, with the exception of an upper crust of wealthy or fairly well-to-do Jews. The bulk of Russian-Polish Jewry seemed outwardly as though petrified in the forms molded by the feudal system of Poland in the 18th century. Underneath, however, disintegration was setting in, accompanied by the germination of new patterns of living and new cultural trends. These did not come to light until the emancipation of the serfs (1861) and the reforms inaugurated by Tsar Alexander II, which stirred the Pale of Settlement, awakened the spiritual energies of the heads of Russian Jewry, shook the young men of the yeshivas and houses of study out of their lethargy, and set in motion that epoch-making emigration which ultimately gave rise to the present American Jewish community.

Unable to cope with political and economic problems, the Czar and the Russian Orthodox Church resorted to instigation against the Jews as a means of distracting the Russian masses from their bitter plight. The notorious pogroms (massacre of Jews) were the consequence.

The first pogrom occurred in Odessa in 1871 and was followed by others in 1881 and 1889. The worst years were 1903 to 1907, starting with the infamous Kishinev pogrom in 1903, following with the Zhitomir massacre of 1904, and culminating in the holocaust that raged in 600 towns and villages in 1905.[4] Now persecution was coupled with economic and social destitution to trigger a tremendous exodus from the eastern countries. Most of the immi-

---

[3] Jacob Lestschinsky, "Economic and Social Development of American Jewry," in *Jewish People: Past and Present* (New York: Jewish Encyclopedic Handbooks [CYCO], Vol. 4, 1955), p. 74.

[4] Nathan Ausubel, *Pictorial History of the Jewish People* (New York: Crown Publishers, 1953), pp. 234–35; and Schappes, p. 145.

grants came to the United States. In the four years (1903 to 1907) over four hundred thousand Jews left Russia for the United States.[5] Another two hundred thousand came to America during those years from the other eastern regions.[6] (See Appendix to this chapter for additional immigration statistics.)

After 1905, there were 1¼ million (1/7th of all Jews in Europe) who were emigrants from Eastern Europe. Some settled in Western Europe and England; others traveled to South America, Palestine, and South Africa; but the greatest numbers came to the United States.[7]

The character of this immigration was different from the others. When several hundred thousand Jews came from Germany prior to 1870, they were a barely significant minority within a large general German migration. But in the eastern countries the Jews were the first to leave, setting an example for some peasants who followed in smaller numbers.

The Jews came to stay, and they did stay. Fully one-third of all who arrived during the general immigration returned to their native countries; but more than 90 percent of the Jewish newcomers remained.[8] Perhaps a Jew felt that he had no "native" country to return to, regardless of strangeness and difficulties in the new world.

In the closing years of the nineteenth century Jewish immigration into the United States already meant not an individual but a family migration, with the intent to settle permanently in the new country. This was the percentage of women who came:[9]

1886–1888	37.1
1889–1896	44.0

---

[5] *Ibid.*, p. 235.
[6] Schappes, p. 119.
[7] Oscar Handlin, *Three Hundred Years of Jewish Life in America* (McGraw-Hill, 1954), p. 85.
[8] Schappes, pp. 120–21.
[9] Jacob Lestschinsky, "Jewish Migrations," in *The Jews*, Louis Finkelstein, ed. (Philadelphia: 1949), p. 1225.

The percentage of children was as follows:

$$1886–1888\ldots\ldots\ldots\ldots\ldots\ 27.9$$
$$1896–1898\ldots\ldots\ldots\ldots\ldots\ 44.0$$

The trend continued into the new century. The following figures (averaged from 1900 to 1925) present an interesting comparison of Jewish family-migration to America as compared to non-Jewish:[10]

women among Jewish immigrants	45.8 percent
women among non-Jewish immigrants	32.9 percent
children among Jewish immigrants	25.3 percent
children among non-Jewish immigrants	12.3 percent

In America, the Jewish immigrant encountered a great contrast to the life he had known in Czarist Russia. Though he was poor and there were many trials and tribulations, there were also new opportunities. Here he found full freedom to practice his religion. He could develop his mother tongue and express his rich cultural heritage.

Jewish immigrant literacy was strikingly higher than that of non-Jewish. Because of the ancient tradition of educating the boy, male literacy was almost twice as high as female. The following tables "1" and "2," adapted from S. Joseph, make the point clearly:[11]

TABLE 1

Illiteracy of Peoples From Eastern Europe, 1899 to 1910

People	Immigrants 14 Years of age and over	Illiterates	
		Number	Per cent
Jewish	806,786	209,507	26.0
Lithuanian	161,441	79,001	48.9
Polish	861,303	304,675	35.4
Russian	77,479	29,777	38.4
Ruthenian	140,775	75,165	63.4

[10] *Ibid.*

[11] *Jewish Immigration to the United States from 1881–1910* (New York: Columbia University, 1914), p. 194.

TABLE 2

Sex of Illiterates of Peoples From Eastern Europe, 1908

Race	Number illiterates 14 years and over		Per Cent	
	Male	Female	Male	Female
Jewish	9,455	13,762	21.9	40.4
Lithuanian	4,215	2,097	53.4	63.4
Polish	14,573	8,813	36.7	42.9
Russian	5,820	828	40.1	50.8
Ruthenian	4,203	1,836	49.6	57.4

There was exploitation but there was also the opportunity to improve one's lot.[12] So the Jewish immigrant brought his family, put his artisan skills to work, and stayed in "Columbus' America." In 1900 there were 1,000,000, by 1917 close to 4,000,000 American Jews.[13]

The new immigrants were not able to spread through the country so easily as those who came prior to 1870. They concentrated largely in the eastern urban centers, mostly in New York City. Those who were interested in commerce started laboriously with small peddling and petty retailing: groceries, dry-goods, stationery, clothing. A few went into banking and real estate and some became distinguished in modern merchandising.

In 1920 the Bureau of Jewish Social Research estimated the American Jewish population as 3,600,800. About half of the number lived in New York City. Some estimates, such as those of David Trietsch, placed the New York figure as high as 2,000,000.[14]

The concentration of the Jewish population in large urban centers is clearly shown in the following table number 3, adapted from the *American Jewish Year Book*. The massive concentration in

[12] Louis Wirth, *The Ghetto* (Chicago: The University of Chicago Press [Phoenix], 1956), p. 148.
[13] Handlin, p. 85.
[14] Wirth, p. 149.

New York is obvious, with only two cities, Chicago and Philadelphia, having a Jewish population running into the hundreds of thousands in 1928.[15]

TABLE 3

Jewish Population in the
Larger Cities (1927–28)

New York City	1,643,012
Chicago	285,000
Philadelphia	240,000
Cleveland	78,996
Boston	77,500
Baltimore	67,500
Newark	55,000
St. Louis	55,000
Los Angeles	43,000
Pittsburgh	42,450

The largest group of newcomers were those who formed the mass of Jewish skilled and unskilled workers. At the turn of the century the Jewish immigrant came with an average of eight dollars in his pocket. Characterizing the group in a brief sentence, one chronicler writes:[16]

Their religion was severely orthodox, their language was Yiddish, their background was poverty and they tended to swell the ranks of the workers here.

Table number 4, below, graphically shows the economic distribution of the Jews during the period when the immigrant community was crystallizing.[17] We note that 3 out of 4 breadwinners filled positions either in industry or as unskilled laborers. There were more individuals employed as house servants than were engaged

---

[15] *American Jewish Year Book, 1927–1928*, pp. 243–46.
[16] Schappes, p. 112.
[17] Lestschinsky, "Jewish Migrations," p. 1230.

in trade. The percentage in the professions was even lower than that for non-Jewish immigrants.

The second half of table 4 shows the occupation distribution in the non-Jewish group of immigrants. The differences are obvious.

TABLE 4

Occupational Structure of the Jewish and Non-Jewish
Gainfully Occupied Immigrants into the United States
(1900–1925)

Occupational Groups	Jews		Non-Jews	
	Absolute Numbers	Percent-age	Absolute Numbers	Percent-age
Industry	596,043	60.1	1,719,361	14.9
Commerce (Trade)	100,147	10.1	475,822	4.1
Husbandry	24,792	2.4	3,059,798	26.6
Liberal professions	19,620	2.0	261,033	2.3
Unskilled laborers	102,739	10.4	3,760,213	32.7
House servants	123,220	12.4	1,779,218	15.4
Miscellaneous	25,769	2.6	456,111	4.0
TOTAL	992,330	100.0	11,511,556	100.0

Most of the Jews landed in New York and stayed in New York. Requiring work at once, they became available to the fast growing ready-to-wear clothing industries. Many utilized their skills at tailoring. The unskilled were taught to be pressers, machine operators, and cutters.

Illustrating the preponderant influx of almost all Jewish immigrants into the clothing industries, Dr. B. Hoffman wrote:[18]

Former Yeshiva students, sales clerks, insurance agents, semi-intellectuals, teachers, bookkeepers, sons-in-law of the well-to-do, storekeepers, merchants, etc. became cloak operators.

[18] *Fuftzig Yohr Klokmacher Yunion* [Yiddish] (New York: 1936), p. 22.

Another chronicler of labor history recalls:[19]

Fortunate were those who had learned a trade in the old country; the tailors, the carpenters, and other artisans would very quickly obtain employment. But the great majority of the Jewish immigrants consisted of non-workers. The committeemen and their friends used to take the newly arrived immigrants to work in their shops, where they were taught a trade. Many immigrants hired out as unskilled laborers, working for stevedore companies, for the railroads, and also in large factories.

The following table number 5, adapted from an article on Jewish migrations by Jacob Lestschinsky,[20] clearly shows the concentration in the clothing industries. Please note that column one lists the number of craftsmen employed, while column two shows percentages.

TABLE 5

Distribution of Jewish Craftsmen According to Industries:
(1900 to 1925)

Clothing industry	362,642	60.8 percent
Lumber and building	84,683	14.2 percent
Metal work	46,336	7.8 percent
Food industries	42,501	7.1 percent
Jewelry and watchmaking	9,582	1.6 percent
Printing	9,282	1.6 percent
Leather workers	8,017	1.4 percent
Miscellaneous	33,000	5.5 percent
Total	596,043	100.0 percent

One "landsman" brought another into the "sweat-shop." Hours were long, the factories were filthy and unventilated, working conditions were miserable, and salaries did not average $12 per week until 1910. It was common for women and children to both work

[19] Bernard Weinstein, *Jewish Unions in America* [Yiddish] (New York: 1929), p. 44.
[20] *Op. cit.,* 1231.

in the shop and take work home. By 1890 there were already 13,000 employed in New York's East Side garment trades, building an industry that was clothing the nation.[21]

Skills and aptitudes took the Jewish worker into other trades as well. They became painters, glaziers, carpenters, printers, jewelry workers, clerks, and salespeople.

Several organized efforts at agriculture failed.

There were, in fact, determined but largely unsuccessful efforts to induce Jews to take up farming as a vocation. . . .

The Yiddish press regularly added its encouragement. Lest traditional prejudices stand in the way, the Morning Journal in 1914 pointed out that the American farmers "are similar to the small noblemen of our old home rather than to the degraded and oppressed peasants."

The sum total of all these efforts was remarkably slim: by 1912, there were less than 4,000 Jewish families on the land. Whatever allowances must be made for poorly chosen sites and for the unforeseen calamities of nature, the fact remains that Jewish immigrants were not tempted by the reality involved in being "small noblemen." The intellectuals were quickly discouraged, and the others failed to make a living.[22]

The professions became attractive to the capable and hard-working immigrant and even more so to his children. For many it became possible to achieve economic security and social status by combining intelligence with ingenuity and hard work. Jews became doctors, dentists, teachers, lawyers. As early as 1905 there were 500 Russian-Jewish doctors practicing medicine in New York City.[23]

During the last decades of the 19th century the tendencies toward liberalism and the efforts at reform crystallized into a permanent movement establishing a Reform community with clear

---

[21] Handlin, pp. 92–98.
[22] Oscar and Mary F. Handlin, "A Century of Jewish Immigration," in *American Jewish Year Book*, Vol. 50 (1948–49), pp. 20-21.
[23] Handlin, *Three Hundred Years. . . .*

identity. The leaders were mostly German rabbis. They succeeded in establishing a clerical body, the Central Conference of American Rabbis and the Union of American Hebrew Congregations, which affiliated the Reform temples.

A number of groups, Americanized in character, had hoped to find common ground with the liberal elements. But they could not accept the Reform tenets and broke away under the leadership of Sabato Morais, orthodox Sephardic rabbi. They differed from the old European orthodoxy but they wanted to retain what they considered "historical" Judaism.

The consequence was the establishment of the Jewish Theological Seminary of America in 1887. In contrast to the liberal reformers, this group developed Conservative Judaism, which aimed to retain traditional concepts and ritual, adapted to American social conditions. The United Synagogue was organized to affiliate the Conservative synagogues.

At the outset the Conservatives developed very slowly. They were groping along with some well-defined concepts but with little working material. Many of their affiliates had divergent ideas and practices. But mainly they lacked substantial mass support. Their appeal was limited largely to the Jews who did not necessarily have German backgrounds but who achieved at least middle- or lower-middle-class status. The early Conservatives were the English-Speaking Orthodox elements.[24]

However, whether they could anticipate it or not, Conservative Judaism was destined to become the fastest-growing Jewish group during the middle of the 20th century. Today the largest Jewish social group, the middle-class, finds Conservatism admirably suited to its purpose. The members of this community are mostly native born. They enjoy considerable economic security; they have acquired education for themselves and their children and have thoroughly absorbed the culture required for adjustment to urban American middle-class society.

Surveys show that this group has abandoned orthodox ritual and

[24] Solomon Graysel, *A History of the Jews* (Philadelphia: The Jewish Publication Society, 1948), p. 696.

restrictions to a very large degree.[25] But most of them "have no feeling" for Reform Judaism. They are "cut from a different clay." Their parentage was Orthodox. They stem mostly from the Eastern European immigration and they feel strange and out of place in a synagogue "without their hats on." The rational Conservative understanding of social needs, respect for tradition, but leniency of enforcement, has been responsible for the attraction of the new large, restratified Jewish community.

The mass of Jews who came from Eastern Europe could not feel at home with either the Reform or Conservative institutions. Neither could they join the American Sephardic groups. Concentrated in the larger cities, they had ample opportunity to recreate a reasonable replica of the synagogue and religious life that had been unique to their specific locality in the Old World.[26]

Kinship, and country or province of origin, became the criterion for unity. Kinsmen and "landsleit" were instrumental in bringing their relatives and friends over here and when the "landsman" arrived he was happy to join the religious and fraternal groups that welcomed him into the fold.

A writer for one encyclopedia, commenting on the societies and landsmanshaften, says:[27]

In most cases the language of the societies has been Yiddish, and their warm spirit has helped members endure adverse circumstances and low economic standards.

To Louis Wirth the concentration of Jewish immigrants in the larger industrial centers appeared as "ghettos without walls." In his classic work on the Chicago ghetto he describes the role of the landsmanshaft.[28]

---

[25] See Marshall Sklare, *Conservative Judaism* (Glencoe, Ill.: The Free Press, 1955).

[26] Wirth, p. 147.

[27] *The Standard Jewish Encyclopedia* (Doubleday & Company, Garden City, 1959), p. 1167.

[28] Wirth, pp. 222–23.

We note that the last sentence of the quotation squarely contra-
dicts Dr. Sachar's position that the immigrants disregarded their
social obligations and broke their ties with the less fortunate brethren
in the old countries:

> The ties of family, of village-community, and of *Landsman-
> schaft* that bind the ghetto inhabitants into little nuclei of more
> or less autonomous units are only partially apparent to the out-
> sider. The ghetto family will survive crises that would tear an
> ordinary family asunder, and a stranger who is able to call him-
> self a Landsmann, not only loosens the purse-strings of the first
> individual he meets, but also has access to his home. Not only
> do the Landsleute belong to the same synagogue, but as a rule
> they engage in similar vocations, become partners in business,
> live in the same neighborhood, and inter-marry within their own
> group. A Landsmannschaft has its own patriarchal leaders, its
> lodges and mutual aid associations, and its celebrations and
> festivities. It has its burial plot in the cemetery. It keeps the
> memories of the group alive through frequent visits and main-
> tains a steady liaison with the remnants of the Jewish community
> in the old world.

The "landsmanschaften" or societies, in addition to caring for
social needs, most often sponsored their own synagogue. The
growth of synagogues was phenomenal. In New York City there
were altogether 14 synagogues in 1854. In 1890 there were already
150; and by 1942, fully 1,200.[29] The ethnicity of this Yiddish-speaking, working-class, orthodox Jew from the old "shtetl"[30] was culturally representative of the millions that constituted the American
community of Jews during the early decades of the 20th century.

A tremendous network of fraternal, cultural, and educational institutions developed during this period.[31] Labor fraternalism became very popular. Right wing (socialist-inclined), left wing (communist oriented) and labor-Zionist orders affiliated hundreds of

[29] Handlin, *Three Hundred Years* . . . .
[30] "Shtetl" means literally: small town. The "Shtetl" identifies the many
Eastern European Jews who lived in, and came from, the small towns and
villages that were included within the limited pale in which Jews were allowed, by the Czar, to live.
[31] Wirth, p. 148.

thousands in the *Workmen's Circle, The Jewish People Fraternal Order,* and *The Farband,* respectively.[32] (See Chapter 8 for full development of this subject.)

The Jewish intellectual from Eastern Europe was swept along with the migration to America.[33] Some were educated in the European yeshivas, others came from a Russian intellectual milieu, and many had received training and experience in the Jewish "Bund."[34] They provided inspired and dynamic leadership to the manifold institutions in Jewish life. Their energies were applied in the fields of journalism and theater, in political, labor, and fraternal and educational movements.

All the mass movements were permeated with Yiddish language, culture, and tradition. Some of the leaders who in the old country were influenced by the Haskala on one hand or by the Zionist nationalist movement on the other, were most adept in the Russian or Hebrew languages. Many of them had to relearn Yiddish in order to integrate with, and provide leadership to, the American Jewish community.

The Jewish world was colorful. The population was drawn from every region and country of eastern Europe. Ausubel says they "brought the characteristic of the *Litvak, Galitzianer, Poilisher, Rumainier, Ukrainer,* and *Bukoviner* patterns."[35] They spoke many dialects and there were some antagonisms and differences. But the dialects blended and the differences were lessened and an "American" Yiddish emerged as the common denominator.

The European "Shtetl" offered a unique background. In spite of poverty there were many joyous features of Jewish life in the village-ghettos. Nathan Ausubel speaks of a transcending "will-to-joy."[36] The community feeling of propinquity and commonness was high. While sorrow was shared, so was festivity.

---

[32] Judah Pilch, *Jewish Life in Our Times* (New York: Behrmans, 1943), p. 163.
[33] Lestschinsky, "Jewish Migrations," p. 1226.
[34] The "Bund" was the organization of Jewish "underground" revolutionaries in Czarist Russia. (See Wirth, p. 10.)
[35] Ausubel, pp. 287–88.
[36] *Ibid.,* p. 235.

Religious and national holidays such as *Succoth, Simchas Torah,* and *Purim* were occasions for communal merriment and festivity. Engagements, weddings, and homecomings were moments for celebration. Jewish weddings were particularly famous for exuberance. Eating, drinking, and dancing would continue for several days. The famous "Klezmorim"[37] provided the indispensable music and color for the folk dancing and for the traditional dances of the "mechutonim."[38]

Much of this spirit and way of life was brought to America by the immigrants. Some of it was "lost in transit"; a great deal had to be modified and adapted to the new world. One of the manifestations of the Jewish impulse for dance, music, and drama was expressed in the establishment of the famous Yiddish theater.

Yiddish theater was started in Romania by Goldfaden in 1876, on the eve of the tidal wave of immigration.[39] By 1880 a Yiddish troupe (the Golubocks) had come to New York from London. At first the material was trash dished up by hack writers and box-office entrepreneurs anxious to capitalize on the thirst of the public for Yiddish entertainment. Musical comedy, "operas," and operettas were presented to please the popular desire for song and dance. However even in the "shund" (hack) productions there was a reflection of the interests of the masses. The plots dealt with biblical-historical stories, and themes of immigration life.

In 1891 the serious dramatist Jacob Gordin came to New York and started a collaboration with the talented actor Jacob Adler. The work of the two "Jacobs" reformed the Yiddish theater and ultimately turned it into a "temple of drama." Eventually the Yiddish theater became a medium for presenting the works of the best Yiddish literary and dramatic talents, such as Sholem Aleichem, Y. L. Peretz, Sholem Asch, David Pinski, Ossip Dymov, Leon Kobrin, H. Leivick, Peretz Hirshbein, and Joseph Opatoshu.

[37] Singular: "Klezmer," plural "Klezmorim." The "Klezmorim" were the small-town musicians who were largely self-taught and whose talent was an indispensable part of the Jewish idiom.
[38] The "Mechutonim"—were the respective relatives of the bride and the groom, whose "in-law" relationship was being established by the marriage.
[39] For source in Yiddish Theatre see B. Gorin, *Die Geschichte Fun Yiddish Theatre,* Vol. 2 (New York: 1923) [In Yiddish].

As a medium of Yiddish culture it was unique in reaching the broadest audiences. Handlin found:[40]

> The relationship between the intellectuals' creative activity and the life of the people emerged still more clearly in the case of the theatre. Yiddish theatre . . . was responsive to the moods, the emotions, and ideas of its audience, to which it therefore supplied an intimate meaningful experience. In those days the stage was a mass medium . . . making no demands of literacy . . . its vivid, dramatic presentation an easy . . . release to thousands of tired people.

The theater created a social bond between the writers, the actors, and the audiences. In addition to the sold-out week-ends, playhouses were full from Monday through Thursday because of the benefit system, whereby societies and organizations distributed blocks of tickets, earning revenue for themselves and simultaneously guaranteeing continuity of the theater. By 1928 there were 24 theaters in 10 cities, with 11 in New York, 4 in Chicago, and 2 in Philadelphia.[41]

Joseph Schildkraut, reminiscing about his youth when his father was a great star of the Yiddish stage, writes:[42]

> It was an exotic world, that lower East Side where the People's Theatre was located . . . not a ghetto . . . a world of contrasts, blending into the city and influencing its life through all the boroughs.

In addition to the professional theater there were many opportunities for nonprofessional creative expression. The fraternal orders, cultural groups, clubs, and societies provided rewarding vehicles for dramatic, musical, and dance groups. Professional talent of high calibre was frequently enlisted to direct the activities of the amateurs. Here the people—workers, housewives, children—enriched their personal lives with the best of the Yiddish culture, and

[40] Handlin, *Three Hundred Years* . . . , p. 138.
[41] Schappes, p. 206.
[42] Joseph Schildkraut, *My Father and I* (New York: Viking Press, 1959), pp. 117–18.

thus enhanced the life of the community with their efforts.

Yiddish amateur as well as professional artistic activities provided the community with a cultural backbone that helped to resist tendencies towards assimilation. This was the Yiddish community's method of stemming dissolution as against the "Americanization" and "Reform" employed by the earlier "German" community.

In his study of Jewish life, Judah Pilch observed that: "Modern Jewish music, theater, literature . . . became an antidote for assimilation and dissolution."[43]

Of all the cultural phenomena, the Yiddish press was probably the most vital. It was the basic medium upon which the community, in all of its aspects, depended for sustenance and continuity.

Ausubel writes that during the early decades of the century more Yiddish was spoken in New York City than in any other locality in the world.[44] It was the first language in most homes, synagogues and organizations. It was often considered the second language of the city.

The daily press and numerous publications responded to the need for popular education in the mother-tongue. In addition to presenting local and international news it was concerned with social, political, and labor problems. There were educational features dealing with history, geography, health, civics, music, art, and drama.

A series of short-lived and experimental efforts at Yiddish journalism started in 1870. The efforts culminated in the first two decades of the new century with a powerful and effective body of publications. The important dailies were: *The Tageblatt, The Daily Forward, The Jewish Morning Journal, Die Wahrheit, The Day,* and *The Freiheit.*[45] The combined circulation was: 716,146 in 1916; 536,346 in 1927; and still 425,000 in 1943.[46]

A wide range of political thought was represented, from Republican and Democratic to Socialist and Communist. Religious orthodoxy and traditionalism, and atheism and free-thinking nationalism were reflected in editorials, news items and features. The greatest

[43] Pilch, p. 6.
[44] Ausubel, pp. 287–88.
[45] Handlin, *Three Hundred Years* . . . , pp. 124–125.
[46] Pilch, p. 46.

intrinsic value of the press was that it served as a cultural tool for the Jewish people in their economic, social, and intellectual struggle for an improved life in the Jewish community and in the American society.[47] (See chapter 7 of this work for a full treatment of this subject.)

Yiddish literature will be dealt with in another section of this work. However, in passing, it is important to point out that a large "Yiddish Kultur" developed during the period. Many of the cultural leaders were integrated in the organizational structure of Jewish life. Others were the mainstay of the world of the "pen," press, publications, literary and political journals, and the like. A large group of gifted writers emerged on the American scene, creating a substantial folk-literature. The works of many are now considered classics. We will mention only a few.

Some poets were: Morris Rosenfeld, David Edelstadt, Morris Winchevsky, Yehoesh, H. Leivick, Abraham Reisen, M. L. Halperin, and Mani Leib. Novelists, playwrights, and short-story writers included Sholem Asch, David Pinski, Ossip Dymov, Peretz Hirshbein, Moishe Nadir, Isaac Raboy, and Joseph Opatashu. Important critics and commentators: Abraham Liessin, Moissaye Olgin, Abraham Cahan, Chaim Zhitlovsky, Abraham Coralnick, and S. Niger.[48]

The Eastern European Jews came to America during a period of rapid industrialization. Most of the newcomers were enlisted into the ranks of the growing working class. The Jewish labor movement became an important factor in the life of the new community.

Earlier in this chapter we noted the process whereby the Jewish immigrants were drawn into the rapidly developing clothing industries. The European Jew was either an artisan or a small "middleman." By background and disposition he was most suited to the work of the light industries.

During the period of the sweat-shop, the social climate created a movement for the organization of labor. Replacing the Knights of Labor, the young American Federation of Labor opened new panoramas for organization of the Jewish Workers.

By 1890 there were thousands of Jewish workers in the gar-

---

[47] Wirth, p. 148.
[48] Ausubel, pp. 287–88.

ment trades. Handlin points out that prior to 1888 the United Hebrew Trades played a significant role in organizing Jewish workers.[49] During that period, through the efforts of such groups, thousands of Jewish workers were led into the early unions in New York, Chicago, Philadelphia, Baltimore, and other centers. They were organized into crafts of cloakmakers, men's tailors, capmakers, furriers, milliners, shirtmakers, printers, and barbers. The very important International Ladies Garment Workers Union, the Amalgamated Clothing Workers, and the Furriers Union grew from the roots that were developed at that time.[50]

Here again Yiddish played a crucial role. The language of the sweat-shop was Yiddish. The Jewish workers were capable of understanding and responding to the *bund*-trained union organizers who spoke to them in their mother-tongue. Economic solidarity and national cultural solidarity became interrelated. Judah Pilch comments that "the growth of the Jewish labor movement . . . created a demand for Yiddish literature."[51] The social-minded writers and publicists gave leadership and lent expression to the problems and sentiments of their fellow-Jews in the shops and factories.

Thus there developed the phenomenon of an integration and unification of the religious, cultural, social, and economic aspects of Jewish life through the forces of the Yiddish language and culture.

Ben Halpern, who also saw the immigrant community as a "ghetto," recognized the deeply national and cultural character of the Jewish society:[52]

There was . . . a very active cultural life and a vivid sense of history in the Jewish Ghetto. That generation, in fact, reached an unsurpassed peak of historical awareness as Jews. And concomitantly, they led a life of high cultural intensity.

[49] Handlin, *Three Hundred Years* . . . , p. 133.
[50] Judith Greenfield, *Yivo Annual of Jewish Social Science*, Vol. II-III (New York: 1947–1948), pp. 180–204.
[51] Pilch, p. 46.
[52] Ben Halpern, "America is Different," in *The Jews*, Marshall Sklare, ed. (Glencoe, Ill.: Free Press, 1958), p. 36.

After the early decades of the century the turbulence in Jewish life began to subside. The workers had achieved a status of economic and social stability. A tendency to white-collar work became evident. Symptoms of a social restratification were beginning to appear. The social life of the now Americanized immigrant was becoming oriented toward stabilizing the future of his American-born children. Economic and religious activities were being modified to conform to a changing world and a "new way of life."[53]

Rapidly increasing numbers sought a solution to economic and social problems by acquiring a higher education and taking their places in the professions and white-collar occupations. It was becoming fundamental for Jewish children to get a good education. By World War I, there were 15,000 Jewish college students; by the middle 20s there were 100,000. This was one-tenth of the national total of college students.[54] This tendency continued and today the percentage is greater still.

With this direction in Jewish life, the dependence of the Jewish community on Yiddish was diminished. The language and the culture were losing their intensity and vitality among great numbers of the people.

At the time when the Nazi blow was struck and the world became embroiled in a battle for democratic survival, an epoch was closing in the life of the American Jews.

[53] See Marshall Sklare, *Conservative Judaism* (Glencoe, Ill.: The Free Press, 1955).
[54] Handlin, *Three Hundred Years* . . . , p. 117.

6

The Development of Yiddish
Language and Literature

Modern Jews are divided into two historical groups: the Sephardic (Spanish-Portuguese), who speak Ladino, and the Ashkenazic (German-European), who speak Yiddish. Yiddish was the mother-tongue of more than ten million Jews (two-thirds of all the Jews of the world) until World War II.

The purpose of this chapter is not to present a comprehensive survey of Yiddish literature, but rather to trace and describe the beginnings and the development of the language and the literature, as a background for understanding modern Yiddish institutions.

There are many misconceptions regarding the Yiddish language. Most people just "don't know." Others, whose interest has become awakened for one reason or another, think that the language goes back only to Mendele[1] (less than one hundred years). Most communal leaders, rabbis, and community workers are greatly preoccupied with the current Hebrew "zeal." They are also consumed with an eagerness to maintain and extend their foothold on the middle and upper-middle rungs of the social ladder. Thus they often relegate the "jargon" (Yiddish) to the junk-heap of a poorly understood and inaccurately evaluated past.

Yiddish evolved from an admixture of several German dialects, through adaptation to environment, under continuous influence of Hebrew (the language of piety), and later through contact with slavic (Eastern European) languages. This process of birth, development, and formation of a modern language began about a thousand years ago.

[1] Mendele Moicher Sforim (Sholem Jacob Abramovich), the grandfather of modern Yiddish literature.

It is difficult to pinpoint the exact birthplace of Yiddish. We do know that Yiddish is the product of the Jewish dispersion. Everything known points to the probability of its origin in the Rhine district.[2]

Dr. A. A. Roback believes that some adventurous group of Jews found their way to the land of the Goths and the Huns, even before the conquest of Palestine by Rome. They made their home first among the Alemanni tribes and later among the Saxons and Franks.

There is practically no record of the cultural and secular activities of the German Jews in the very early medieval period. According to Roback the German Jews before Charlemagne's reign spoke a language that was a mixture of German dialects, strongly influenced by Hebrew and Aramaic.[3] While Medieval Yiddish (and even modern Yiddish) has been referred to as "Judeo-German"[4] it should be, and has almost universally become, adjudged a separate language.

At the very beginning, the new Germanic Yiddish developed a cultural identity of its own. The language reflected and served the needs of the people. To quote Roback:[5]

> To begin with it may be stated at the outset that much of the medieval Yiddish literature had nothing in common with Gentile writings. The barrier which separated the ghetto from the outside world served too, in more than one way, to divide the Jews and their neighbors.

The Jew lived in a "separate world." He was not a participant in the issues that concerned the Germans in the Middle Ages. While he was too often the victim, he took no part in the conflicts, of the feudal system. The Ghetto absorbed its scars and found expression through its own culture. The new Yiddish language reflected the religion, morality, and economic individuality of the Jews.

---

[2] A. A. Roback, *The Story of Yiddish Literature* (New York: Yiddish Scientific Institute, 1940), p. 36.

[3] *Ibid.*, p. 37.

[4] Nathaniel Buchwald, "Yiddish Literature," in the *Cambridge History of American Literature*, p. 599.

[5] A. A. Roback, p. 44.

Edward Sapir considered language and literature so closely related that he believed that "Language is the medium of literature as marble or bronze or clay are the materials of the sculptor."[6]

Just as the precise beginnings of the Yiddish language are somewhat misty, so the exact birth date of Yiddish literature can only be approximated. But most researchers agree that the literature is only slightly younger than the language.

S. J. Dorfsohn quotes the sociologist and historian Jindrick Kohn as having produced documentary evidence showing that Jews of the Siebenburgen area (Transylvania), more than a thousand years ago, developed and used a Swabian dialect that was an ancestor of Yiddish.[7]

Two of the earliest Yiddish manuscripts that have come to our attention are: 1) a medical leaflet on phlebotomy, written in 1396 and discovered in the archives of Cologne and, 2) a psalter of the year 1490.[8]

Constant persecutions and subsequent wanderings of the Jews accounts for the scarcity of ancient documents in Yiddish. Because of the secular nature of the writings, the language of the common people evidently did not find a place of importance in the synagogue libraries.[9]

Wherever the Ashkenazic Jews traveled they carried the Yiddish language and culture. Sixteenth-century Italy was briefly a center of Yiddish literature. During the 17th century, Amsterdam was a haven for Ashkenazic Jews. That city became a principal center for book publishing. In Amsterdam the first Yiddish newspaper was founded and there was a development of Yiddish theatrical art.

During the 17th century a shift of Jewish population from West to East was started. In the latter half of the 18th century and during the 19th century, Jewish life was more strongly oriented to the Slavic countries. Eastern Europe became the center of Yiddish

---

[6] *Language* (New York: Harcourt Brace and Co. [Harvest Book], 1949), p. 22.
[7] J. Dorfsohn, "Yiches Briv fun Yiddish fonem Tzentn Yorhundert," *Literarishe Bletter* (Yivo), July 22, 1932, Vol. 9, no. 30 [in Yiddish].
[8] Roback, p. 54.
[9] *Ibid.*, p. 55.

literature. The subsequent mass immigrations to America brought a stream of Yiddish cultural creativeness to these shores.[10]

Dissemination of early Yiddish literature was expensive. Wealthy women would engage scribes to copy, translate, and adapt material for special occasions. These scribes often went beyond the simple tasks of copying and authored some original passages and works. These were conglomerates of biblical stories, amusing sketches, and songs.

Since women were not obligated to learn Hebrew and participate in the affairs of the synagogue, the Yiddish stories provided them with biblical information, important rules of religious ritual to be observed by their sex, and miscellaneous hints and instructions for proper conduct and behavior.

Bards, minstrels, jesters, and troubadours carried the products of Yiddish literature farther and wider than the scribes. They brought romance and fanciful tales based on biblical and folkloristic themes into the homes and communities with pageantry and color.

Two popular biblical stories that were presented were the romantic and adventurous story about David in the *Samuel Book* and the eighty-stanza poem called *The Sacrifice of Isaac, or Jewish Descent.*

The beginnings of Jewish theater may also be traced back to those days. Lyrical material, humorous skits, and monologues were performed on festive occasions such as Purim and Chanukkah in the homes of wealthy Jewish families. A popular presentation was the *Dance of Death.*[11]

The invention of printing created a literary upswing in the 16th and early 17th centuries. The anonymous works of the scribes, bards, and jesters now took on authorship and reached hundreds of thousands of readers.[12]

The most interesting and dynamic figure of that period was the versatile scholar Elye Bocher (Elia Levita), 1469–1549. He was a

---

[10] Yudel Mark, "Yiddish Literature," in *The Jews: Their History, Culture and Religion*, Louis Finkelstein, ed. (New York: Harper & Brothers, 1949), p. 859.

[11] *Ibid.*, p. 862.

[12] *Ibid.*

Hebrew scholar, philologist, lexicographer, and wandering Yiddish poet. His distinction earned a call to the University of Paris and he served for thirteen years as Hebrew tutor to the eminent Cardinal Egidio de Viterbo.[13]

Professor Roback considers Bocher to be the "father of Yiddish literature." His two important romances were the *Bovo-Buch (Buovo d'Antona)* and *Paris un Viene.* As a result of wide popular usage Bovo became confused with *Bobbe* (Grandmother) and the *Bovo-Buch* became known as the *Bobbe-Maasse,* which contributed to the modern Yiddish expression denoting an old-wives' tale.[14]

The *Maasse-Buch* (Story Book), which appeared toward the end of the 16th century, was a collection of more than 250 stories, including talmudic legends and folk-tales. This work, which was first printed in Basle in 1602, had an important literary quality and replaced such lighter and less significant opuses of the bard-period as the *Kuh-Buch* (Cow-Book).[15]

During this period Prague developed as the center for Yiddish poetry. The best known lyricist of that city was Solomon Zinger. The poetry and legendry of the time were rich in imagination and dramatic content but there is no record of any emergence of significant dramatic works. However, Purim plays were developing, and we know of a rollicking comedy called *A Play About Deaf Yeklein, His Wife Kendlein and His Two Sons Fine.*[16]

To some degree the development of Yiddish literature paralleled the craving for entertainment of the Jewish masses. It was not surprising that the rabbis and preachers reacted negatively to this tendency. Many saw frivolity as a danger to piousness and the rigid precepts of the sacred law.

However, in large measure we are indebted, for the growth and survival of Yiddish as an independent language, to Rabbi Jacob of Janow. He met the need of those who lacked literacy in Hebrew (mostly women) by completing his *Tzehno-Urehno* toward the end

---

[13] Roback, p. 59. See also N. B. Minkoff, *Elye Bokher and His Bove-Bukh* (New York: M. Vaxer, Publishing, 1950).
[14] *Ibid.*, p. 60.
[15] Mark, p. 863.
[16] *Ibid.*, p. 865.

of the 16th century. This work, later known as the *Teitch-Chumesh,* became the pious women's Bible and simultaneously a story book to be read aloud in appropriate sections *(Sedra)* every Saturday. This book has been reprinted year after year since the early 17th century. Dr. Roback observes that this work "may easily take its place as the *best-seller* of all times in Yiddish, having reached some three hundred editions in less than three and a-half centuries. . . ."[17]

Social consciousness was expressed in the 17th century in the first publicistic book in Yiddish by Zalmen Ufenhausen, *Der Yiddisher Teriak (The Jewish Anti-Dote),* which was written in a dynamic style as a defence of the Jews against the libels of the apostate Friedrich (Samuel) Bronz.[18]

Amsterdam, the center of Jewish printing and publishing, was the birthplace, in 1686, of the first Yiddish newspaper, the *Kurant,* which appeared semi-weekly, on Tuesdays and Fridays.[19] (It is interesting to note that the first English daily newspaper, *The Postboy,* was not published until 1695, although an English weekly was inaugurated in 1622.)

During the latter half of the 17th and the early part of the 18th centuries the aura of the Cabbala, with its mystical and ascetic overtones, spread through Jewish life in Eastern Europe. The holy book of the Cabbala was the *Zohar,* not the Bible. An explanation of the *Zohar* appeared in Frankfort in 1711, by the Cracow cabbalist Zevi Hirsh Chotscz, as a morality book entitled *The Wealth of Israel.* There were also other works in Yiddish promulgated by the mystical Sabbatai Zevi movement; but no new literary forms or important works were produced to supplant the old favorites.[20]

Enlightenment was the mode in the eighteenth and nineteenth centuries. Among the Jews of that period the Haskalah movement was developing. While Yiddish originated in Western Europe, the cultural interchange of books and authors between East and West

---

[17] Roback, pp. 64–65.
[18] *Ibid.,* p. 68.
[19] *Ibid.,* p. 70.
[20] Mark, pp. 865–66.

continued to enrich the language and expand the culture until the middle of the 18th century. Then a break was evident. The Haskalah (Enlightenment) movement began in the western countries with the objective of freeing the Jew from the *spiritual Ghetto*. The Jewish intelligentsia of the West set out to become the saviors of the downtrodden people. While it was their objective to refine the manners, develop secular education, and improve the standard of living of their brothers, actually a serious blow was struck at the social existence of the Jew by weakening the status of his language.[21]

Jewish scholars destroyed and disparaged their own language. Contradicting its purpose, the Enlightenment movement in the West gave impetus to assimilation. Yiddish literature, language, and culture declined rapidly in Western Europe. It was, however, preserved in the East, where it later reached new heights of development.[22]

In traveling from West to East the Haskala movement took two roads. One went directly to Lithuania, the other (the principal one) went through Galicia to southern Russia and Poland.

The more realistic Maskilim (followers of Haskala) of the East were aware of the inevitable need to make use of Yiddish to disseminate their thought. But writers such as Mordecai Aaron Ginsburg attempted to re-Germanify the Yiddish. They were not very effective. Those who wrote in an idiomatic, spoken Yiddish were more successful. Examples are the works of the Barditchever Maskil Chaim Chaikl Hurvits and the famous Galician Mendl Satanover (1749–1826), whose influence was most extensive at the time.[23]

The Maskilim, seeking to elevate and improve the lot of the poor masses, directed their sharpest attack against the Chasidim. They used every type of literary form to accomplish their purpose, including witty comedies, satirical stories, and collections of "letters."

One consequence of this literary activity was the beginning of the dynamic and militant social writing in Yiddish that ran through the 19th century. Isaac Baer Levinson, the philosopher of Russian

---

[21] Roback, pp. 72–73.
[22] Mark, p. 868.
[23] *Ibid.*, pp. 870–71.

Haskala, wrote the *Heedless World,* an attack against the injustice within the Jewish community against the poor masses. The dramatic form was employed when the Polish Maskil, Efraim Fishlzon, wrote *Theatre of Chasidim,* a three-act, anti-Chasidic satirical comedy.[24]

While the Western European Jew was being drawn into the maelstrom of assimilation, and creativeness in Yiddish was dying, Eastern European Jewry was experiencing the surge of Chasidism. The Chasidic rabbi was the center of mystical, religious self-expression. Yiddish was most frequently the tongue of the Chasidic "courts." Famous Chasidic rabbis prayed and taught in Yiddish. The Chasidic rabbi became the subject of a rich, fanciful literature of praise. The great Bael Shem Tov (the *Besht*) had unique genius in telling allegorical stories and anecdotes. To the Chasidim these were elevated to a level of recited Torah.

The fervor of the *Chosid* was expressed through artistic creativeness in poetry, music, and dance. One of the most active courts was that of the Maggid of Mazaritscz, Reb Levi Yitchok Barditshever. He was an allegorical poet whose creations revealed great lyricism and a religious feeling of personal worth.[25]

Reb Nachman Brathslever (1772–1840), a grandson of the *Besht,* was one of the greatest Jewish narrators and mystic dreamers. He created a literature of mystical fantasy and ethical romanticism. His disciples believed that their leader revealed the secrets of the Torah and of life itself. After his death his pupil Nathan Brathslever published the stories of the teacher in a collection called *Narrative Tales* (1815).

Yudel Mark sees:

In the Narrative Tales . . . a link in the chain of the centuries-old narrative tradition begun with the Maaseh Book and to be continued in the works of Isaac Leibush Peretz.[26]

The Chasidic movement, with its emphasis on self-searching artistic creativeness through language, movement, music, and dance

---

[24] *Ibid.,* p. 871.
[25] *Ibid.,* p. 869.
[26] *Ibid.*

laid a strong foundation for subsequent Yiddish artistic expression in literature, music, and theater. In modern Yiddish theater the Chasidic breath was felt in the acting of Maurice Schwartz, in the staging and direction of Schwartz and Benno Schneider, and in the theatrical dancing of B. Zemach and Lillian Shapiro.

The grass-root strength of the Yiddish language possessed such unique power that it influenced the Maskillim of Eastern Europe. While Moses Mendelssohn, determined to eradicate the effects of Yiddish, translated and interpreted the Bible into German, Mendel Levin created a sensation with his translation of Proverbs and Psalms into the colloquial Yiddish of the Russian Jews. Levin's *Proverbs*, published in 1817, was considered an important step in the development of Yiddish, since he accomplished the self-appointed task of clearing the language of pretentious and stultifying Germanisms.

Y. Bick and J. Y. Perl supported Levin's position when it was attacked by the bitter foe of Yiddish, Tovye Feder. Feder, who was an extremist in the Enlightenment camp, was outnumbered, and he reluctantly agreed to withdraw his controversial pamphlets from circulation.[27]

There were many shadings and gradations falling between the two extremes in the Haskala. Numerous individuals were devoted to expressing their lofty philosophy and idealism in the language of the people. In doing so they often enriched, improved, and modernized Yiddish.

The two important writers of the early half of the 19th century who wrote exclusively in Yiddish were Yisroel Aksenfeld and Dr. Solomon Ettinger.

Aksenfeld (1787–1866) started writing in 1832 and by 1862 had completed more than thirty works. He was considered the first great storyteller of the Enlightenment. While he was prolific, he was not very effective in having his stories published. His dramatic works, however, caught on and were published. The play *The First Jewish Recruit* (a story about forced conscription into the Czarist army) was popular and was performed successfully as late as the 1920s and 1930s.

---

[27] Roback, p. 84.

Solomon Ettinger (1800–1865), a product of the Haskala, was important to Yiddish literature. He mustered his talent for the purpose of the literary art itself rather than for cultural or social ideology. He was the first to do important work in refining the language, creating new words and terms and polishing the literary style. Ettinger was one of the earliest authors to be concerned with the problems and feelings of the individual rather than the group. His style broadened the scope of Yiddish literature.

Dr. Ettinger's most important work is the dramatic comedy *Serkele* (*Little Sarah*). The central character is realistically and clearly drawn. The capable and valiant heroine dominates her household in a lusty drive for wealth and power. The style reflects folklore, idiom, and Jewish atmosphere. Ettinger borrowed some of the more primitive methods of the earlier Haskala comedies of Eichl and Wolfson. But his plot and technique were original and set a pattern for some of the important works for the Yiddish Theater to come later from the pens of Jacob Gordin and Abraham Goldfaden. Because Ettinger refused to compromise with the censorship of the Czarist regime, his works were not published until after his death.[28]

Isaac Meir Dyk (1814–1893) of Vilna reached a reading public of many tens of thousands. His style was that of a teacher and morality writer. He had a German obsession and felt that he could refine the people by translating German expressions and idiom into good Yiddish. But he was also an effective storyteller and he served as a link toward the later literature.

Eliezer Tzvi Tsveifl, a Haskala conservative, stirred up his colleagues at the Zhitomir rabbinical school to write in Yiddish. He created good narratives in that language. He was influenced considerably by Mendl Satanover, and in turn affected the later work of the great Mendele Moicher Sforim. Abraham Gotlober, the wandering Haskala writer, contributed a comedy to the dramatic literature, *The Veil, or Two Weddings in One Night,* which was clearly influenced by Ettinger's *Serkele.*

Bringing to a close, as it were, the many generations of bardic singers, was the work of Velvl Zbarazer and Berl Broder. Zbarazer's

---

[28] Mark, pp. 872–73.

songs were a combination of old lyric balladry and modern Yiddish writing. Broder was a bardic entrepreneur. He organized a cabaret troupe, singing his repertory, dispensing his minstrelsy all over Galicia, southern Russia, and Poland.

The Singers of Brody were the beginning of Yiddish "Little-Theater." In Warsaw there were attempts at organization of theatrical companies (1838–39 and 1866–70). But there was not yet a permanent professional Yiddish Theater. However the drive to create for a theater in Yiddish was continuously given expression. Many of the plays were performed by amateur groups or were read aloud for entertainment at various small gatherings.[29]

Although we shall not here deal with the very vital factor of the Yiddish press and journalism, it is important to mention that in 1862 the Yiddish publication, *Voices of the Messenger,* appeared in Odessa. From that time on the rapid development of Yiddish journalism became an integral part of the development of the language, the literature, and the drama.[30]

Up to this point we were concerned with the nascent and developmental stages of the Yiddish language. We now come to the last decades of the 19th and the beginning of the 20th centuries.

Jewish life and Yiddish cultural development were subject to the vicissitudes of history. The last part of the 19th century brought many changes to the Eastern European countries where the Jewish population was heavily concentrated.

"Emancipation" of the Russian peasant (1861) and industrial and economic development, encouraged a shift of population from the smaller towns to the larger cities. New commerce and trade created some opportunities for Jewish participation. The devlopment of a working class brought new thought and a struggle for more freedom and a vision of a better life.

These factors, coupled with the new life in America set the

29 *Ibid.*, p. 874.
30 *Ibid.*

stage for a tremendous advance and growth of Yiddish literature and artistic creativeness, serving the millions of Jews then concentrated on both sides of the Atlantic, for whom Yiddish was the mother-tongue.

The most vital creators and molders of the Yiddish language were the "Big Three" of Yiddish literature: Mendele Moicher Sforim, Sholem Aleichem, and Yitschok Leibush Peretz. Each of these writers would warrant many pages in any evaluation of the Yiddish language and literature.

Our object was to sketch the genesis and metamorphosis of the language. Since the scope of our work does not include a complete survey of the literature *per se,* we must regrettably conclude this section of the essay with a brutally reduced summary of the three "greats."

Sholem Jacob Abramovich (1835–1917), when he began writing in Yiddish (1864), took the pen name of Mendele Moicher Sforim, which is somewhat more than just a pseudonym since it means literally Mendele the book-seller. Mendele, known as the grandfather of Yiddish literature, is responsible for the standardization of modern literary Yiddish. He integrated the Ukrainian and Lithuanian dialects, blending words and word-usages to produce an even language pattern. Up until Mendele, style and technique were neglected in favor of plot and dialogue. Mendele's stories were rewritten, polished, and revised. His language structure is still accepted as a standard.

Mendele was a satirist, a humorist, a social critic, a story-teller. He exposed the ugliness that resulted from oppression and persecution. The motifs of the *Haskala* are reflected in his work. We see the backwardness of the ghetto. But his personalities are realistic figures. His aim is to serve, not disparage, the people.

Mendele did not start writing in Yiddish until he was almost thirty years old. It is most interesting that he, who is considered to be more responsible than any other individual for the emergence of modern Yiddish as a standardized literary language, came to his task not because of his idealization of the language but rather because of his deep desire to contribute to the welfare of his poor people. This is pointedly illustrated in a brief autobiographical quotation from Mendele by A. A. Roback:[31]

> I closely observe the mode of life of our people and want to relate it afterwards in the sacred tongue. But the majority of the people don't understand this language and speak Yiddish. Of what good then are the writer's efforts and his soul's desire if he cannot serve the people? This question, 'For whom am I laboring?' did not give me any peace and caused me a good deal of embarrassment. . . . Our writers, the linguists, looked at Yiddish disdainfully, and with the greatest contempt. . . . The thought that I should humiliate myself by writing in Yiddish distressed me considerably, but the eagerness to be of service overcame my false pride, and I said to myself 'Come what may, I shall take the part of the outcast Yiddish and I will be of some use to my people.'

Mendele's important works are: *Die Takse* (The Meat Tax); *The Little Man; The Wishing Ring; Fishke The Lame; The Travels of Benjamin The Third; The Old Mare;* and his autobiography: *Schloime, Son of Reb Chaim.*[32]

Sholem Aleichem was born Sholem Rabinowitch (1859–1916), in the Ukraine. He was easily the most popular and beloved of the Yiddish writers. His writing was characterized by graphic, colorful expression and wealth of *spoken* idiom.

Sholem Aleichem gave life and folk character to the Yiddish language. He breathed the soul of the Jewish people into literary form. He was a humorist; but his was a Jewish humor. He found the key, and richly adapted the language to express social and economic oppression and historical lamentation, through humor and laughter.

He was a master of characterization and drew his characters from every social group, always with a philosophical depth of understanding, never belittling life.[33]

---

[31] Roback, pp. 99–100.
[32] Yudel Mark, pp. 875–77.
[33] Roback, pp. 107–24.

Sholem Aleichem's important works are: *Stempeniu; Yossele Solovay; Little People With Little Ideas; Menachem Mendl; Tevya the Dairyman; Song of Songs; Mottl Paysie, the Cantor's Son;* and the autobiographical novel, *From the Fair.*

His style was admirably suited to dramatization. His dramatic works that were most performed were *The Great Winnings;* and *Scattered Far and Wide.*[34]

The last of the three classicists, Yitschok Leibush Peretz (1852–1915), born in the Polish city of Zamosc, was the most worldly and intellectual of the trio. His greatest medium was the short story. He also created drama and poetry.

Peretz's contribution to Yiddish was that he elevated the language to a cultural plane equal to the major European languages. He "crashed the barrier" between East and West, between Jew and non-Jew. His work is very widely translated and is more easily translatable because of its greater universal character and style. His more advanced work is woven in a romantic and symbolical style.

At the height of his career Peretz embellished the Chasidic theme. But while he idealized the Chasidic rabbi, his own saintly Jews were a wood-cutter and a water-carrier.

Peretz devoted his organizational, as well as his literary talents, to modernizing and advancing Jewish life through the use of the Yiddish language. His popular dramas are: *The Golden Chain;* and *A Night at the Old Market-Place.* His *Folk-Tales* are most memorable. *Bontche Shveig;* and *If Not Higher* are examples of his best writing. Peretz's contemporary younger writers honored him with the title "Father of Modern Yiddish Literature."[35]

Yudel Mark writes that[36]

the constellation of Mendele, Sholem Aleichem and Peretz is a happy combination of mutually complementary temperaments. . . . All three created a new centripetal force linking, through literature, the present and the past, the intellectual and the untutored, the Jew of one region and the Jew of another.

[34] Mark, pp. 880–81.
[35] Roback, pp. 125–47; and Mark, pp. 881–83.
[36] Pp. 882–83.

Mendele created a linguistic structure, giving Yiddish a form so that it could be brought up to contemporary standards of creative literature. He was truly the "grandfather," setting the child on its feet so that it might continue to grow and stride into the 20th century, under the loving and expert parentage of Sholem Aleichem, Y. L. Peretz, and hundreds of talented and devoted creators of prose, poetry, and drama on both sides of the Atlantic Ocean.

Thus Yiddish, which started as a daily tool, meeting the needs of the Jews in Medieval Europe, became an instrument for religious education and ideological and secular enlightenment, evolving into the national mother-tongue and medium of creative expression for millions of Jews.

7

The Social Role of The
Yiddish Press

There are in the United States about 1,500 foreign language newspapers and magazines with an aggregate circulation of about eight million, which are printed in 33 languages and are found in every State in the Union.[1]

No other foreign-language press has succeeded in reflecting so much of the intimate life of the people which it represents, or reacted so powerfully upon the opinion, thought, and aspirations of the public for which it exists. This is particularly true of the Yiddish daily newspapers in New York City.[2]

A young scholar studying the life of Louis Marshall tells us that when Marshall settled down to his busy life in New York he learned Yiddish so that he could regularly read one or two Yiddish papers.[3]

The Yiddish press in the United States is about ninety years old; and for all the gloomy forecasts which have been repeated periodically, indeed almost annually, it is here to stay.[4]

---

[1] Mordecai Soltes, "The Yiddish Press—An Americanizing Agency," in the *American Jewish Year Book*, 26: 167. The reference in the quotation is to the year 1920.

[2] Robert Ezra Park, *The Immigrant Press and its Control* (New York: 1922), p. 89.

[3] Morton Rosenstock, *Louis Marshall, Defender of Jewish Rights* (Detroit: Wayne State University Press, 1965), p. 46.

[4] A. A. Roback, "The Epic of Yiddish Periodicals," in the *Chicago Jewish Forum* (Chicago, 1959), p. 221.

W. I. Thomas learned Yiddish about ten years before he died so that he could read the Yiddish press.[5] Obviously the Yiddish press has been a subject of serious interest to community leaders, journalists, and social scientists.

This chapter of our work is devoted to a study of the Yiddish press as an integral part of the life of the immigrant community. The press is seen here as a product of the old culture adapted to a new environment and new needs. In the process of this adaptation the culture and the language grew and developed as part of the fabric of the new life.

As did everything else in American Jewish life, the American Yiddish press had its beginning in Europe. Two important publications should be mentioned as early predecessors:

Kol Mevasser was established as a weekly journal in Odessa, October, 1862, by Alexander Zederbaum. As this chapter develops we will see that one of the unique functions of the Yiddish press was to "make a home" for the contemporary writers. This publication played an important role in that respect. It carried the first works of Mendele Moicher Sforim, I. Y. Linetski, J. L. Gordon, and Yehoshuo Lifshitz.

> *Kol Mevasser* brought to the fore many readers . . . the number of writers also increased, and their influence became stronger and more noticeable.[6]

The *Warshaver Yiddishe Zeitung* was organized five years later (1867) and concerned itself particularly with the encouragement of young Yiddish poets. It published much of their verse. Notable among the poets were Eliyokum Zunser and Abraham Goldfaden (who later played an important role in bringing Yiddish theater to America). Much of their lyrical work was set to music, creating a body of ever-popular Yiddish folkloristic balladry, which is still remembered today.[7]

---

[5] *Ibid.*, p. 228.
[6] Samuel Niger, "Yiddish Literature in the Past Two Hundred Years," in *Jewish People: Past and Present* (New York: Jewish Encyclopedic Handbooks [CYCO], 1952), 3: 178.
[7] *Ibid.*, p. 180.

Mendele (the "grandfather" of modern Yiddish literature) described the 1860's as the "springtime," a period that encouraged Jews with hopes of education and emancipation. However, the reactionary period of the 80's in Russia, the anti-Jewish decrees, the bloody pogroms, undermined the old ideals of the "Enlightenment." Yiddish literature took a new turn. S. Niger describes it thus:

> Some intellectuals started a return to the people, and in part also to its language and literature. Nor did they return to awaken and enlighten the people. They came back to find a spiritual home for themselves. The new intelligentsia did not go to the people to rid it of its faults, as the Maskilim had gone. Instead they returned to nourish their spirits on the people's customs and traditions. They came not to preach, but to comfort and encourage, and thus to find comfort and courage themselves. . . .[8]

In a period of political reaction, the Jewish literature experienced a national resurgence. This movement found expression through new literary outlets. Three Yiddish Journals were important in that period:

1. The *Yiddishes Folksblatt* (the Jewish People's Weekly, A. Zederbaum, ed.) St. Petersburg, 1881–1890. Formerly *Kol Mevasser*.
2. *Der Hoiz-Fraind* (Friend of the Home; publisher: Mordecai Spector) Warsaw, 1888–89, 1894–96.
3. *Di Yiddishe Folks-Bibliotek* (A review of literature and popular science, issued by Sholem Aleichem) Kiev, 1888–89. Y. L. Peretz made his debut in this publication.

These publications helped to crystallize a new Yiddish literature. Many who previously wrote in Hebrew or Russian were creating in *Yiddish*.

During the early years of migration from Eastern Europe, London was sometimes a way station for Jewish writers and intellectuals who eventually came to America. This was the course taken by Morris Winchevsky, who later became an important personality in

---

[8] *Ibid.*, p. 184.

American Yiddish literature, education, and the labor movement. In London, 1884, Winchevsky published the weekly: *Dos Poilishe Yidl.* I have encountered speculative comments questioning the use of the term "Yidl" by Winchevsky. The thought expressed was that "Yidl" had a derogatory or cynical meaning. I do not read it that way, but rather as I would read "Yingl" for a "youth." In other words "Yidl" here would carry the feeling of a sympathetic diminutive for "Yid"—a Jew.

One year later Winchevsky also published the monthly journal, *Der Arbeter Fraind.* This publication was read with interest and eagerness in the United States, where the Yiddish labor movement was taking form. In a sense, it paved the way for that type of labor journalism in America.

In the 1870s the Jewish community in America represented a cultural potpourri. The Russian-Polish immigration was still just a trickle, but it was beginning to bring to America Jews who were exclusively Yiddish speaking. Hebrew was used and understood by the few who were learned. German was still an important conversational language.

Thus, the press in the very early 70s had a utilitarian purpose and a commercial character. It is well expressed in the editorial of the quadri-lingual (English, German, Hebrew, and Yiddish) *Hebrew News,* of April 5, 1871:

> Hundreds of thousands of our brothers live here. Those arriving every day speak no other language but the one spoken among our brothers in Russia and Poland. Despite their intelligence and civic spirit, these Jews cannot express their desires in matters of state, for they know no other language. For this reason and because they want to know what is going on in their old home, they need a newspaper in their own language. The publishers therefore plan to issue this paper in a clear and easy Hebrew, a simple *Jewish-German,* and a lucid English.[9]

---

[9] Cited by Kalman Marmor, article in the *Morning Freiheit* (Yiddish), Oct. 26, 1946.

This Hebrew editorial states clearly the purpose of reaching *all* Jews. The interesting social phenomenon is the acknowledgment of the need for a "simple Jewish-German" (that is, Yiddish) together with the other more prestigious languages.

Two exclusively Yiddish publications made their appearance at that time:

Di Yiddishe Zeitung, March 1, 1870, edited and published by J. K. Buchner; and

Di Post, August, 1871, published by Henry Hirsh Berenstein and edited by Zevi Gershuni.[10]

K. Z. Sarasohn, who was destined to play an active role in Yiddish newspaper publishing for several decades, created the weekly newspaper *Yiddishe Gazetten* in 1874. (This publication later became the weekly supplement of Sarasohn's daily *Tageblatt*.) Its language was simple, "primitive," Germanized Yiddish. However, it made a unique contribution to Yiddish literature in America because it led to the publication of the first Yiddish book in the United States.[11]

The *Gazetten* encouraged the printing of poetry in its columns. Among several poetic contributors, Jacob Zvi Sobol attracted some attention in 1876. The next year Sobol published his book of Hebrew and Yiddish verses. The book was also notable because it contained at least one long poem dealing with the *social position* of the new Jewish immigrant. This was the first literary reaction to the problems of the newcomers.[12]

The decade of the 80s represented an early turning point in the development of the Yiddish press. There was a proliferation of weeklies. In addition to the *New Yorker Yiddishe Folkzeitunq*,

10 Kalman Marmor, *Der Onhoib Fun Der Yiddisher Literature in Amerike* (Yiddish) (New York: 1944), pp. 10–11; and Morris Schappes, *The Jews in the United States* (New York: 1958), p. 270.
11 Samuel Niger, "Yiddish Culture," in *Jewish People: Past and Present*, 4 (New York: Jewish Encyclopedic Handbooks [CYCO], 1955): 276.
12 Ber Green, "Di Yiddishe Literatur in Amerike" in *Ykuf Almanach*, Nachman Meisel, ed., New York, 1967, p. 182; and Hasye Cooperman, "Yiddish Literature in the United States," in *The American Jews: a Reappraisal*, Oscar I. Janowsky, ed. (Philadelphia: 1964), p. 194.

there appeared the *Yiddishes Vochnblatt*, the *New Yorker Yiddishe Illustrirte Zeitunq*, and the *Folks-Advokat*.[13]

The advent of the *New Yorker Yiddishe Folkzeitunq* was the most meaningful because it represented a serious effort at publishing a labor socialist weekly. The two editors, Breslawsky and Mintz earnestly endeavored to advance the cause of socialism and Jewish nationalism simultaneously.[14] The *Folkzeitunq* supported the young United Hebrew Trades, and its popularity among the Yiddish workers caught on. One contemporary writer tells us that the paper had a circulation of 5,000 readers.[15]

The most militant effort at publication lasted only a few weeks. The young fiery socialist, Abraham Cahan, collaborated with Charles Rayefsky to publish *Di Naie Zeit*. They ran out of financial resources since the "money partner" (Rayefsky) was only a worker in a soap factory at a salary of $6 per week.[16]

It is important to remember that these early efforts at a labor press occurred against a social background where the sweat shop was developing at its ugliest and the condition of Jewish labor was probably at its worst.[17] Thus, the first noteworthy contribution of the 80s was the beginning of a labor press.

The second milestone of the 80s was the general improvement of the language, the establishment of Yiddish as the legitimate language of the people, and the use of the language as a stated goal for reaching the people. This attitude was also reflected in the less literary weeklies; as stated by the simple, but popular writer Getzel Zelikovitch (1863–1926), in one of his columns in the *Yiddishes Vochnblatt*:

We must speak to the reader in the language he understands best, the language in which lullabies were sung to him, the language in which he mumbled his first words before he was weaned, the

13 Niger, 4: 284–85.
14 J. M. Budish and George Soule, *The New Unionism in the Clothing Industry* (New York: Harcourt, Brace & Howe, 1920), p. 240.
15 Melech Epstein, *Jewish Labor in the U.S.A.*, 1 (New York: 1950) : 144.
16 *Ibid.*, and Budish.
17 See Marmor.

language with which he took his first step into the everyday world, the language in which he conducts his daily affairs and in which he sighed, flattered, mourned, rejoiced and loved.[18]

There was a conscious attempt at a "cleansing process" of the language. Socially it was now representative of a larger, ethnically definable, Yiddish population, deserving of a more refined language of its own. There was less dependence on German; Yiddish was becoming less "Daitchmerish."

In 1886, six years before he started work on the *Yiddish Dictionary*, Alexander Harkavy published the little book *Di Yiddishe-Daitshe Shprach*, in which he took the position that Yiddish was as good as any other language. This attracted responses in the press and was prominently featured in the *Folkzeitunq*.[19]

Regarding the painful process of its becoming a self-sufficient language, the journalist and critic Samuel Niger writes of Yiddish:

The Yiddish periodicals gradually began to free themselves from the German and Germanized Yiddish which had contaminated the American Yiddish press in its first period. Though they did not recover from this protracted disease very easily, the fear of "*Yiddish* Yiddish" began to vanish.[20]

The third event of the decade was historically important to Yiddish journalism, namely the establishment of a continuously functioning daily newspaper. Sarasohn's founding of the *Yiddishes Tageblatt* in 1885 marked the beginning of a vital institution in the society of American Jews—the daily newspaper.

The *Tageblatt* (sometimes called the *Jewish Daily News*), a conservative, traditional, orthodox paper continued publication until it merged with Sapperstein's ideologically similar *Morgn Zhurnal*

---

[18] A. R. Malachi, "Yiddishes Vochnblatt," in J. Shatsky, ed., *Zamlbuch Lekoved dem 250-tn Yovyl far der Yiddisher Presse* (Yiddish) (New York: 1937), p. 181.
[19] Shlomo Noble, "The Image of the American Jews," in *Vivo Annual of Jewish Social Studies*, no. 9 (1954), p. 96; and *New Yorker Yiddishe Folks Zeitunq*, Sept. 18, 1889.
[20] 4: 283.

in 1928. The *Morgn Zhurnal, Jewish Morning Journal,* had been
started in 1902.[21]

A fourth important fact was that, very early, Yiddish literature
became identified with the press. Each was dependent upon, and
part of, the other. The literary personalities were also the journalists:

> . . . Yiddish literature was virtually synonymous with the Yiddish
> press, and it was the press that paved the way for purely literary
> creation and enjoyment. The press helped develop the language;
> it taught the writers to write and the readers to read.
> . . . Nearly all novels, short stories, poems and critical essays were
> published in the press before appearing in book form—if they
> ever attained this distinction.[22]

This characteristic of the press and the literature continued. In
1902 a contemporary American journalist studying the Ghetto
wrote:

> . . . The Yiddish press, particularly the socialist branch of it, is
> an educative element of great value in the Ghetto. It . . . has
> largely replaced the rabbi in the position of teacher of the
> people. . . .
> They give more space proportionately than any American paper
> to pure literature . . . and to scientific articles of popular char-
> acter.[23]

This unique relationship of press to literature, and of the public
to its writers has been illustrated many times. For example when
the celebrated Sholem Aleichem came to America in 1915, he was
given a staff position in the *Tog* with a regular weekly salary. Many
other noted writers published first in the press. Some outstanding
examples are: Jacob Gordin, Sholem Asch, Abraham Reisen, Z.
Shneur, I. J. Singer, David Pinski, Leon Kobrin, Z. Libin, and
Joseph Opatoshu.

[21] Oscar and Mary F. Handlin, "A Century of Jewish Immigration to the
United States," in the *American Jewish Year Book,* 50: 9, and Samuel Niger,
4: 282–83.
[22] Niger, 3: 191–92.
[23] Hutchins Hapgood, *The Spirit of the Ghetto* (New York: Funk & Wag-
nall, 1902), pp. 178–79.

Culturally, the 90s were the years when traditional piety and conservatism were challenged by secularism and socialism in American Yiddish society. S. Niger feels that this "revolution" against the existing order was most sharply expressed by the press of that period.[24]

Accepting that premise, a study of the Yiddish press from the 90s on, would really entail an analysis of the Yiddish labor press and its relationship to the labor movement. Therefore a separate section of this chapter is categorically devoted to that task. However for chronological purposes we will here list the most important publications of that period:

The dailies were the *Abendblatt* (1894–1902): *Morgn Zhurnal* (founded 1902); *Forverts* (founded 1897); and in Chicago, the *Yiddisher Kurier* (1892–1944). There were several minor, ephemeral dailies. One recent chronicler says that at the turn of the century there were as many as six dailies competing for readers.[25]

The following periodicals should be mentioned:

Di Zukunft: Edited by Philip Krantz for the Yiddish-speaking section of the Socialist Workers Party (1892–93); edited by Abraham Cahan (1894–97); then it appeared irregularly and with interruption until 1913, at which time it was taken over by the Forward Association and edited by A. Liessin, until his death.

Di Freie Geselshaft: A monthly journal dedicated to advanced ideas in literature and science; (1895–1902 and again in 1910); Editors: L. Moisseiff, M. Katz, and S. Yanovski.

Di Naie Zeit: (1898–99) published by the Yiddish socialists who sided with the *Abendblatt* against the *Forverts*. Editors: B. Feigenbaum and Philip Krantz.

Der Naier Geist: (1897–98) A monthly, edited by the scholar Alexander Harkavy, and devoted to science, literature, and art.

Folkskalender, also edited and published by Harkavy, (1895–1900). *Emes*, appeared briefly in Boston (1895–96).

---

[24] 4: 288.
[25] Moses Rischin, *The Promised City: New York's Jews 1870–1914* (Cambridge: Harvard University Press, 1962), p. 123.

To this list should be added the radical weeklies *Arbeterzeitung* and *Freie Arbeter Shtimme*, which are discussed more fully in another part of this chapter.[26]

After 1905, in addition to the socially conservative and the radical journals, a third type began to appear. The new publications were reflections of the nationalistic, zionistic, or "culturistic" thought. A partial list is:

Dos Yiddishe Folk (1909). A Zionist periodical

Der Arbeter (1904). National, cultural, socialist orientation

Dos Folk (1905) Jewish Territorialist. (The *Territorialists* were militant socialist-nationalists who believed in the principle of establishing an independent, autonomous, Jewish state but that it did not necessarily have to be in Palestine.)

Der Yiddisher Kemfer (1906) Socialist-Zionist ideology.

Dos Naie Lebn (1908), edited and guided by Chaim Zhitlowsky.

Dos Naie Land (1911), edited and guided by Abraham Reisen.

Literatur un Lebn (1915), edited and guided by Abraham Reisen.

In an earlier chapter we have dealt with the 19th-century movement of "Enlightenment" among European Jews. At the outset Yiddish did not come to play a role in that process. At first many Jewish "emancipated" intellectuals became deeply involved in German, Hebrew, and Russian culture. Some intellectuals had to learn or re-learn Yiddish to conquer their estrangement from the Jewish people and Jewish culture. The case of Vladimir Medem is classic.[27]

During the decades of Eastern European immigration, the drama of a developing culture was stimulating an intellectual leadership that was itself seeking a framework or format within which it could

---

26 Niger, 4: 288.
27 See Vladimir Medem, "The Youth of a Bundist," in Lucy S. Dawidowicz, ed., *The Golden Tradition* (New York: Holt, Rinehart & Winston, 1967), pp. 426–34.

shape itself so that it could live and breathe, and infuse the mass of people with their life and spirit.

The Yiddish labor press played a special role in that drama. I find the following quotation from a leading authority on Yiddish literature and culture most expressive:

> Attracting intellectuals previously alienated from the Jewish environment and the Yiddish language to Jewish cultural activity was a substantial accomplishment. For this accomplishment we are indebted to the radical Yiddish press and social ideas and ideals it propagated. Writers and speakers whose medium of expression had been Russian, Hebrew or German studied to become Yiddish writers or speakers. Where once there had been an intelligentsia without a people and a people without an intelligentsia, the Yiddish press and the social movement it represented gave the intelligentsia a people and the people an intellectual leadership. Both, the intellectuals and the people, benefited greatly. Creative individuals found an audience, and the spiritually thirsty masses found an opportunity to quench their thirst.[28]

In that sense, Yiddish language, culture, labor press, and social movements are interrelated phenomena. With that thought in mind, it should be meaningful to devote the following pages to an examination of the Yiddish radical press and the umbilical cord that tied it to the Jewish labor movement.

"The year [1886] of labor's supreme effort to gain its basic rights through industrial warfare, was also marked by a concerted effort to achieve the same results through the ballot."[29]

In that year an interesting crystallization of organized labor political action developed: the formation of the New York State United Labor Party. This was a uniquely broad coalition of trade unionists, Socialists, German Social Laborites, united in a common program with Henry George (the native American "single-taxer") as the standard bearer. The Jewish Workers' Verein, an organization of

---

[28] Niger, 4: 289.
[29] Melech Epstein, *Jewish Labor in the U.S.A.*, 2 vols., (New York: 1950 and 1953), 1: 147.

young intellectual Jewish socialists, threw themselves into the work enthusiastically.

The labor groups (A. F. of L. and Knights of Labor) and the German socialists had their press organs. The young Yiddish weekly, the *New Yorker Yiddishe Folkszeitung*, assumed that role for the Yiddish socialists. It conducted a campaign urging workers to become citizens so that they would not remain disenfranchised. It appealed to its readers:

> Seize the bright ray, Jewish workers, lend your ears to the sound of liberty, merge yourselves with the representatives of the labor movement and join the fighters for general human rights.[30]

It was an energizing stimulus. The Jewish Workers' Verein went on to form a Henry George Political Committee. They organized Jewish storekeepers and peddlers, as well as workers, into an active string of Henry George Clubs.

The non-Yiddish American Jewish press was hostile to the Jewish Workers Verein. The *American Hebrew* attacked it as a harmful anarchist organization.[31] This, under the shadow of the *Haymarket Affair*, was a bitter and dangerous accusation.

In the Yiddish press the *Folkszeitung*'s opposite was Sarasohn's conservative *Yiddishe Gazetten*, which attempted to alienate the conservative and orthodox Jew against the socialists. Epstein sees the *Gazetten* attack against the *Verein* as having been "vulgar . . . and loudmouthed." Among other things they attacked the socialists as being "no better than Christian missionaries."[32]

Henry George lost the mayoralty campaign to Tammany's Abraham Hewitt by only 22,000 votes (with Tammany men as vote-counters), and Teddy Roosevelt ran third.

Although the dynamic and productive work of the coalition was hailed as a victory, it broke up after the election because of basic theoretical differences among the constituent groups. The Yiddish socialists parted ways with Henry George. But they had received

30 *Ibid.*, p. 150.
31 *Ibid.*, pp. 154–55.
32 *Ibid.*, pp. 163–65.

their political "baptism," and a young Yiddish press had already begun to play a role in the life of the Jewish community and its social and political struggles.

Through Branch No. 8 and through the "Russian" Branch No. 17, the Jewish Socialists became, after the split with the mid-western German Social Democrats, integrally involved in the work of the Socialist Labor Party.

The orientation was to merge political, trade union, and cultural-educational activities into a single basic Marxist context. Here again the new Yiddish press was continuing to play a part. The United Hebrew Trades was organized in 1888; two years later it had its Yiddish organ, the *Arbeter Zeitung*; in 1892 the monthly *Zukunft* made its appearance.[33]

When the *Yiddishe Geverkshaften* (United Hebrew Trades) joined with the Socialist Labor Party in an effective May Day demonstration in 1890, involving almost ten thousand Jewish workers, the *Arbeter Zeitung* reported through the enthusiastic pen of the revolutionary Abraham Cahan:

This imposing demonstration is the beginning of the great revolution which will overthrow the capitalist system and erect a new society on the foundation of genuine liberty, equality and fraternity. Standing here, between the palaces of the millionaires on Fifth Avenue, the rich stores of Broadway on one side and the dark miserable tenement section on the other side, let us swear, brothers, that we will lay down our lives to abolish the present inequality.[34]

With intensification of Yiddish Socialist activity (participation in the International Congress in Paris, 1889; the extension of the *Geverkshaften* activities to the formation of the Hebrew Labor Federation of the United States and Canada), press reactions became stronger and partisanship sharper. For example, in the *Arbeter*

[33] *Ibid.*, pp. 163–65.
[34] *Arbeter Zeitung* (Yiddish), May 9, 1890.

Zeitung, December 5, 1890, Louis Miller sharply attacked the "capitalist press for hiding behind socialist trappings."

Epstein interprets this as an attack against the benign and friendly pro-labor weeklies, *Folks Advokat* and *Folkszeitung*.[35] This may be so, but it would seem more reasonable to assume that when Miller was referring to "capitalist papers" he was more likely thinking of the real hostility of the Anglo-Jewish press and the conservative *Tageblatt*.

There was considerable opposition in labor circles to the Jewish socialists' policy of organizing Jewish workers separately. When Joseph Barondess split with his Jewish comrades on this question of "segregation," his views were published by the monthly *Zukunft*:

> The Central Labor Union has accused us of dishonesty. . . . You preach, "Workers of all lands unite," and in practice you split the strength of organized labor by segregating our German and Jewish co-workers into separate bodies. If we permit this segregation, then the Irish, the English and workers of other nationalities will also separate, the measure of unity that the American workers have achieved after so many years will be entirely destroyed.[36]

However, Jewish labor organization, politically and in the unions, continued, and ultimately became an important force in the American labor movement, and in the American Jewish community, because of a cultural factor—Yiddish.

When the *Hebrew Labor Federation* was organized in 1890 there was not yet a *Yiddishist* movement in America. There were only the beginnings of a young literature and a new theater. It was only four years since Alexander Harkavy had taken the courageous position that "Yiddish was as good as any other language."[37] It was two years before he started his labors on the *Yiddish Dictionary*.

Yiddish and Yiddish organization was not then approached either as an ideal, nor as an ideology, but rather as a cultural (utilitarian, if you wish) tool. As the simple journalist and novelist, Zelikovitch,

---

[35] P. 184.
[36] *Zukunft* (Yiddish), April, 1906.
[37] Alexander Harkavy, *Di Yiddishe—Daitshe Shprach* (Yiddish) (New York: 1886).

pleaded in the *Vochnblatt* to ". . . speak to the reader in the language he knows best . . . the language in which he mumbled his first words before he was weaned . . . the language in which he conducts his daily affairs," the *Hebrew Labor Federation* proclaimed:

> . . . we, Yiddish-speaking citizens, are able to work amongst Jewish immigrants, only because we speak their language and are acquainted with their lives, solely for that reason are we creating this Jewish body. The Yiddish language is our tool . . .[38]

The Yiddish labor press was diligently and effectively dedicated to serving this principle.

During the early and middle years of the 90s, bitter fratricidal battles developed between the Jewish socialists and their anarchist counterparts in the unions. At this point it is inappropriate to develop the details of the conflict. But in brief, starting with ideological differences and quickly spreading to jurisdictional competition, the conflict spread from Hebrew typographical workers to the garment trades and wherever there were Jewish workers. Strange coalitions developed where anarchists cooperated with the conservative American Federation of Labor, while the socialists worked through the Knights of Labor.

What is of interest to us here is that out of this vehement strife another Yiddish labor publication was born. The anarchist *Freie Arbeter Shtimme* started publication in July, 1890, four months after the appearance of the *Arbeter Zeitung*.

Jewish labor now had two Yiddish weeklies that were dedicated to the ideal and purpose of educating, teaching, and organizing the poor working masses. However, it would appear that they both spent the greater part of their energies in efforts to annihilate each other.[39] (This precedent seems to have persisted for many crucial decades after the turn of the century during each period of division and splintering in Jewish labor ranks.)

---

[38] Herz Burgin, *History of the Jewish Labor Movement* (New York: United Hebrew Trades, 1915), p. 167; and Epstein, p. 183.
[39] Epstein, p. 207.

In response to the Anarchists' successful organization of Jewish printers in the A. F. of L., the *Arbeter Zeitung* exploded:

> Gompers with his collector 'Yoshke' [reference to *Joseph* Barondess] of the cloakmakers, together with the scab boss, a member of the Central Labor Union, are making the rounds of the printers and publishers of Jewish papers and demanding that they fire the typesetters of the old bona fide Hebrew American Printers Union, and employ the scabs of the fake union.[40]

Though the anarchists participated in the May Day demonstration in 1892, one year earlier the *Freie Arbeter Shtimme* grotesquely described a spirited May Day march of thousands of Jews through the East Side as follows:

> . . . Poor little Jews, shriveled and withered, march, wearing comic colored caps. American ruffians meet them with pebbles. . . . The street cars do not want to stop in front of this ridiculous procession. The chosen marshals, with red bands, sit hunched on the emaciated nags and remind one of poor Don Quixote.[41]

The battle became even more bitter during the economic crisis of 1893. Regrettably, neither the anarchists nor the socialists had an effective program of leadership for the country's unemployed at a time when "General Coxey" led his "army" to Washington.

The anarchists' *Freie Arbeter Shtimme* foundered and ceased publication after a couple of years. The new *Freie Arbeter Shtimme*, edited by S. Yanofsky, was reorganized in 1899. Ostensibly it was still anarchist but its character had changed, for indeed the character and role of the Yiddish anarchists had been altered at the turn of the century. The weekly devoted itself to the publication of theoretical, classical, and literary works.[42] It went on to become an important vehicle for some of the most interesting Yiddish literary contributions in America.

After the *Freie Arbeter Shtimme* suspended publication, the

---

40 *Arbeter Zeitung* (Yiddish), no. 29, 1893.

41 *Freie Arbeter Shtimme* (Yiddish), no. 46, May 8, 1891.

42 See Hapgood, pp. 190–94, for a contemporary's description of the Jewish anarchists.

Yiddish labor press consisted of the following: the weekly *Arbeter Zeitung* (1890), the daily *Abendblatt* (1894), and the monthly magazine *Zukunft* (1892).

The *Arbeter Zeitung* and the *Abendblatt* (essentially the organs of DeLeon's S. L. P.) were published and controlled by a small group of militants organized as the Arbeter Zeitung Publishing Association. A schism was developing in the ranks of the S. L. P. that was sharpened by "DeLeon's dogmatism and his peremptory behavior towards his opponents."[43]

The publishing association was controlled by militant Yiddish labor leaders who had risen from the ranks of shop workers. They were loyal to DeLeon and were influential in decision-making in the U. H. T., in the unions, and in the party. The journalists and writers (the intellectuals) were not admitted to policy-making positions. Under the leadership of Abraham Cahan and L. Miller they revolted, demanding greater freedom of action (Winchevsky spoke in verse of a "free spirit") and that "the press be turned over to a delegated body of all labor organization."[44]

In 1894, locally (in New York) and at a convention in Boston of Jewish Social Laborites, Cahan openly challenged DeLeon's policies. Though he was defeated, he was permitted to continue as editor of *Zukunft*. Compromises were attempted but it was becoming clearer that a new split in the ranks of the Yiddish socialists was imminent. This time the struggle was destined to give birth to a new daily, which ultimately wielded great power and exercised unique influence over the Jewish labor movement during its most crucial decades of development.

At a meeting of the association, January, 1897, the die was cast. Under the leadership of Cahan, Miller, Winchevsky, and Zametkin, a minority of 52 walked out, issuing a call to a convention to found a new daily "based on socialism, and of trade unions, based on class struggle . . . to launch a paper that shall honestly serve the movement and not be the property of a clique with income for a dozen business socialists."[45]

---

[43] Epstein, p. 259.
[44] Hapgood, pp. 186–89; and *ibid.*
[45] Burgin, p. 167.

The *Tageblatt* gleefully took its swipe at the labor press commenting, "The *genossen* are now revealing the rottenness of those who want to improve the world."[46]

Socialists throughout the country were dumbfounded and confused. To many this seemed to be a battle between rival cliques for personal power. Efforts to patch things up notwithstanding, on the 22nd of April, 1897 the first issue of the *Forverts* (Jewish Daily Forward) appeared on the streets of the East Side.[47]

The battle was on. The old *Abendblatt* and the new *Forverts* engaged in a duel of verbiage that included personal slander, accusations of heinous crimes against labor, and general vituperative mudslinging. Both sides were well skilled in these techniques, having been experienced veterans of the recent battles with the anarchists.

Abraham Cahan, who was selected as the first editor of the new publication, believed in fighting the enemy more subtly, with strategies of silent contempt. He left the helm of the paper after eight months; then he returned in four years and eight months to edit the *Forverts* for the rest of his long life.

The defection of the New York Jewish Socialists coincided with the national rift that pitted the Victor Berger-Eugene Debs coalition against DeLeon. After being expelled from the S. L. P., the Jewish group, headed by Dr. I. A. Hourvich and Meyer London organized their group as Branch No. 1 of the Social Democratic Party. The *Forverts* continued in this political camp, following the currents eventually into the new Socialist Party under the leadership of Eugene V. Debs.

The *Abendblatt* fought a losing battle with the *Forverts*. Aside from the overall reasons for the decline of the S. L. P. (which cannot here be considered) the position of the *Abendblatt* on two issues of interest to the Jewish population helped to seal its doom.

The first was the Spanish-American War (1898), the second the Dreyfus affair (1894–1904). In each case the *Abendblatt* "played it ideologically"; the *Forverts* "played it by ear."

The *Abendblatt*, as well as the S. L. P., correctly pointed to the

---

[46] Quoted by Epstein, p. 265.
[47] *Ibid.*, p. 266.

imperialistic interests, rather than the altruistic motives of the United States in driving Spain out of the Western Hemisphere. However the Jewish press and public opinion were handily mobilized in the war against Spain because of the historic Jewish hatred (four centuries) for Spain.

The *Forverts* cleverly glossed over the investment capital aspects of the war, stressing the inhuman character of Spanish rule. They threw themselves into the war propaganda, stressing the unity-in-war-time theme and even attacked DeLeon as being a "Spaniard."

In the Dreyfus affair the *Forverts* took advantage of the Social Laborites' floundering over the issues.

At first the Social Laborites took a cool position on the question because as they saw it, it had no direct bearing on the class struggle in France. When they finally brought themselves to supporting Emile Zola in his fight for Justice in 1898, this is what the *Abendblatt* wrote:

> We cannot join in the trumpeting of all Jewish papers who are of the opinion that because Dreyfus is a Jew, they must shout that he is innocent, that he is a victim of intrigue by the enemies of Israel. . . .

> However, although Dreyfus' honorable origin as an offspring of Jacob is for us no proof of his innocence, there is nevertheless another witness to whose testimony we cannot remain lukewarm,—this is Emile Zola.

> From the depths of our hearts we wish success to Emile Zola in his unceasing endeavors to expose the injustices committed by the military. Not so much to free the unjustly accused man, Dreyfus. Oh! How can you compare a single instance of the wrongs suffered by one man from capitalism and its main support, militarism, with the wrongs that millions of workers suffer day and night? Still, we wish Zola success in his efforts to destroy that unrestrained idolatry for all things military, the mightiest mainstay of capitalism and all prevailing injustices, compared to which the entire Dreyfus scandal is as unimportant as a drop in the sea.[48]

---

[48] *Abendblatt* (Yiddish), Jan. 4, 1898.

This, in 1898 when the Dreyfus affair was the burning *cause
célèbre* to Jews all over the world, helped seal the fate of the *Abendblatt*. (The *Forverts* played this and all other popular issues to the
hilt.) Melech Epstein closes a chapter on the *Abendblatt*:

> The position of the *Abendblatt* became untenable. Its repeated
> calls for support met but little response. On the 23rd of April,
> 1902, five years after the appearance of its rival, it had to cease
> publication.[49]

The *Forverts* was born in a "battle" against "Association" control
of the *Abendblatt*. After a few months of an attempt at manage-
ment by a committee of organizations, they found this method far
from ideal and promptly founded a *Forverts Association*. When
Cahan returned to the editorship he was given a free hand. That
was his condition.[50]

Friends and foes alike concede that the *Forverts* was built around
a "Cahan cult." This is not strange because Cahan's acknowledged
pragmatism was completely compatible with the early statements
of policy of the newspaper, even when Cahan was out as editor.

The paper was gaining readers but still desperately needed funds
for expansion. In a policy statement, appealing for public support,
it announced:

> . . . Inasmuch as there are various trends within the socialist
> movement itself, the *Forverts* will remain an organ for free dis-
> cussion of all the views arising from the common belief in so-
> cialism.

> However, the *Forverts* will support *that* socialist movement which
> will, under the prevailing conditions, prove itself to be the best;
> that is, which will more reflect the free, flexible principles of
> the *Forverts*.[51]

Thus, the *Forverts* would decide hereafter what is good socialism
and what is not. And when Cahan returned, he decided, more often

---

49 P. 272.
50 *Ibid.*, p. 324.
51 *Forverts* (Yiddish), April 21, 1901.

than not, that "that which succeeds is good" and that "nothing succeeds like success." And when often, what resulted was not "socialism" at all, it was still good, if it was good for Cahan and good for *Forverts* circulation.

It appears that cunning and pragmatic leadership alone was not responsible for the phenomenal growth of this institution. As the paper was struggling to get out of its financial straits, the floodgates of Eastern European, Yiddish immigration were opening wide.

Between 1901 and 1910 almost one million Jews arrived from Russia, Austria-Hungary, and Rumania. The peak years were 1905 with 129,910; 1906 with 153,748; and 1907 with 149,182.[52]

When the paper triumphantly announced a paid circulation of 60,000 in 1906, it was a year when 153,748 new prospective readers arrived.

Also, the type of immigrant was changing. Up until 1905 a substantial number came to work a few years and return home with some money. They were less stable. "Only in 1905, after the failure of the premature revolution in Russia, did a new type of Jewish immigrant begin to reach the United States, one who had destroyed all his bridges behind him. Almost at once did these newcomers, disappointed in the Russian revolution, eagerly respond to the appeal of the American rhythm and to the very breadth of the land. . . ."[53]

These were the immigrants who began swelling the ranks of Jewish skilled and semi-skilled workers; they became the backbone of the *Forverts'* strength.

Cahan's bureaucracy still had a major stumbling block to overcome in its steady and phenomenal growth. It came very soon.

The feud with Jacob Gordin (discussed elsewhere in this chapter) and the break with his old friend and collaborator, L. Miller,

---

[52] S. Joseph, *Jewish Immigration to the United States from 1881 to 1910* (New York: Columbia University Press, 1914), p. 162; and Mark Wischnitzer, "The Impact of American Jewry on Jewish Life Abroad," in *Jewish People: Past and Present* (New York), 4: 289.

[53] Joseph Opatoshu, "Fifty Years of Yiddish Literature in the United States," in *Yivo Annual of Jewish Social Studies*, no. 9, 1954, p. 76; and Niger, p. 297.

were manifestations of Cahan's inability to share the stage with those of equal stature.

"Gradually, Zametkin, Winchefsky and Feigenbaum, veterans who deserved well of the movement, were relegated to the background, to the displeasure of their admirers, and a breach with L. Miller, the most ambitious, became inevitable."[54]

This break resulted in the formation of still another Yiddish daily newspaper. Miller, supported by Morris Winchefsky, Jacob Gordin and others, left the *Forverts* and in 1905 organized the *Warheit* with himself as editor.[55]

S. Niger seems to think that though the *Warheit* changed from socialist to a non-partisan orientation, it still was a vital and fiery publication.[56] However, there is some evidence to support Epstein's contention that Miller was opportunistic in offering his paper to Tammany Hall for election publicity and advertising, and that "Miller, anxious to beat Cahan, soon surpassed the *Forverts* in human interest topics, both in amount and in low quality."[57] The fact that the impeccable Morris Winchefsky and some of his better supporters left Miller very early would help to bear out that position.

The Warheit continued to appear as an independent publication with nationalistic and Zionist excursions. But after declining popularity it was sold to the new *Day* (*Der Tog*), which was organized in 1914.

The split in the socialist ranks that earlier isolated Daniel DeLeon from the dissident Social-Democrats and Socialists, ultimately leaving him with a small Socialist Labor Party, did not prevent him from militantly opposing the otherwise unified effort of Socialists to elect Morris Hillquit to the U. S. Congress from the 9th district in 1908. Hillquit subsequently charged that DeLeon's rival candidacy was responsible for his defeat.

The *Forverts* campaigned ardently for Hillquit and for Socialism,

[54] Epstein, p. 329.
[55] *Ibid.*, p. 332.
[56] Niger, p. 297.
[57] Epstein, p. 332.

with broad support of many important independent and reform personalities. But the other two Yiddish dailies (The *Tageblatt* and the *Warheit*) concerted their efforts in a special anti-Hillquit campaign charging that Hillquit was not truly representative of Judaism and Jewish interests.[58] It would appear reasonable that this strong opposition of the conservative press was the real factor in Socialism's defeat on the East side that year, rather than DeLeon's dissident one percent of the total vote.[59]

In 1914, the time and the man were different. Meyer London was the Socialist standard bearer and the campaigners were organized workers in the garment industry, the Workmen's Circle, and the *Forverts*. The Jewish immigrants of the lower East Side knew London intimately. He was their neighbor, their labor lawyer, who waived his fees and helped them pay their rent when they could not. But it took more than that to break the Tammany control in the 12th Congressional District.

The conservative *Tageblatt*, which had opposed London, came out with an "extra" edition announcing Tammany's victory. But two o'clock in the morning Tammany conceded the election to London.

London's immense popularity alone could never have beaten the Tammany machine. The victory was a consequence of meticulous and arduous organization. Rischin feels that the "lion's share" of the credit goes to the *Forverts*:

The *Forward's* house-to-house electioneering in three consecutive Congressional campaigns (with its pages listing the names and addresses of every one of the district's 12,000 registered voters) finally brought victory to the East Side's beloved labor tribune whose devotion to the cause of the workingman was matched only by his passion for knowledge. . . .[60]

Epstein describes the scene that election night:

At dusk, crowds had begun moving towards Rutger's Square, facing the *Forward* building. . . . Seward Park and the side

58 *Ibid.*, pp. 344–47.
59 Rischin, p. 234.
60 *Ibid.*, p. 235.

streets were jammed with people waiting impatiently for the election returns to be flashed on a screen in front of the *Forward*. About eleven o'clock, the *Tageblatt* published an extra, announcing the victory of M. Goldfogle, the Tammany candidate. The crowds refused to accept the finality of the announcement. . . . Thousands remained on the square . . . Tammany leaders conceded London's election . . . joy broke out. . . . London was brought to the square at four o'clock in the morning.[61]

The *Forverts* building mentioned in the above citation was probably the "crowning glory" in the growth of that institution, both physically and symbolically. The ten-story impressive building was erected in 1912 at 175 East Broadway, towering over the old tenements in that neighborhood.

The Yiddish labor movement, swelled by the crest of the immigration wave, flocked to the spacious halls and meeting rooms of the new edifice for meetings, concerts, lectures, and campaign functions. The building served as headquarters of the United Hebrew Trades and the Workmen's Circle, and many other organizations. It was the site for the most festive balls and also the most important funeral gatherings for Jewish labor leaders. The building became the hub of the Yiddish labor movement and the newspaper went up to a circulation of 200,000 in 1917.[62]

The next political conflict and split in the ranks of Jewish labor again deeply involved the *Forverts* and resulted in the founding of still another Yiddish daily. This development carries us into the 20s and 30s, a period that falls outside the scope of this present work. To deal with this subject properly, we would also be obliged to go deeply into the role of the *Forverts* and the Socialists during World War I. To do this, in addition to the areas of study already selected for analysis by the writer, would involve us in a rambling work. Obviously, we must draw our lines of limitation. Thus, the following "mini-sketch" must suffice:

Majority American Jewish opinion was for noninvolvement in

---

61 Epstein, pp. 359–60.
62 *Ibid.*, p. 323; also see N. W. Ayer & Son, Newspaper Directory.

the war, for neutrality. Some of the opinion was interpreted as being pro-German, while in reality it was strongly anti-Czarist.

On December 10th, 1914, Cahan stated in the *Forverts* that a Russian defeat would represent progress for Jews and that it would be fortunate for all of Europe (especially the Jews) if Germany would take Lithuania and Poland. This anti-Czarist approach was almost universal in the Yiddish press.

American socialists were militantly anti-war. Jewish socialist groups, including unions and the Workmen's Circle, were all against the war. While the *Forverts* had some reservations it went along for neutrality.

With the overthrow of the Czar, March, 1917, American Jewish attitudes changed, they became pro-Ally. The entire Yiddish press: the *Tageblatt*, the *Morgn Zhurnal*, the *Tog*, and the *Warheit* urged American and Jewish preparedness and organized the Jewish League of American Patriots to advance their pro-war cause.

The *Forverts*, supporting the socialist position, remained anti-war. But after the United States declared war, even while the Socialist Party stood by its St. Louis Convention anti-war position, the *Forverts* mildly and inconspicuously printed a little front-page box statement announcing that the position on the war must be altered since we are now in it.

While the overthrow of the Czar and the Russian Revolution were received jubilantly, the conservative Yiddish press strongly opposed the subsequent Bolshevik victories. Although the *Forverts* staff included pro-Menshevik elements, Cahan's position and that of the *Forverts* was at the outset friendly to the new revolutionary Leninist regime.

The Menshevik-Bolshevik split had its repercussion in the American socialist movement. The prolonged battle between "left-wing" and "right-wing" Jewish socialists reached a breaking point in 1919. The Jewish Socialist Federation (left) split with the Socialist Party, which was led by Morris Hillquit. The Federation leadership included most of the writers and intellectuals. When they left they took such important *Forverts* contributors as B. Hoffman, H. Rogoff, and M. Olgin.[63]

---

[63] Epstein, 2: 111-13.

In Cahan's absence (he was in Europe) the *Forverts* Association fired the six important writers who had sided with the "left" majority in the Jewish Socialist Federation.

The stage was set for the founding of a new Yiddish daily. On April 22, 1922 the *Freiheit* (or *Morning Freiheit*) appeared as the organ of the Jewish Federation of the Workers Party. After several months Rogoff and Hoffman went back to the *Forverts*; Olgin remained as editor with a dedicated staff of writers and workers.[64]

This new daily ultimately became the Yiddish organ of the Jewish communists and sympathizers. The battle of the next two decades in the Jewish labor movement, with the "right" polarized around Cahan and the *Forverts* and the "left" grouped around Olgin and the *Freiheit*, are now part of well documented recent history.

The Yiddish theater played a unique role in the life of the community. An analysis of this institution must be undertaken separately. It should be mentioned, however, that some of the most important writers for the theater (notably Jacob Gordin) were also journalists. There was a functional bond that tied the institutions of press and theater together.

Of course, the press "reviewed" the theater and assigned this task to its best journalists. Certainly, the press carried the advertising and announcements of the theater world. It is also interesting that the young radical (and financially poor) press used the theater for "fund raising" purposes, as did all the societies, fraternal orders, labor unions, and so on of the day.

Hapgood describes the process whereby on Mondays through Thursdays the theaters would sell all their tickets only to organizations (at reduced rates) that would resell them to its members and the general public at a profit. (This obviously was the beginning of the "theater benefit" practice that has persisted until today.) He notes that: ". . . the *newspapers* of the Ghetto have their constituency, which sometimes hires the theater. Two or three hundred dollars is

---

[64] Morris Schappes, *The Jews in the United States* (New York: Tercentenary Book Committee, 1958), p. 191.

paid to the theater by the guild, which then sells the tickets among the faithful for a good price."[65]

He cites an example:

"The anarchistic propaganda (group) hired the Windsor Theater for the establishment of a fund to start the *Freie Arbeiter Shtimme*, an anarchistic newspaper." He obviously is referring to the year 1899 when the weekly was re-established after a few years of suspended publication.[66]

The following may be an illuminating example of how the papers used the theater in their "smear" competition with each other:

During the early years of the new century the ideological hostility and competition for readers between the *Forverts* and the *Tageblatt* had hit a peak. Sarasohn's paper, of course, was a business venture. It had a profit motive, but it did have an ideological orientation: that of traditional, conservative Judaism—the maintenance of the status quo in society as well as in religion. The *Forverts* was technically not a "party organ" as the *Arbeter Zeitung* and the *Abendblatt* had been, but as a free institution it was publicly committed to represent the interests of labor and socialism.

Thus, in every area of Jewish life, cultural as well as political and economic, the two large journals fought each other tooth and nail. The domain of the theater and drama was no exception.

Jacob Gordin, the "reformer" of the Yiddish theater, was a controversial figure. His prolific work went off into many directions but he was determined to become the dramatist of the people. He was a critic of society, of the established rich, and of the status quo. Gordin became the prime target of the *Tageblatt* and the other conservative Jewish papers. At the same time his popularity grew tremendously with the workers and radical intellectuals. Hapgood wrote: "The thinking element of the Ghetto is largely Socialistic, and the Socialists flock to the theater when the Gordin type of play is produced."[67]

---

[65] Hapgood, pp. 114–15.
[66] *Ibid.*, p. 141.
[67] *Ibid.*

However, labor press reaction to Gordin was mixed. When his classic "Mirele Efros" was produced on August 19, 1898, Morris Winchevsky expressed the greatest emotional enthusiasm in the *Forverts*. The editor (then L. Miller) allowed the publication of six enthusiastic articles about the drama.[68]

Cahan's reactions to Gordin were strange. At first the two writers were collaborating journalists on the new *Forverts* at its founding, in 1897. Then, while Gordin was building his reputation, during his own years away from the *Forverts*, Cahan remained rather quiet and aloof. When Cahan returned to the editorship, he alternated between silence and bitter attack and criticism. Marmor attributes this to a personal feud between the two men that started with a verbal exchange at one of Gordin's performances in 1895, and a critical review that Gordin later wrote about Cahan's "Yekel."[69]

Despite the Cahan-Gordin feud, the *Forverts* contrived a situation where it would use a Gordin play that was being bitterly smeared by the *Tageblatt* to sensationally attack its journalistic rival and create dramatic publicity for itself. Thus it would prove its strength among the people, and conduct a profitable "theater benefit" to boost its financial resources. It engaged the Thalia Theater for a performance of Gordin's "Yoisaime" (Orphan Girl) with the following front-page publicity:

HOW THE ARROGANCE AND CHEAPNESS OF THE APOSTATE AND THE ALMS-BOX, WILL BE EXHIBITED ON THE STAGE OF THE THALIA THEATRE. A DEMONSTRATION IN FAVOR OF THE *FORVERTS*.

It continues:

The pigs and piglings of the "sewer-rag" (Tageblatt) are squealing that the "Yoisaime" is a sacrilegious play, no person, no Jew will ever again permit himself to view it. All are running from it as if from a pestilence. The Forverts is therefore arranging the production of the "Yoisaime" for its "benefit" to expose the

68 Kalman Marmor, *Yakov Gordin* (Yiddish), (New York: Ykuf, 1953), pp. 100–6.
69 *Ibid.*, pp. 96–99.

cheapness and arrogance of this slander, to express our deepest disdain against the "pen-and-ink cadets" of the Tageblatt . . . and to prove which of us is the most powerful in the (Jewish) quarter.[70]

Of course the "benefit" was a sellout. It was a great success for the *Forverts*!

The Yiddish press was virtually a mirror of the day-to-day activities in the community, in the unions, in the fraternal groups and landsmanshaften. A random copy of the *Forverts* of November 28, 1909 offers a good example:

On page six there is a featured column headed: *IN THE UNIONS AND IN THE FARAINS*, in which there is complete listing of all meetings and functions involving union and landsmanshaft organizations. On the same page there are paid advertisements and announcements:

1. Mattress Makers Union of Greater New York
2. Minsker group
3. Tarashter Literary Circle—Literary evening
4. Socialist Party sponsors class in physics
5. Workmen's Circle meeting
6. Brooklyn Butchers workers meeting
7. United Hebrew Trades meeting
8. Landsmanshaft Balls
9. Concert and Literary Evening in support of striking clerks
10. Concert sponsored by the Socialist-Territorialists
11. Emma Goldman will lecture (in Yiddish) on "Is the Family Holy?"
12. Morris Hillquit will lecture (in Yiddish) "Principal Problems of American Socialism"

On another page large ads featured the forthcoming:

1. FORVERTS BALL
2. BUND BALL

---

[70] Quoted by Marmor, pp. 141–42.

3. PINSKER RADICAL ASSOCIATION BALL
4. POALE ZION BALL

On the same page with a column entitled *Meetings and Lectures of the Evening*, there was a prominent column headed: *"Farshvundene Menner"* (men who are lost or have deserted), with pictures of the missing "culprits."

Thus the newspaper columns became a directory for the reader. In his favorite Yiddish paper he could locate the meeting, the lecture, the concert, or the ball that suited his social, intellectual, and emotional needs.

A scholar who made a study of letter-writing to the Yiddish press interviewed an editorial secretary of a Yiddish daily on the question of reader involvement with the press regarding their personal lives and problems. The following replies to the interviewer are interesting:[71]

> When one comes here he is in a strange country. He has friends who are busy and occupied. They cannot pay much attention to him. He reads the *Forverts*, sees that the *Forverts* answers so many questions, so he comes, he comes here. It is friendly here. Russian immigrants and Polish immigrants come here. Those looking for landsleit can locate them through the *Forverts*.

> They look upon it (their newspaper) as their best friend and advisor. They have faith in their newspaper. Only today we got 20 calls on whether to say 'Yiskor' today. . . . They call about their mother's 'Yohrtzeit.' They get all the information from the paper. Once there was a fake insurance company. We printed the news. We had avalanches of fire insurance policies, hundreds of people waiting to see if they had the right policy. . . . If he needs something he calls up the *Forverts* or sends a telegram or a letter. What form of a monument should he make for a 'matzeivah.' The paper always plays a remarkable role in their lives.

The writer of the same study further confirmed that the readers come freely to the "open offices" of the Yiddish dailies:[72]

---

[71] George Wolfe, *The Bintl Brief of the Jewish Daily Forward as an Immigrant Institution and a Research Source* (New York: Graduate School for Jewish Social Work, 1933). (Interview with Mr. Gottlieb, Editorial Secretary of the *Forverts*.) PP. 190–91.
[72] *Ibid.*, p. 187.

The offices of New York's Yiddish newspapers . . . are open to all, and the readers take advantage of it. Perhaps even more frequent than personal visits are the numerous letters requesting information, advice, financial assistance, etc., received by every Yiddish newspaper daily, some of which are answered privately. . . . Then too, the relationship between writer and reader is close. Staff members of every Yiddish newspaper appear daily as speakers at meetings and can be seen and talked to.

Of course, not all letters could be answered personally. Consequently most of the papers developed regularly featured sections or columns devoted to mail that evoked general interest.

The *Warheit,* mentioned earlier in this study, which often tried to out-do the *Forverts* in sensationalism and popular appeal, developed two features in 1906:

1. a column, "Shtimmen fun Folk" (the Voice of the People)
2. a feature rather fully called, "Tragedyess, Komedyess un Poshete Tzoress fun Emmesn Lebn" (Tragedies, Comedies and just Plain Trouble Taken From Real Life)

Both were "letters-to-the-editor" departments.

The *Morgn Zhurnal* started a "Bintl Brief"-type column, edited by Meyer Sunshine in the 1920s, which was taken over by Dr. Klorman in 1926. Dr. Klorman made a serious effort to answer questions relating to courtship problems, economic problems, and questions involving religion, Sabbath observance, and education.

The *Day* (*Tog*) had a staff member whose chief function it was to answer questions and give advice orally and personally. But this became too popular, therefore in January, 1930, a written column called "Men and Women" was established. From the name of the column one can see that here too was an effort to deal with the universally popular personal and family problems that obviously interested the readers so much.[73]

The most successful column of this type, the one that has attracted the greatest attention of readers and critics, students and scholars, is the *Forverts'* famous Bintl Brief (Packet of Letters), which was started in 1906.

In the Appendix to this chapter we have reproduced a small

---

[73] *Ibid.,* pp. 163–69.

representative number of letters, selected from some of the earliest
written. The samples are preceded by our analysis of Wolfe's "Analytic Index." This should help throw into tighter focus the range
of subject matter contained in the letters.

The Bintl Brief is a bit of journalistic and sociological "curiosa."
It has, at one and the same time, attracted the greatest reader-
response and the strongest literary cynicism. It has evoked the contempt of the intelligentsia, but has attracted W. I. Thomas to translate and study 1,000 letters (study unpublished) before his death.

For the purpose of this study, no further analysis of this feature
of the Yiddish press is necessary. The Bintl Brief column stands
as a comment on itself. It is presented here as evidence of the
tremendous degree to which the readers feel personally involved
with their favorite Yiddish newspapers.

One of the fundamental social facts that must be considered is
that during the developmental decades of the Yiddish press there
were not one but two Jewish communities in New York. One was
the older: the established, the middle and upper class, the German.
Its members were the "up-towners." The other was the new: the
Yiddish immigrants, the sweat-shop workers, the Eastern Europeans.
Those were the "down-towners."

It will be illuminating to look at some of the descriptive comments regarding the two communities and how they related to each
other:

Moses Rischin quotes Mencken as saying:[74]

'Uptown' and 'downtown' separated employers from employees,
desirable from undesirables, 'classes' from 'masses,' 'Americans'
from 'foreigners.'

Recently Stephen Birmingham drew a composite profile of the
uptowners in his *Our Crowd*. A few comments follow:[75]

---

[74] Rischin, p. 97.
[75] Birmingham, *Our Crowd* (New York: Harper & Row, 1967), pp. 295-96.

 וולאד.מעדעם

1879 – 1923

Vladimir Medem, Russian Socialist intellectual who learned Yiddish so that he could offer leadership to the Jewish masses (About 1920)

Abraham Cahan, young and fiery Marxist agitator in the early 1890s, later editor of the Forverts

Kalman Marmor standing alongside the legendary Morris Winchevsky (1926)

These four pictures represent "shtetl" (village) types. The East European "shtetl" was the main source of Jewish immigration to the United States during the period 1880–1920.

The village coppersmith

Yeshiva "bocher" (Young Talmudic scholar)

"Bal-Agole" (*Literally, man of the road*), *the hauler of the road*

The "shtetl" marketplace

Aspects of New York's Lower East Side

Editorial offices of the Freie Arbeter Shtimme *in the 90s* (*An East-Side basement*)

Sholem's Café (A popular Yiddish writers' meeting place on the East Side's Division Street, at the turn of the century)

Cloakmakers' strike meeting near the Forverts *building (During the strike of 1910)*

New arrivals dressed for a holiday occasion (Posed on the steps of the HIAS building on East Broadway during World War I)

"Succoth" on the East Side

ארבייטער !

ווי-לט איהר וויסען יעדע האלבע שטונדע דיא עלעק־

שיאן רעטוירנס פון דער ס. ד. פ. ? וויללט איהר ער־

פאהרען אין צייט דעם אויספאהל פון דעם עלעקצּיאן

פיר אלֶלע אנֶדערע פארטייען און אין דער זעלבער צייט

הערען דיא בעסטע יודישע רעדנער וויא דיא נֶאנֶאסען:

ב. פיינֶגענֶבוים, מ. ווינֶטשעוֶוסקי, זאמעֶטֶקין, בֶאראנֶדעֶסֶס, דר. גירזֶדֶאנֶסקי, עדֶלין און אנֶדערע ?

דֶאן קומֶמֶט אין מאסֶסֶען אין

נֶיו אירוֶוינֶג הֶאלל

214-220 ברום ססטרים

אנֶפֶאנֶגֶס פֶונֶקט 8 אוֶהר אבֶענֶדֶס,

דיעֶנֶסֶטֶאג, דֶען 6טֶען נֶאוֶועֶמֶבער, 1900

איינֶטֶריט:

אום צו דעקֶען דיא אויסֶגֶאבֶען, 5 סעֶנֶט.

דֶאס קֶאמֶיטֶעֶע.

Political circulars during the election campaign in New York City in 1900. The Yiddish circular appeals to the workers to join the "best Yiddish speakers" at an election eve rally in support of the Social Democratic Party at the New Irving Hall on Broome St.

SOCIAL
DEMOCRATIC PARTY.

GRAND
MASS-MEETING

to be held at

Pleasure Palace Hall,
62 PITT ST.,

On Friday, October 19th, 1900
AT 8 P. M.

Alexander Jonas, candidate for Congress, William Edlin, candidate for Assembly and M. Sametkin will address the meeting.

COME ONE, COME ALL.

Julius Litwak, Printer. 24 Delancey St., N. Y.

William Edlin, active socialist who later became editor of The Tog (The Jewish Day), was a featured "speaker" at each of the meetings.

פאַרלאַמענטאַרישע װולם

וויא צו פיהרען מיטיננען פון יוניאָנס, לאָדזשען
און אַנדערע פעראיינען.

❖

בעאַרבייטעט נאך דיא בעסטע ביכער
מכח פּאַרלאַמענטאַריזמוס.

הערוויסגינעבען פון דיא „אַרבייטער צייטונג".

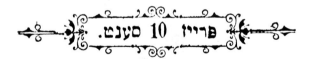

פּרייז 10 סענט.

NEW YORK.
ARBEITER-ZEITUNG Union Printing,
81 Ludlow Street.
1891

Cover of a brochure entitled: Parliamentary Rules—How to Conduct meetings of Unions, lodges, and other societies, published by the radical Yiddish Arbeter Zeitung as a service to the Jewish workers (1891)

Schiff, for all his giving, lacked the common touch. His buttoned, German sense of superiority was too great. When faced with a Russian (Jew), his blue eyes glazed.

Uptown, at Mount Sinai Hospital, though 90 percent of the patients were Eastern European Jews, there was a rule that no Eastern European could be admitted to the staff.

Though the Germans gave away millions to the Russian immigrants, they never invited them to their dinner parties, clubs, dances.

The uptowners were stricken with a fear that identification with the uncouth East Side Jew would threaten their social position. This was echoed in the Anglo-Jewish press where the Russian Jews were sometimes referred to with racist overtones, as "wild Asiatics":

Are we waiting for the natural process of assimilation between Orientalism and Americanism? This will perhaps never take place.[76]
The thoroughly acclimated American Jew . . . has no religious, social or intellectual sympathies with them (the Russian Jews). He is closer to the Christian sentiment around him than to the Judaism of these miserable darkened Hebrews.[77]

But the uptowners did come downtown. They came to help their coreligionists through relief, reform, education, and social work. Birmingham's colorful description follows:[78]

. . . Clearly the Germans would have preferred it if the Russians had not come, but there they were. . . . The next logical step, as far as the Germans were concerned, was to try, if possible, to reshape those shabby immigrants along what the Germans considered "acceptable" German lines—to clean the immigrants up, dust them off, and get them to behave and look as much like Americans as possible. The East Side settlement houses, originally little more than delousing stations, were set up.

---

[76] *American Hebrew*, December 6, 1889.
[77] *Hebrew Standard*, June 15, 1894.
[78] Birmingham, p. 298.

In 1902 Hapgood wrote his sweet, colorful, but sometimes naïve little book about the Jewish Ghetto. In a summary of the daily Yiddish newspapers appearing at that time he says:[79]

> Recently a sixth daily, *The Jewish World,* has been organized under favorable auspices. Its avowed policy is to bridge the chasm which exists between fathers and sons in the Ghetto; to make the sons more Hebraic and the fathers more American; the sons more conservative and the fathers more progressive.

It would be more precise to say that if the publishers of *Di Yiddishe Velt (The Jewish World)* intended to "bridge a chasm" or fill a hiatus, it was the closing of the cultural gap that separated "uptown" from "downtown." The details of this enterprise on the part of the legendary "uptowner," Louis Marshall, are described in a fascinating article by Lucy S. Dawidowicz.[80]

Louis Marshall was earnestly involved with reform on the lower East Side. The institution that he and the other native "uptown" Jews were sponsoring in the Ghetto for this purpose was the Educational Alliance, directed professionally by David Blaustein. Through Blaustein, Marshall learned that the East Side Maggid (orator) Zvi Hirsch Masliansky had acquired the plant of the defunct *Abendblatt.* Marshall organized a fund to establish a new paper, *The Jewish World,* for the avowed purpose of Americanizing and elevating the Jews of the quarter. Masliansky was publisher, with a unique staff (or "motley crew") of writers consisting of socialists, Hebraists, anarchists, Zionists, and poets.

"Among the twenty-five original subscribers to the fund for the *Jewish World* at least half were millionaires."[81] Donations ranged from $500 to $5,000 and the list was headed by Schiff, Warburg, Lewisohn, Marshall, and Guggenheim. "The board consisted of five uptown trustees, with one vote each, and three downtown trustees,

---

[79] Hapgood, pp. 188–89.
[80] Lucy S. Dawidowicz, "Louis Marshall's Yiddish Newspaper, *The Jewish World*—A Study in Contrasts," in *Jewish Social Studies,* no. 25 (1963), pp. 102–32.
[81] *Ibid.,* p. 105.

presumably sharing two votes."[82] Without subterfuge, Marshall made it clear that he aimed to control the publication and set its policy:[83]

> It is understood that the people whom I represent are to have control of the newspaper and to dictate its policy which is to make the paper everything that the existing papers are not, namely clean, wholesome, religious in tone; the advocate of all that makes good citizenship, and so far as politics are concerned, absolutely independent.

If Hapgood's description of the contemporary Yiddish newspapers had validity, then Marshall and his "maggid" were faced with a formidable job:

> They are controlled by passion rather than by wealth. It is their joy to pounce on controlling wealth and to take the side of the laborer against the employer. . . . The remark by one of the Jewish editors, that the 'Yiddish newspaper's freedom of expression is limited by the penal code alone,' has its relative truth.[84]

Marshall wanted to change this, to become "clean, wholesome, and religious in tone." He believed in the high-minded idea of a Yiddish newspaper to serve as an Americanizing agency. There was an unreality about the undertaking: an attempt to reconcile two conflicting worlds and two opposites in social attitudes.

Marshall hoped that his "clean journalism" would not only reform the people's manners but that it would have a wholesome influence on the Yiddish press as a whole. Here is an example of how a contemporary Yiddish journalist saw the *Jewish World*:[85]

> It was too tidy . . . every line was written carefully without teasing exaggeration. . . . In addition Marshall's heavy hand lay on the editorials . . . preaching refinement to the immigrant

---

[82] *Ibid.*
[83] Letter of Louis Marshall to Cyrus Sulzberger, June 14, 1902.
[84] Hapgood, p. 179.
[85] J. Chaikin, *Yiddishe Bleter in America* (Yiddish) (New York: 1946) p. 142.

readers . . . and teaching respect for the rich Yahudim ('uptown' German Jews). Little wonder that the *Jewish World* was too dull for the immigrant crowd.

According to Mrs. Dawidowicz, the paper never caught on. In its two years of publication it never acquired any substantial circulation and was not a threat to the existing Yiddish press. It was founded on socially unsound premises. The greatest incongruity lay in the fact that the sponsors of the paper wanted to use Yiddish, not because they believed in the language and its culture, but to *alter* the tastes, habits and manners of the people so that they would eventually *abandon* Yiddish. Commenting on the irony of the situation Lucy Dawidowicz states:[86]

. . . The Yiddish language was often the target of a venomous hostility on the part of the American ('uptown') Jews, and the Yiddish press was for many decades an object of their scorn and derision . . . to reach the people . . . they were obliged to use . . . the language of the people.

The effort artificially to superimpose one culture over another through the facilities of a wealthy (about $100,000 was spent on the *Jewish World*) newspaper failed, and on May 11, 1904, Marshall sold the paper to Ezekial Sarasohn with the words. "Let us get rid of this incubus as quickly as possible."[87]

We see this episode as an excellent illustration of the validity and viability of the native Yiddish culture and its power to resist and destroy attempts at conquest from an "outside world."

The *Jewish World* failed because it could not encompass the worlds of uptown and downtown. Jews in America . . . were divided by the walls of two cultures and two classes. The American and German Jews considered themselves superior to the Russian Jewish immigrants largely by virtue of their social position, education, and wealth. They mistook the immigrants' inferior economic status and his ignorance of American ways for intellectual and spiritual inferiority. . . . At best it was a conflict

86 Dawidowicz, p. 105.
87 *Ibid.*, p. 123.

between those who prized the accommodation of their Jewishness to America and those who wanted to transplant their culture from Eastern Europe.[88]

There is ample evidence that Marshall gained from the experience of his contact with the East Side. Much more than most of his German Jewish friends, he learned about the problems of acculturation. He even got to get along with, and respect, labor leaders.[89]

Some years later, evaluating the general failure of the uptowners in their work in the Ghetto (in this case particularly the Educational Alliance), Marshall wrote to a colleague:

They held themselves aloof from the people. They did not associate with them socially, religiously, or otherwise. They acted as Lords and Ladies Bountiful bringing gifts to people who did not seek for gifts. They frankly avowed the purpose of bettering those among whom they labored, and of dealing with them as a problem, and the work was done in such a manner as not only to give offense, but to arouse suspicion of the motives which inspired the action contemplated.[90]

The scholarly author of the article mentioned at the outset of this discussion concludes:

In that miniature struggle between East and West, the immigrants had won, and the Yiddish press returned to its rightful owners. The East Side vanquished the uptown world of power and wealth. The values and standards of the downtown immigrants had prevailed. But their success was temporary. In the long run, Marshall's Jewish world conquered. The irony is that time and the more natural forces of acculturation accomplished in two generations what the uptown Jews tried to bring about overnight.[91]

While this may be largely true, we think that certain modifications must be added. Two generations of acculturation did not

---

[88] *Ibid.*, p. 124.
[89] For study of Louis Marshall, see Morton Rosenstock, *Louis Marshall, Defender of Jewish Rights* (Detroit: Wayne State University Press, 1965).
[90] Letter of Louis Marshall to Judge Samuel Greenbaum, 3 February, 1919.
[91] Dawidowicz, p. 125.

accomplish assimilation. (Which is what many of the uptown *Yahudim* aimed at; and many succeeded at.)

Marshall and the honest reformers did not aim at assimilation. But had their methods succeeded when they first tried, they would have perpetrated cultural genocide.

Did Marshall's world really conquer? Why? Because the East Side Ghetto disappeared? Because the Yiddish press has shrunk? Because Jews speak English in their synagogues? Because very few wear ear-locks; and all appear to be deloused and clean? And because socialism is not so popular among them?

I think that there are deeper social explanations. As developed in the first section of this work, we see the "two generations of acculturation" mentioned in the quotation above as characterized by a uniquely rapid restratification of a whole people. The "sweatshop" population has been altered to a middle- and upper-class national minority. But the contemporary group is the offspring of the earlier one, and the marks of its original culture are stamped indelibly on its face.

As a matter of fact, upon closer scrutiny, is it not possible we may find that the original German, uptown culture has also been drastically altered? Perhaps this group has really been impressed into the larger one—the one derived from the downtowners, and today substantially shares the same culture. The old elite has possibly also experienced a unique "acculturation"!

The history of the American Yiddish press appears to this writer to reflect well the sociology of American Jews during the era of 1880 to 1924. The formation and transformations of the Yiddish press intimately involved all the other Yiddish cultural institutions, notably the literature, the theater, trade union, labor, and political life.

The press was a mirror of the strivings of the people and the day-to-day activities of the Jewish community. As was pointed out by Robert Ezra Park, it represented an unusually high degree of involvement with the life of the people. We have seen that the people, collectively and individually, were highly involved with their Yiddish press. The press became an early vehicle for purifying, and establishing status for, a language that was often denigrated and described as a "mongrel-language" or at best a "jargon."

Landsmanshaften and Fraternal Organization

Landsmanshaften

One important aspect of Jewish life may be broadly called fraternal organization and activity. This term turns somewhat pale and colorless when compared with the ideas and emotions that are aroused at mention of the words "landsman," "landsleit," and "landsmanshaft" to those familiar with the American Yiddish idiom. Louis Wirth knew the meaning of the words:

> The ties of family, of village-community, and of 'Landsmanshaft' that binds the ghetto inhabitants into little nuclei of more or less autonomous units are only partially apparent to the outsider. The ghetto family will survive crises that would tear an ordinary family asunder, and a stranger who is able to call himself a *Landsman*, not only loosens the purse-strings of the first individual he meets, but also has access to his home. Not only do the *Landsleit* belong to the same synagogue, but as a rule they engage in similar vocations, become partners in business, live in the same neighborhood, and intermarry within their own group. A *Landsmanshaft* has its own patriarchal leaders, its lodges and mutual aid associations, and its celebrations and festivities. It has its burial plot in the cemetery. It keeps the memories of the group alive through frequent visits, and maintains a steady liaison with the remnants of the Jewish community in the Old World.[1]

A Yiddish writer describes the social and emotional function of the Landsmanshaft, spilling it out, as if in one long breath:

---

[1] *The Ghetto* (Chicago: University of Chicago Press [Phoenix Books], 1928 and 1956), pp. 222–23.

Under the pressure of his initial wearying problems of transition, confused by his sudden jump from one world into another, the first: almost feudal, the second: at the highest level of industrial development, the Jewish immigrant created a social nest, the Landsmanshaft Society, which gave him a measure of social sureness and salved his pains-of-transition, returning to him at least a ray of his forsaken home atmosphere, and serving him as a bridge between his past and his future life.[2]

According to available records the oldest American Jewish landsmanshaften were two: one Dutch, the other Polish, going back to the founding dates of 1859 and 1870 respectively.[3]

The well known B'nai B'rith, however, was organized in 1843. Thus, in order properly to understand the development of the Jewish fraternal movement we should consider first the national Jewish orders, which were the forerunners of the Landsmanshaften.

Before the massive immigration of the final decades of the 19th century, the relatively small Jewish population organized fraternally according to countries of origin rather than small towns, provinces, or regions. That is: German Jews, Hungarian Jews, Austrian Jews banded together in groups organized on the basis of their respective origins.

When the B'nai B'rith was established, the American Jewish population numbered less than 50,000. The founders included a group of German Jews who were refused admission to the Odd Fellows. Amongst them were a chazan (cantor), a synagogue-clerk, two shop-keepers, two jewelers, a tailor, a shoemaker, and a barber.[4]

The order included provisions for aid to the needy, to widows, and to orphans, and insurance benefits. But there were also "loftier" ideals, such as "the inculcation of the purest principles of philanthropy . . . to unite the Israelites for the purpose of advancing their own interests and the interests of humanity . . . the defense and rescue

---

[2] M. Blechman, "Landsmanshaften and the Central Relief Organizations," in I. E. Rontch, ed., *Di Yiddishe Landsmanshaften fun New York* (Yiddish) (New York: Yiddish Writers Union, 1938), p. 33.

[3] Rontch, p. 15.

[4] Morris U. Schappes, *The Jews in the United States* (New York: Tercentenary Book Committee, 1958), p. 71.

of the victims of persecution . . . the advancement of patriotism
. . . the support of science and art."[5]

B. A. Weinrebe sees the broad purpose in the establishment of
the order as an effort of the newer immigrants, the German Jews,
to create a medium for the "gathering of prestige" so that their
position in American society could be established against the resist-
ance of the earlier, more prestigious, Sephardic community.[6]

The B'nai B'rith took fertile root and grew rapidly. By 1850
there were 10 lodges, with a total membership of 1,032. Four lodges
in New York counted 532 members, and there were two lodges
each in Philadelphia, Baltimore, and Cincinnati, totaling 500 members. All conducted their business in German, except Lodge No. 9,
in New York, which was the first Jewish lodge to conduct its business in English.[7]

The history of growth and work of this order is well documented.
What is interesting to us is that during this period of growth and
development a notable process of change and adaptation to the
American scene and the needs of the American Jewish community
took place. The principles and needs of the "loftier" ideals (mentioned above) crowded out the earlier needs of mutual aid (which
became less important as the status of the German Jews became
more secure).

The B'nai B'rith became an organization primarily devoted to
cultural and community relations activities.[8] Rather than to self-help
or mutual aid, which became the cornerstone principle of the fraternal societies and landsmanshaften, the B'nai B'rith is devoted to
the interests of the Jewish community at-large and special functions,
as are expressed through its Hillel Foundation on the American
college campuses, the Anti-Defamation League and so on.[9]

There are incomplete records of the organization of some smaller

[5] Translated from the Yiddish, as quoted by B. A. Weinrebe, "Social Role
of the Landsmanshaften," in Rontch, p. 69.
[6] Ibid., p. 69.
[7] Schappes, p. 71.
[8] Jacob Rader Marcus, "Background for the History of American Jewry,"
in Oscar I. Janowsky, ed., The American Jew; a Reappraisal (Philadelphia:
The Jewish Publication Society of America, 1964), pp. 18, 21, 23.
[9] Harold Weisberg, "Ideologies of American Jews," in Janowsky, p. 35; and
Judah J. Shapiro, "Jewish Culture," in Janowsky, p. 379.

orders. One such was the *Kesher Shel Barzel* (Iron Band), founded by Polish Jews in 1860, showing a membership of 1,000 only in New York and California in 1871.[10] We have not seen any recent reference to this order in our research.

The second oldest of the large important orders, *Brith Abraham*, was organized in 1859, the better part of the two decades later than the B'nai B'rith, when the status position of the earlier German immigrants was already fairly well established. This order affiliated newer and poorer immigrants. Here mutual aid was the dominant impulse. Health and death benefits (as in the later Landsmanshaften) were serious concerns. Most of the founders were Austrian Jews who felt more comfortable on their own social level. They soon attracted additional membership from the increasing influx of needier, lower-class German Jewish immigrants.

Their lodges started to take on some of the character of the Landsmanshaften that were to come. It was normally typical of the lodges to carry prestigious-sounding names. In *Brith Abraham*, in the 1880s, when they began to attract large numbers of Eastern European Jews, some of the lodges adopted *home-town names*, such as: *Kiev, Suwalk, Ostrolenko*, and so forth.[11]

The founding date of the Independent Order Brith Abraham was 1888. Now the character of the Jewish community was changing sharply, and was reflected in the composition and character of the order. The founders were Hungarians who were conscious of their lower position in the social "pecking order" in relation to the "superior" German and Austrian brethren. They opened their doors wide to the flood of Eastern European Jews and consequently became the largest order of the period. Their lodges were now beginning to resemble the Yiddish "Farain" or "Society," sporting such shtetl names as, *"Poltaver," "Stanislaver," "Stoliner,"* and the like. Their growth was impressive. It is estimated that they achieved a membership of 200,000.[12]

Records are not clear as to the exact dates, but during the successful growth, this order caused its competitive "younger brother" to

---

[10] Schappes, p. 109.
[11] Weinrebe, p. 69.
[12] *Ibid.*

peter out of existence and merge with the new organization. Eventually the term "Independent" was dropped and only one large *Brith Abraham* remained.

The following Table No. 1 shows the founding dates, membership, and number of lodges as of 1924, of the various fraternal orders.

TABLE 1

JEWISH FRATERNAL ORDERS IN 1924

(Adapted from *American Jewish Year Book*, Vol. 26, 1924–25)

Organized	Name	Membership	No. of Lodges
1843	Independent Order of B'nai B'rith	74,490	500
1887	Independent Order of Brith Abraham	142,555	600
1905	Independent Order of Brith Sholom	28,960	228
1849	Independent Order Free Sons of Israel	8,429	83
1905	Independent Order Sons of David	1,360	13*
1894	Independent Western Star Order	17,924	128
1906	Independent Workmen's Circle of America	5,576	50*
1912	Jewish National Workers' Alliance	6,100	112
1921	Jewish Valor Legion	638	
1900	Jewish Veterans of Wars of the Republic	6,000	16
1919	Jewish War Veterans of America	264	5*
1859	Order Brith Abraham	35,000	365
1896	Order Knights of Joseph	14,556	75
1915	Order of the United Hebrew Brothers	4,132	10*
1908	Order Sons of Zion	7,000	101
1896	Progressive Order of the West	19,721	20*
1846	United Order "True Sisters"	9,800	27
1900	The Workmen's Circle	82,824	500*
	Totals:	465,329	2,833

* Estimate.

The Landsmanshaft described by Louis Wirth at the beginning of this chapter must be understood as a product of the Eastern European Jewish immigration. It stands as one of the sharpest examples of Yiddish culture. It has not only integrated the lives of millions of Jews into the American Jewish Ghetto society, but has itself become institutionalized as a basic and integral part of Jewish culture in America.

In 1917 the New York Jewish Kehilla made a survey of founding dates of Landsmanshaften, similar to the survey made later by the Jewish Writers' Project, to which this study makes numerous references. Despite small discrepancies in the figures,[13] both show conclusively that the greatest period of Landsmanshaft organization was during the years of 1901 to 1917—the period of heaviest Eastern European immigration.[14]

The term *Landsmanshaft organization* applies broadly to a large variety of groups. I do not believe that I can improve upon the description by Louis Wirth quoted at the beginning of this chapter. However, for purposes of a shorter definition we will consider a Landsmanshaft any organization of men, women, or youth, organized fraternally, structured to provide means for its members for religious observance and ritual, and/or mutual aid and benefits for health and death, and/or educational and social activities, drawing its membership primarily on the basis of kinship or common origin in a European *Shtetl,* city or province.

However, there are different types of Landsmanshaften, each group identified by a special emphasis on one or more of the functions or characteristics included in the above definition. Seven clear categories can be established:

1. Anshes or Chevras
2. Societies
3. Ladies Aid Societies and Ladies Auxiliaries

---

[13] Kehilla Study: 395 unaffiliated landsmanshaften. Writers' Study: 491 unaffiliated landsmanshaften.
[14] See tables in *Appendix B* to this chapter.

4. National Orders (containing Landsman-type lodges or branches)
5. Family Circles and "Name" societies
6. Groups organized primarily for overseas relief (Relief Committees)
7. Miscellaneous Centers and Clubs

We will briefly examine each of the above:

1. Anshes and Chevras. This type of organization is based very strictly on kinship and Shtetl of origin. It is organized primarily for religious purposes and always constitutes itself as a congregation. The Anshes were found to be the earliest form of Yiddish Landsmanshaft in New York. As the tables in Appendix B show, 118 such congregations were formed thru the year 1897, as against only 86 strictly mutual aid societies for the same period. Although the Dutch mutual aid society was formed (in 1859) before the very first Anshe appeared three years later (1862). The following breakdown may be noted:

Period	Number of Anshes Founded
1862–64	2
1868–77	5
1877–87	25
1888–97	66

The landsmanshaft congregation was one of the most colorful phenomena of the early ghetto period. For an interesting description by a contemporary of that period see chapter one in Hapgood's little book on the ghetto.[15] Most of the Anshes were crowded into narrow areas on the lower East Side. Sometimes 20 or 30 landsmanshaft congregations would share one building, each occupying a small room or corner of a room. In 1938, the Writers' Study still found 100 Anshes crowded into one block on Henry Street.[16]

The primary function of those little groups was the meticulous

---

[15] Hutchins Hapgood, *Spirit of the Ghetto* (New York: Funk and Wagnal, 1902).
[16] Rontch, p. 13.

preservation of the traditional Orthodox service. Their by-laws and constitutions often specifically provided for the orderly carrying out of the Sabbath service, with proper priorities for Bar Mitzvas. One of their most prestigious "committees" was the "Chevra Kadisha," the group within the congregation that was responsible for the proper provisions for ritual burial.[17]

2. The Societies (or Farains). The Societies or "Farainen" were a more modern and more secularized form of Landsmanshaft. While they could sponsor a synagogue, their primary concern and purpose was mutual aid and insurance benefits. Each Society carried the name of a town or shtetl modified by such terms as "Independent"; "First"; "Progressive"; "Mutual Aid"; "Progressive Mutual Aid"; "Young Men's," and various redundant combinations of the above terms.

Rontch cites three typical answers to the question, "How was your society organized?", which illuminates the idea of need and purpose for a mutual aid and benefit society:[18]

a) The men here, who left their wives, or brides-to-be at home, were lonely. They would therefor gather at the home of a married landsman to drink tea, play cards, and read letters describing the continuing life at home, in the shtetl.

b) A landsman was being deported because of bad health, thus the landsleit became aware of the importance of a "Farain" for mutual aid, to combat need and illness.

c) A landsman suddenly dies in the factory. He is mistaken to be a Greek and is buried in Potter's Field. The landsleit become aware of this, dig up the deceased, bury him properly, and decide to establish their own "Farain," with appropriate cemetery and burial privileges.

Table No. 2, showing the disbursements of a typical society, offers a good picture of their activities.

---

[17] See reference to Paneweczer Progressive Constitution later in this chapter.
[18] Rontch, p. 14.

TABLE 2

Example of Expenses of a Local Society

Disbursements of 1906–1931 of Independent First Pillover K.U.V.
(From their *25th Anniversary Journal*, N.Y., 1931)

Sick Benefit	6,888.00
Shiva Benefit	339.00
Support to Brothers	3,635.00
Endowments	5,200.00
Undertakers	2,333.85
Salaries	2,782.00
Entertainments	1,120.00
Committee Expenses	535.00
Rent	1,848.25
Wedding Presents	615.00
Presents to Brothers	688.00
Printing and Postage	1,864.84
Buttons	52.00
Theater Tickets	2,908.00
Charity	4,266.25
Framing Pictures	125.00
Lost in Banks	485.00
Doctors	7,456.45
10th Anniversary	897.80
20th Anniversary	4,176.75
Baron Hirsch Cemetery	1,600.00
Fence for our Cemetery	1,200.00

3. Ladies' Societies. Basically there are two types of Ladies' Societies: one is the "Ladies' Benevolent Society." As the name implies, this is an organization of women devoted to the functions normally expected of a benevolent society. They will concern themselves, as a men's benevolent society would, with functions relating to their social needs and activities of benevolence among their landsleit-ladies and the community at large. The other type is the ladies' branch of an aid society, or what is more often known as a

"Ladies' Auxiliary" of a men's society. The latter has always been the more popular form of ladies' Landsmanshaft. In 1938 there were 237 such groups in New York, with a total membership of 22,431. The first type had only 71 societies in the same city with a membership of 1,788. However, it is interesting that the first "Ladies' Benevolent Society" predates the founding of the first "Ladies' Auxiliary" by three years (1895). Yet there were no years from 1895 to 1935 that showed a founding of more than one, two, or three groups in any one year. The "Auxiliaries" started slowly, but beginning with the 1920's many years showed the founding of more than 20 groups in one year.[19]

The ladies' groups were treasured by the men's societies. There was great unity in activity and purpose, and often the men's group selected a secretary to help the ladies run their business. The emotional solidarity seems to have been very important to the life of the organizations. With the organization of the ladies, the landsleit-family seems to have been made complete. An excerpt from the introduction to the printed constitution of the *Mezritcher Ladies' Aid Society,* written by the male secretary, illustrates the point:[20]

> We may now consider our "Farain" a large growing family. We are confident that our *Mezritcher Ladies Aid Society* will continue its existence for ever and always. Our experience has taught us to value and respect the many good deeds and work of our *farain.* We must therefor maintain our sacred duty to support our rules, so that our "sister-love" may under no circumstance be disrupted."

4. Yiddish Fraternal Orders (Landsman Branches). Three Yiddish fraternal orders, totaling a membership well over 100,000, were organized between 1900 and 1930. About half of their branches were Landsmanshaft Branches. (A large section, at the end of this chapter, is devoted to a study of these organizations.)

5. Family Circles. The *Family Circle* is the newest form of organization. It represents a much more closed type of group. Qualification

---

[19] See Tables Nos. 5 and 6 in *Appendix B* to this chapter.
[20] Rontch, p. 15.

for membership calls for kinship (even though the kinship may be "distant" or "by marriage.") They have gained in popularity in recent years. Although the first recorded group was founded in New York as early as 1887, by 1916 there were still only 9 groups. In 1938 there were 78 "Circles."[21] However, the United Jewish Appeal of Greater New York reports that it has contact with about 1,200 "circles" totaling a membership of about 75,000.[22]

6. Relief Organizations. This category covers landsmanshaft groups organized specifically for the purpose of overseas relief, particularly to the needy in their respective towns and villages back home, or special committees (sometimes federations) for the purpose of providing organized aid to victimized landsleit overseas. The impetus to this type of grouping was the years of war and revolution in Europe—1914 to 1921. The Writers' group gathered information on 39 relief organizations functioning between 1914 and 1938. More will be said about this type of activity later.

The 1938 study of New York Landsmanshaften, based upon a very large sample (1,840), concludes that in that year there were about 3,000 landsmanshaft groups of all types in the city with a total membership of almost one-half million. The conclusion would be that in New York in 1938, one out of every four Jews in the population was Landsmanshift-affiliated.[23]

The Landsmanshaft, a product of the Eastern European immigration was always a working class phenomenon. It was born during the sweatshop era. The most dynamic years in the founding of landsman groups were from 1903 to 1909. In 1938 (when the process of restratification of American Jews was already under way) the landsmanshaften in New York were still predominantly working class. It was revealed that 75% of the membership were employed workers; 15% were in small business; and 10% were

---

21 See Table No. 7, *Appendix B* to this chapter.
22 Philip Friedman, "Political and Social Movements and Organizations," in *Jewish People: Past and Present* (New York: Jewish Encyclopedic Handbooks (CYCO), 1955, Vol. 4), p. 163.
23 Rontch, p. 16.

professionals. Most of the workers were in the clothing industries, and the majority of the businessmen were merchants.[24]

What should be added, parenthetically, to the above analysis is that a study of "out-of-town" landsmanshaften, particularly those representing Jewish populations in the smaller towns (cities other than Philadelphia, Boston, Chicago) would probably reveal a higher percentage of members in business and self-employed.[25]

We quoted Louis Wirth as saying that landsleit often engage in similar vocations. As one landsman brought over another from the old shtetl he took him into his home and most often also into his shop. Most of them learned the new trade (many had tailoring skills from home) and stayed in the shop. Thus many crafts are characterized by consisting of landsleit from one special shtetl or province. A Society reports that it still had a membership in 1938 made up almost entirely of mens' vest-makers. Rontch states that "to this day there are still a large number 'Marmoresher' landsleit in the necktie industry."[26]

One can easily observe today that "Family Circles" are frequently representative of a special field of business endeavor. It is very common to find certain families (often spanning two or three generations, and including in-laws) in the food businesses such as delicatessens, restaurants, catering, and the like.

We repeatedly refer to the "*Yiddish* Landsmanshaften." The language of the immigrants, of the ghetto, and of the vital institutions which they established in the new society, was of course Yiddish. The landsmanshaft organizations were most typical.[27]

The Writers' Project study found that in 1938, 76% of all societies still recorded their proceedings in Yiddish. It is worth noting that the landsman-branches of the fraternal labor orders showed the highest percentage of Yiddish usage—96%. The figures for language usage at the lodges were: 70% Yiddish; 15% English; 15% German.

---

[24] *Ibid.*, p. 17.
[25] Refer to earlier section of this book devoted to the restratification of American Jews.
[26] Rontch, p. 17.
[27] See *Appendix A,* Landsmanshaft Constitutions.

Another significant discovery was that there is a high correlation between the use of Yiddish and the degree of cultural or educational activity conducted at the organizations. In reply to the question, "Do you conduct cultural activities?", the answers in the total group surveyed were divided just about evenly between the affirmative and the negative. However the independent societies and the lodges answered about two to one in favor of the negative; while the fraternal labor branches (who showed 96% of Yiddish usage in recording their proceedings) answered more than ten to one in the affirmative.[28]

A study of the character of the Yiddish used in the early societies and of the metamorphosis of the language form and usage would in itself require a long study of linguistics. A few brief comments on the subject may be made here, however.

At the beginning, the Eastern European landsleit made an effort to structure the format and procedures, and consequently the language, of their societies (particularly the secular groups), as replicas of the earlier Jewish lodges and societies, which were German. Of course their knowledge of German was limited and its usage was garbled. It was fashionable (particularly at formal occasions) to use the "German" forms of speech. What emerged was a Germanized ("Daitchmerish") form of Yiddish. (It is interesting that this "prestigious" use of "Daitchmerish" was limited to the societies, theatres, and somewhat in the press, but did not penetrate the daily vernacular very deeply.) In time, through the influence of educational institutions, the press, and the more literate theater, Yiddish usage became "purer" and its forms more grammatically regulated. The people and their language became more literate and eventually independent of German.[29]

This transition is graphically portrayed in three (chronologically different) editions of the Constitution of the Kolomear Friends Association, organized on January 31, 1904.

The first edition provides (in crippled, Germanized Yiddish) that all accounting and bookkeeping must be kept "in the German

---

28 Rontch, p. 19.
29 See *Appendix A,* Landsmanshaft Constitutions.

language," and assigns priority to the use of German as the conversational language at meetings.

The second edition still provides that records be kept in German, but clearly stipulates that "if any members do not understand German, then the records will be kept in Yiddish or English."

The third edition (in greatly improved Yiddish) provides plainly that "all proceedings and records be kept in Yiddish."[30]

A study of the printed constitutions of the societies is most revealing and interesting.[31] They are all similarly structured. The name, purpose, and language are always stated. Some include an elaborate pledge of fraternal fidelity to the organization and to all its members individually. There is tremendous emphasis on the name of the society. In each case the "shtetl" of origin is conspicuously included and there are provisions that the name "shall never be altered," and that the landsmanshaft shall never be dissolved as long as there are at least "seven" (sometimes "ten") remaining members.

Many constitutions are printed in both English and Yiddish. But Yiddish is the language of priority. The constitution of The First Turover Aid Society states the matter concisely:

> If there are any discrepancies between the English and Yiddish versions, the constitutional interpretation shall be consistent with the Yiddish form.

The constitutions also provide for regular meetings (generally monthly or semi-monthly), duties of members, and election of officers. Uniquely, officers are generally elected for periods of only six months, and in many cases office-holders are restricted to no more than two consecutive terms.

In addition to the normal slate of officers there are two characteristic offices, "der Inner-Vacher" (the inside guard) and "der Hospitaler." The guard is a "shomer" or sort of sergeant-at-arms, who

---

30 Rontch, pp. 18, 19.
31 The Writers' Project has studied about 100 examples and we have reviewed a sizable file at the Yivo library. See *Appendix A,* Landsmanshaft Constitutions.

is in charge of orderliness and must decide on admittance of late-comers and outsiders at the meetings. The Hospitaler has the vital job of visiting each "brother" who reports an illness. He must meticulously see that the patient receives proper medical attention and sick-benefits, and he is expected personally to visit the sick "brother" at least once or twice a week until he recovers, and then make a report to the membership.

Benefits are provided for needy members, for those "sitting Shiva" (observance of the week of mourning), and there are elaborate ritual and benefits in cases of death. Provision for burial is one of the strongest motives for affiliation with a landsmanshaft.

All societies acquire cemetery sections, all pay the costs of funeral and burial, and all have special funds and levy special taxes to provide funds and endowments for the bereaved. Special com-mittees and officers take meticulous care of all arrangements and the needs of the bereaved.

The landsmanshaften that are called "Anshes," which are or-ganized specifically as orthodox congregations, pay special attention to the function of burial. The commitee devoted to that duty is traditionally called the "Chevra Kadisha." The constitutions of the Anshes elaborate and emphasize the great importance of the death and burial ritual. They stress the sacred duty of perpetuating names and memories.

The president of the Paneweczer Progressive Y. M. B. A. indulges in a bit of dramatic prose: "To die, or not to die. Each person strives not to 'die away,' strives that his memory may survive on this earth as long as possible." He goes on to say that the "Chevra Kadisha" accomplishes just that by repeating the "Yiskor" and by repeating the name of the deceased in the religious ritual. He concludes with an appeal:

> It is desirable that our younger members should join the ranks of the "Chevra Kadisha" so that this vital institutional function may always continue—because we are, after all, only mortal.[32]

---

32 E. Verschleisser, "Landsmanshaft Constitutions," in Rontch, p. 51.

Thus the Landsmanshaft takes on the duty or function of perpetuating Jewish tradition. It creates in the new world a continuity of language, religion, and family and shtetl name and culture.

The social purpose of the landsmanshaften in providing a structure for immigrants to turn to their fellow countrymen for aid has been fairly well acknowledged.[33] But one author sees the assistance offered by the landsmanshaft as being much more than a financial or physical factor in the lives of the members. Emotional associations are very strong. Most members knew each other and their respective families far back to the days in the "old home." Ties were deep, strong, and sincere.[34] Every meeting and function of the society offered an opportunity for "brother" to share with "brother" the emotional fulfillment gained through sentimental and colorful recollections of common experiences in the romantic past of one's youthful years.

The following quotation may serve as a concise statement on the role the landsmanshaften played in establishing a social and emotional bridge for the immigrants to the new society:[35]

The imagination is staggered to think of the role played by the landsmanshaften in the early years of immigration, before the establishment of the institutions devoted to dealing with the immigrants. They served as the 'stations of arrival.' They were the gathering points, the family-centers, helping the 'green' one to find himself at home and plant his roots in the new 'medina' (country).

The very nature and genealogy of the landsmanshaft tend to orient them narrowly. That is, they are inner-directed; each group is concerned massively with its own "small" problems. Yet, the survey in 1938 showed that large numbers of the landsmanshaften support to some degree most of the important centralized national Jewish

[33] See Moses Rischin, *The Promised City* (Cambridge: Harvard University Press, 1962), pp. 104–105.

[34] Blechman, p. 33.

[35] Weinrebe, p. 33 (translated from Yiddish).

organizations devoted to the social needs of American and European Jews. The following partial list is revealing:[36]

1. *HIAS* (Hebrew Sheltering and Immigrant Aid Society). Organized in 1889 (reorganized in 1909) for the purpose of supplying material, moral and legal aid to Jewish immigrants. This organization is supported by about 800 New York landsmanshaften (annual payments ranging from $5 to $25).

2. *American Jewish Joint Distribution Committee* (known as "Joint"). Organized in 1914 by the American Jewish Committee and the wealthier philanthropists for the purpose of large-scale planning and aid for needy Jews suffering from persecution in all parts of the world. They are supported nationally by 2,000 landsmanshaften.

3. *ORT*—An organization devoted to the advancement of agricultural skills and labor among the Jews. Organized first in Russia in 1880; in the U.S.A. in 1921. One thousand landsmanshaften are nationally affiliated; but in special campaigns and appeals as many as 1,500 have given them support in New York City alone.

4. *American Jewish Congress.* Organized in 1918 for the purpose of developing activities in defense of Jewish rights in America and throughout the world and developing the Jewish homeland in Israel. About half of their affiliated organizations (about 1,000) are landsmanshaften.

It is very common for the "local" or "independent" society to become involved in a variety of centralized organizations and in functions outside of the "narrow" needs of their own institution. A striking example is the Independent First Pillover K.U.V., which is a member of the Linas Hazedek (Aid to the Sick) society in Pilov, of the Federation of Polish Jews in America, of HIAS, of the Denver Sanatarium, of Chesed Shel Emes, of Gon Yeludim of

[36] Blechman, pp. 33–42.

Montgomery Street, and the Haim Solomon Home for the Aged.[37]

Political, labor, and community leaders were interested and involved in coordination of the work and activities of the societies. For example, the late B. Charney Vladeck (former Minsker Bundist) manager of the *Forverts* and a most active labor, civic, and political leader, found some time to concern himself with the activities of his old landsleit.

Examination of an extensive exchange of Yiddish correspondence between Vladeck and various Minsker societies about functions and meetings in his office relating to Minsker Landsmanshaft activities disclosed, in the 1929 file, a letter addressed to Vladeck from the Minsker Progressive Branch No. 99 of the Workmen's Circle, obviously reporting on the state of activities of the Minsker organizations in the city. The Branch reported the following:

1. *Minsker Independent* has an office at 100–104 W. 40th Street.
2. *Minsker United* meets every second and fourth Monday at the Clinton Hotel.
3. *Minsker American* meets every second and fourth Monday at the Forward Hall.
4. *Minsker Old Men* meets every Sunday at 56 Henry Street.
5. *Minsker Young Friends* meets at Broadway Central Hotel.
6. *Minsker Chae Odom* meets every Sunday at 22 Rutgers Street.
7. *Minsker Branch 507 A. R.* meets at Brownsville Labor Lyceum every second and fourth Saturday.
8. *Minsker Prog. Br. 99* meets every first and third Saturday at the Forward Hall.[38]

Of course, in recent years all the national Jewish campaigns, such as the United Jewish Appeal, Bonds for Israel, and the various local federated appeals have devoted considerable energy to establishing Landsmanshaft Divisions through which they involve the landsman-

[37] *25th Anniversary Journal* of the Independent First Pillover K. U. V. (New York: 1931).
[38] B. Charney Vladeck, *Personal Papers,* (Collection-archive) New York University Tamiment Library, New York.

shaften individually and collectively in support of their fund-raising efforts.

The Federations

There have been repeated attempts at centralizing or "federating" landsman groups on the basis of country of origin, such as, Poland, Hungary, and so on. This did not develop in the early years of migration but came later, after the landsmanshaft movement was already well grounded on American soil. The concept of federation naturally developed during a period of maturity in the movement, when leadership emerged, dedicated to the larger scope of affiliation, with energies directed beyond the confines of the immediate needs of the individual society and its members.

A number of federations were organized, dissolved, merged, and re-organized. Some have remained on the scene and have made contributions towards the life of the Jewish community, but have not altered the fundamental character of the landsmanshaft phenomenon, namely, the relatively small intimate group, fostering highly primary relationships, based on close, tight cultural and kinship ties.

Here follow the names of a few federations:

The earliest was "Der Poilisher Farband" (organized in 1908) which later became "The Federation of Polish Jews in America." Two hundred delegates met in the old Beethoven Hall, on East 5th Street, in New York City "for the purpose of strengthening the feelings of kinship between the Polish Jews of America and those who were left behind in the old home; to help the newcomers materially and socially; and to build their own hospital."[39]

This federation was very successful in raising large sums of money for Polish relief during the two World Wars.

Anti-semitic agitation and persecution of Jews in Rumania caused the organization of the Federation of Rumanian Jews in

---

[39] Samuel Schwartz, "Landsmanshaft Federations in New York," in Rontch, p. 52.

America (1909). In 1916 they merged with the United Rumanian Jews in America. This group was oriented primarily toward helping Jews in Rumania. However they developed considerable energy toward political activities as well as the usual fund-raising responsibilities.

Other federations did not form until the twenties and the thirties. The following two should be mentioned:

The Association of Hungarian Jews in America was formed in 1933. The motivation was dually inspired by a desire to aid the Zionist goals of a homeland in Palestine and "to organize for the purpose of saving the Jews in their homeland from the Fascist pestilence."[40]

The "United Galician Jews of America" was organized at a convention in New York City in 1937, with the following statement directed to their kinsmen in Europe:

"In the name of the 'United Galician Jews of America,' we are hereby creating for you, the Jews of Galicia, an address to which you may at all times direct your needs." The reference here was to the needs created by prewar Nazi and anti-Semitic persecution. This federation became very active in cooperation with the Joint Distribution Committee in its overseas relief work.

S. Margoshes, well-known Yiddish journalist and president of The Federation of Galician and Bucoviner Jews of America, in an article in the *Jewish Communal Register* of 1917–1918, noted seriously the development of communities of landsmanshaften— Spanish-Portuguese, German, Russian, Galician, Hungarian, Rumanian—each with its own synagogues and charitable and educational institutions.[41]

The *Register* for that same year published the information on the following federations:[42]

1. American Union of Roumanian Jews

    Established and incorporated, 1916
    Membership: 69 organizations

40 *Ibid.*, p. 59.
41 *Jewish Communal Register* (New York: 1917–1918), pp. 1328–1336.
42 *Ibid.*, pp. 1337–1339.

Purpose: "To defend the interests of the Jews in Roumania, to work for their civic and political emancipation and for their economic reconstruction and rehabilitation; and to represent and further the interests of the Roumanian Jews in the U.S. and Canada."

President: Born in Roumania, came to U.S. in 1885.

2. Federation of Bessarabian Organizations

Established, 1911
Membership: over 3000
Purpose: "To organize the Jews coming from the provinces of Bessarabia and the southern part of Russia for cooperative social effort."

President: Born in Russia, came to U.S. in 1891.

3. Federation of Galician and Bucovinian Jews of America

Organized, 1903
Membership: 60,000
Purpose: "To study the political, economic and social conditions of the Jews in Galicia and Bucovina, and to devise ways and means of ameliorating those conditions through the exercise of the collective influence and energy of the Galician Jews of America."

"To work toward the fusion of Galician Jews of America into the larger Jewish community in this country, thus making possible the solution of communal problems that affect Galician Jews equally with the Jews hailing from other countries.

"To further the interests of the Jewish people the world over."

President: Born in Galicia, came to U.S. 1905.

4. Federation of Roumanian Jews of America

Established, 1908
Purpose: "To work for the security of equal civil and political rights for the Jews in Roumania and to participate in all movements of Jewish national character."

President: Born in Roumania, came to U.S. 1889.

5. Federation of Russian-Polish Hebrews of America

Established, 1908
Membership: about 40,000
Purpose: "To assist Jews arriving to this country from Russian Poland."

The Yiddish Labor Fraternal Orders

A major element in the social complex of Jewish landsmanshaft and fraternal organizations is the Yiddish labor fraternal order. Three important orders were established during the first 30 years of this century: The Workmen's Circle (Arbeter Ring); The Jewish National Workers Alliance (Yiddisher Nazionaler Arbeter Farband); and the International Workers Order (Internazionaler Arbeter Ordn).

The Yiddish labor order is a dichotomous creature. On the one hand it is a federation of branches (lodges) devoted to the typical interests of societies; fraternalism, kinship, mutual aid, various types of insurance and benefits, death benefits, and cemetery. On the other hand, it has an ideological foundation. The ideology is grounded in the labor movement or in the Zionist labor movement. Thus in Yiddish literature or journalism a discussion of the Yiddish fraternal orders was as likely to appear within the context of "di Yiddishe arbeter bavegung" (Jewish labor movement) as in the category of fraternalism. For example, chapter 17 of Melech Epstein's work on the Jewish labor movement is entitled "The Arbeiter Ring" and deals with the founding of that order as a Jewish labor phenomenon.[43]

This may seem strange to the reader who normally identifies American labor only with the trade-union movement and its institutions. But in the Jewish world it is a reality that so many of its institutions have evolved from the activities of the American Jewish immigrant working class, and are treated as phenomena of the "Arbeter Bavegung" (Labor Movement). The Yiddish labor orders are an example of this approach.

[43] Melech Epstein, Jewish Labor in the United States, 2 vols. (New York: 1950 and 1953) 1:298-317.

As has been shown, the heavy Eastern European immigration after 1880 resulted in the formation of large working class, sweat-shop ghettos in New York and in several other larger cities. Socialist, "Bundist," and anarchist-inspired trade unionism became an integral part of the life of the Jewish community. The Yiddish press, theater, and educational institutions all reflected this fact. The fraternal movement was no exception.

The landsmanshaft organization has been properly described as being specifically concerned with religious function, mutual aid, and kinship fraternalism. Their early character was largely working class. Their membership was drawn from the sweat-shops; many became involved in trade-union activity. Some brought their socialist "Bund-ism" from the old country. An interesting illustration follows:

Kolomea was a "Galitzianer shtetl" that had developed a militant socialist movement among the Jewish population. Yet the people were orthodox and traditional bearded Jews. The important industry was production of ritual articles used in the synagogue, particularly prayer shawls. This did not make them immune to the influence of the socialist "Bund," which taught them to conduct strikes to improve their lot materially.[44]

By 1904 a number of "Kolomear" had found their way to America and secured work at their familiar occupation of weaving "tallaisim" (prayer shawls). During that year, 25 of them founded the "Kolomear Friends Association." This group became known as a socialist oriented society, supporting strikers here and abroad, and cooperating with the Socialist Party in political activities in the Eighth Assembly District in New York. The organization grew to a membership of 400 in the 1930's.[45]

During the turbulent years of trade-union organization in the Jewish trades, the Kolomear and many other societies supported their striking members with special strike funds before the young unions had their own resources for strike relief. Many of the

---

[44] Weinrebe, pp. 85, 86.
[45] *Ibid.*, p. 86.

landsmanshaft constitutions stipulated that "scabs" or strike-breakers were barred from membership.[46]

The Yiddish East Side was hit heavily by the depression in 1893. The numbers of unemployed were high among the Jewish clothing workers. The Yiddish press and community leaders appealed to the general public for support of the workers' struggle. The landsmanshaften responded. One historian reports, ". . . even conservative landsmanshaften allowed strike benefits to members."[47]

Thus, while very few societies were categorically or principally politically oriented, the climate was decidedly pro-union.

The Yiddish fraternal movement reached a peak of development and activity during the first decade of this century. The tenement and sweat-shop culture was a breeder of social and cultural problems and disease as well as physical illness. The *anshes,* the *farainen,* the societies, and the lodges filled many of the vital needs of the newcomers, but something more was apparently needed. A clear subculture was taking form. The new large Jewish working class was involved in a struggle in the trade-union movement; a labor press and socialist leaders were educating and agitating the masses of the people to win a secure place for themselves in this new society. The children of the immigrants, born in "Columbus' America," required education and orientation that would make it possible for them to bridge the old world to the new.

The cloakmakers, dressmakers, waistmakers, cigarmakers, and tallis-weavers had a common bond that brought them together by virtue of similar origins and kinship into their respective landsmanshaft societies and lodges. Yet there was another commonness, complementing the first, and perhaps even transcending it, namely the binding ties of class interest.

At the same time there were social, recreational, and educational needs that could not always be met under the existing structure

---

[46] See *Appendix A,* Constitution of the Progressive Slutzker Young Men's Benevolent Association, New York; also see file of Constitutions at Yivo archives, New York.
[47] Rischin, p. 180.

of the societies. There was a vacuum that could be filled by a labor fraternal movement.

A Yiddish labor order could fulfil a threefold need of the day: mutual aid, an amiable social and educational environment, and the advancement of basically socialist and labor ideology.

According to Melech Epstein,[48] two cloakmakers, Sam Greenberg and Harry Lasker, confided their ideas of an organization that would be a "workingmen's circle" to a third friend, M. Goldreich. They had a vision of an "arbeter kreiz," an intimate circle of workers. Under their leadership the first meeting of the Workingmen's Circle was held at Greenberg's home, 151 Essex Street, in Manhattan's Lower East Side, on April 4th, 1892.[49]

Branches of this circle spread to Harlem and to Brooklyn, as the Jewish population migrated to these areas. Officially, the Arbeter Ring was founded in September, 1900. After a year, the new Yiddish labor order had nine branches; at the convention in 1902, 27 branches reported a membership of 1,500, covering several cities.

TABLE 3

Growth of the Workmen's Circle Membership During First 15 Years

(From *Arbeter Ring Almanach* [Yiddish], 1940)

Year	No. of Members
1901	872
1902	1,042
1903	1,883
1904	4,352
1905	6,776
1906	8,840
1907	14,158
1908	19,324
1909	31,581

[48] P. 299.
[49] *Arbeter Ring Boiyer un Tuyer* (Yiddish), I. Yeshurin, (ed.) (New York: 1962), p. 443.

1910	38,866
1911	38,295
1912	41,725
1913	45,662
1914	47,817
1915	49,913

A sound fraternal basis was established for the order in the early years. Moses Rischin notes that their constitution copies very closely the features of the established German *Arbeter Kranken und Sterbe Kasse* (Workers' Sickness and Death Fund). He seems to suggest that this was an effort to emulate German culture.[50]

It would appear to be more accurate to conclude that borrowing the features of the existing German constitution was an effort of a fledgling workers' order to learn from the technical experience of the functioning "Kasse" rather than to follow their culture. We know that Yiddish socialism was far from German in form, as Rischin seems to think.

Indeed, the new organization did rapidly become involved in fraternal, socialist, and trade-union life. In 1907, when the order was only seven years old, it was a major participant in a successful effort, raising a $10,000 strike fund that helped win one of the earliest significant victories for the ILGWU.

In 1915 the *Arbeter Ring* reached a national membership figure of 49,913.[51] This period of astounding growth coincided with the great exodus of Jews from Eastern Europe, after the Czarist pogroms of 1905. Immigrants thrown into the strangeness of New York, Philadelphia, Chicago, Boston, and Cleveland were met by *Arbeter Ring* landsmanshaft branches.

Many of the Jewish immigrants of this period were socialists or socialist-oriented. Substantial numbers were members or sympathizers of the "Bund," which played a conspicuous role in the revolutionary movement against the Czarist government.

The "Bund" was an organization of Russian, Lithuanian, and Polish, Jewish Social Democrats dedicated to the emancipation of

---

50 P. 151.
51 Epstein, p. 304.

the peoples suffering under Czarist tyranny. It performed a unique function in crystallizing a young generation of Russian Jewish intellectuals, during a period of "enlightenment," into a movement of secular, anti-religious, and later Yiddishist, radicals.

Der Algemainer Yiddisher Arbeter Bund was organized in Vilna in 1897. Rischin translates the name as "The General League of Jewish Workers."[52] Melech Epstein refers to "The General Jewish Workers' Union," and Louis Greenberg calls it "The General Jewish Workingmen's Party of Russia, Poland and Lithuania." In his chronicle of Jewish struggles in Russia, Dr. Greenberg states:

> . . . Arkady Kremer, a founder of the Bund . . . furnished information . . . that although the Bund came into existence in 1897, it had actually existed since *1895*. From that time or earlier the Jewish socialist circles acted as a group, with Vilna as their center.[53]

Some of the Bundists ran off to America to escape Siberian exile and Czarist prisons, others to escape their personal and social frustrations. When they came to America they naturally banded together in formal and informal social groupings, orienting their interests and activities (within the framework of their basically socialist ideology) to their needs and the needs of their fellow workers and landsleit in the new society. However, emotionally they were still tied to their comrades in the home towns, who were still suffering persecution and deprivation. Consequently Bundist landsleit leagues were created for the purpose of advancing the ideology of Bundism in America, but also (very importantly) to send material aid and provide means of rescue for those in their home "shtetls" who were still caught in the net of reaction. Weinrebe tells us:

> Such leagues numbered about 40 throughout the country. They were united thru a central 'farband' in New York. Their chief

---

[52] Pp. 43, 44.
[53] Louis Greenberg, *The Jews in Russia* (2 Vols.) (New Haven: Yale University Press, 1941 and 1951, Vol. 2), p. 147; and *Bund Almanach* (Yiddish) (Warsaw: 1922).

function was to popularize the philosophy of the Bund and to conduct fund raising efforts for purposes of defense.[54]

A. Liessin, who was an early "Minsker Bundist," was then creating some of the best majestic and heroic poetry in the American Yiddish press and periodicals.[55] He was also a very successful journalist. Because of his initiative, effort, and influence, the central organization of the Bundist leagues agreed to join the Workmen's Circle en masse in 1907. Responding to Liessin's dramatic appeal in the *Jewish Daily Forward,* each of the 40 Bundist leagues joined the order as a landsmanshaft branch.[56] This added greatly to the impetus of growth of the first and largest of the Yiddish labor orders.

TABLE 4

Example of Typical Workmen's Circle Branch Expenditures

(From *Thirty-Five-Year Jubilee Journal* of Branch No. 1, A.R., p. 63.)

Branch No. 1 (1927)
Paid out benefits by Branch No. 1 since its existence

Aid to members	$16,436.00
Sick benefit	23,386.00
Funeral expenses	3,519.00
Aid to Societies	1,327.00
Aid to Unions and Strikers	1,833.00
To Socialist Party	740.00
To Socialist Press	800.00
Spent for Lectures	653.00
Paid out Endowments	23,600.00
Total	72,344.00

Branch No. 1 Loan Fund loaned to members from 1909–1926—$41,205.00

---

[54] Pp. 83, 84.
[55] Hasye Cooperman, "Yiddish Literature in the United States," in Janowsky, ed., pp. 196, 199.
[56] Weinrebe, p. 84.

Another type of idealism was also rapidly taking root among many of the "enlightened" or "worldly" Jewish youth in Russia and in the Eastern countries. This was the fervor of Jewish nationalism and the zeal for political self-determination of the Jewish people. Zionism, the ideal of reestablishing Palestine as the modern and permanent political homeland of the Jews, was developing into an international movement. There were many "shades" of Zionism. One of the most dynamic took the form of Labor Zionism or Socialist-Zionism. In the United States they organized in the party of the Poale Zion. The Poale Zion educated and agitated for the establishment of a Jewish State based entirely upon a socialist economic and political order.[57]

As a "political" party they faced all the problems of competition with the other groups in American Jewish life. Their progress was slow. But in several respects they were different from other Jewish socialists and labor idealists. For example, they did not concentrate organizationally in the areas of trade unionism. Many started to gravitate rather early toward the very small business enterprises like candy stores, groceries, and hand laundries.

But they had certain other notable characteristics. While they were Yiddish speaking and Yiddishist ideologically, their Yiddish idiom had to "move over" in their hearts to make place for another linguistic partner, Hebrew. Modern conversational Hebrew was very important to them. While Yiddish was the language of their immediate secular cultural heritage, Hebrew was intermeshed with their Zionist idealism.

Many of the American Poale Zionists had lived in British-mandated Palestine, had worked the soil with their bare hands in the early kibbutzim, and some had fought in World War I for the British in the Jewish Legion. They knew modern conversational and literary Hebrew well. Some had to learn the language. Their unique ideology and unpretentious, pioneer-like kind of intellectuality, created a great social common bond amongst them. When one moved among them, a *fraternalism* could be felt in the air. It became apparent that they could be most successful and achieve

---

[57] Epstein, 2:270.

greatest gratification within the framework of a labor fraternal order.

The Yiddisher Nazionaler Arbeter Farband (Jewish National Workers Alliance) was founded in 1910 with an exclusively labor Zionist membership. The Writers' Project report states that two years later, chartered in Albany, they had a membership of 500. In 1938 they affiliated 200 branches in more than 100 cities, with a national membership of 18,000.[58]

There are some interesting structural differences between the Farband (as they are popularly called) and the Workmen's Circle. Their branches are far less landsman-oriented. While more than half of the Workmen's Circle branches in New York are landsman branches, less than one-quarter of the Farband branches are so organized. Also, in 1938 only one-third of their membership (6,000) were in New York City, where more than half of the American Jewish population lived. These facts can be explained in part by the characteristics of their members described above and also probably because by 1938 they had become slightly more restratified toward the middle class than most labor groups. This would favor a higher proportion of provincial membership in this fraternal order.

Since this study is concerned with the period of mass immigration ending in 1924, when our gates were closed to the newcomers from Eastern Europe, it would appear that the "story" of the founding of Yiddish labor orders would end here. However the composite picture would not be complete unless we referred briefly to the founding and the subsequent demise of a large order that basically, historically, was an offshoot of the Workmen's Circle.

The course of Yiddish organizational life in America has typically reflected events in the "old country," in Russia. The turmoil of 1905 triggered Jewish immigration and subsequent organization of Jewish communal life in the United States; the revolution of 1917 and the years of civil war in Russia, had a dramatic effect on Jewish labor and fraternal life, and its various realignments in America.

---

58 Weinrebe, p. 90.

The detailed development and analysis of this phenomenon as it affected the Jewish labor movement generally is not appropriate at this point, but its consequence and effect on the Yiddish fraternal movement should be noted. The cleavage in the Jewish labor movement reflected broadly the differences between the "left" and the "right." Alignments and realignments were not always clear cut. In the most general sense the "left" represented tolerance and friendship, and often partisanship to a communist and pro-Soviet position on world affairs generally, and on Jewish and labor affairs in America particularly. The "right" was generally represented by the later *Forverts* position on the Soviet Union, which was typified by the *Menshevik,* Social Democratic approach, and broadly included most of the established "old time" Jewish labor leaders and institutions.

This struggle between "left" and "right" in the fraternal movement found sharp focus in the Workmen's Circle and culminated in a "split," with the subsequent founding of a new Yiddish order.[59] According to Weinrebe, the issues were mainly over pro- or anti-Soviet policy among the membership.

Rubin Saltzman says that it was mainly a question of "class struggle." He quotes the manifesto, which was drawn by the left wing group (108 branches and 22 minority groups from other branches) at a national conference in New York City, October, 1929:[60]

> The time has come when each person, who takes the interests of the working class seriously, must shake from his shoe, the dust of the Workmen's Circle.
>
> The Workmen's Circle, which was created under the flying banner of the class-struggle, which wrote into its program the abolition of the capitalist system, and thus won the love and respect of the broad masses of the United States, has in recent years become transformed into an organization serving the interests of capitalism.

---

[59] *Ibid.,* p. 92.
[60] Rubin Saltzman, *Tsu der Geshichte fun der Fraternaler Arbeter Bavegung* (Yiddish) (New York: 1936), pp. 44–53.

After months of hectic deliberations and activity, involving a prospect of merger with the small existing Independent Workmen's Circle of Massachusetts, court intervention, and injunctions, the dissident group, at a conference March 30, 1930 formed the new order called the *International Workers Order.*

M. Epstein takes another view of the new order. While he commends the soundness of the organization's modern insurance and medical programs, he critically describes the fluctuations of their political policy as following that of the Russian and American communist policies.[61]

Regardless of political perspective or partisanship, Weinrebe documents the numerical growth of the Jewish Section of the I. W. O. as having developed from a membership of 7,625 in 1933 to 36,000 (260 branches) in 1938.[62]

During the years of the "united front" the IWO even made serious efforts toward unity with the Workmen's Circle. Eventually the Jewish section was renamed Jewish Peoples Fraternal Order, as a unit of a multi-national order containing sections of Italian, Russian, Ukrainian, and other groups. The activity and growth of this large order was phenomenal. To quote M. Epstein:[63]

On the eve of World War II, the IWO numbered about 110,000 members, of which about 35,000 belonged to the Jewish section. In 1944 the general membership rose to 140,998, and in 1948, to 163,802. From then on the order began to feel the effect of the intensified antagonism towards Communism in the community.

It should be noted that the "intensified antagonism towards Communism" referred to by Epstein occurred during a period in our postwar history referred to as the "McCarthy Era," when so many individuals and groups in our society who were politically "left of center" found their existence untenable.

The IWO was particularly vulnerable. For example, it supported

---

[61] Epstein, pp. 272–75.
[62] Weinrebe, p. 93.
[63] Epstein, p. 273.

financially, and participated in the publication of, the *Morning Freiheit*, the Yiddish press organ of the communist movement. It became a target of government enforcement agencies, and in 1951 the New York State Superintendent of Banking and Insurance (which has jurisdiction over chartered fraternal orders) asked the New York State Supreme Court to revoke the charter of the IWO. The charges were that the order spent unwarranted sums on communist publications, especially the *Freiheit*. Justice Steinberg granted the request. After two years of unsuccessful appeals, the order was disbanded in 1953.

In describing and analyzing the various types of fraternal organizations in Jewish life that developed as a result of the needs of the immigrants in a new society, it becomes apparent that the unifying characteristic of all the forms of organization described in the preceding pages is that they always came to life as manifestations of two basic needs of the Jewish immigrants: the necessity of adjusting to the problems of life and work in a new (often hostile) world; and the apparently powerful social drive to retain as much as possible of the old culture.

Both needs, though often seemingly antagonistic, found a compatibility of expression in the formation of the various fraternal and landsmanshaft organizations.

The earliest groups based on country of origin (mostly German, Austrian, or Hungarian) developed the large national fraternal orders such as B'nai B'rith and Brith Abraham. In sharp contrast to this, the Eastern European, Yiddish-speaking Jews initiated the tremendous network of landsmanshaft organizations based on the culture of the shtetl.

While the societies and landsmanshaften were ethnocentric and "local" in their interests, we have demonstrated that when the needs of their brothers in the old country required aid and relief, the American groups formed federations to unite them in doing the job.

Particularly after 1905, most Jewish immigrants came to stay, and were eventually drawn into the economic, labor, and political life of the ghetto. Socialism and labor fraternalism became very popular. This was manifested in the form of national Yiddish fraternal labor orders. Here also, the shtetl culture played an important role and many of the orders' branches (lodges) were organized on the basis of city or shtetl of origin.

Thus we see the national fraternal orders, the labor orders, and the various landsmanshaften (religious, mutual aid, social, familial, ladies, etc.) tied together broadly as a social category by virtue of the fact that in one form or another they developed on the American scene as a response to the need of the Jewish immigrants for a bridge from the old world to the new.

9

Conclusion

We have attempted to answer the question set forth at the outset of this work about the state of identification and community character of the American Jews of the period of Eastern European (Yiddish) immigration. In our analysis of Jewish life during that period we were cognizant of an observation made, and a conclusion drawn, by Louis Wirth in his famous study of the Chicago "Ghetto-community" 40 years ago:[1]

> What makes the Jewish community—composed, as it is in our metropolitan centers in America, of so many heterogeneous elements—a community is its ability to act corporately. It has a common set of attitudes and values based upon common traditions, similar experiences and common problems. The Jewish community is a cultural community. It is as near an approach to communal life as the modern city has to offer.

We believe that the broad range of social functions covered by the Yiddish cultural institutions, as described above, meets the description of Wirth's "cultural community" and refutes the positions of Drs. Sachar and Marcus.

The historical section of this essay (chapter four) has briefly described two other American Jewish communities: the early Sephardic and the 19th-century German groups. While each of these migrations had formed an identifiable and characteristic Jewish community, neither has produced the historical or social impact on American Jewish life that has been effected by the later Eastern European migration.

---

[1] Louis Wirth, *The Ghetto* (Chicago: University of Chicago Press [Phoenix Edition], 1956), p. 290.

170

It is generally agreed by historians and sociologists today that the "typical" American Jew today is a product largely of the Eastern European migration. This view is clearly illustrated, for example, by Marshall Sklare when he writes: "Jewish life as it is commonly encountered in the metropolitan community is a derivation chiefly from East European patterns."[2] Later, in a footnote, Dr. Sklare specifies: "From this point on, except where the content specifically indicates otherwise, 'Jews' will mean East-European Jews."[3]

Why is this so; what were the forces that favored the "community of the poor and the uncouth" against the economic superiority and social refinement of the earlier migrants? There were two obvious factors: One was the massive numerical superiority of the last wave of immigration; another was that each group came to a different America, historically and economically speaking.

But we are here interested in, and concerned with, still a third phenomenon, namely, that each of the Jewish immigrant groups had evolved its own characteristic cultural pattern. Bernard D. Weinryb, in speaking of the earliest Sephardic immigrants, the Marranos, observes that they had little regard for cultural tradition. Their prayers were in the vernacular. He writes:[4]

In Amsterdam, where the Marranos could return openly to their Jewishness, Spanish and Portuguese remained the official languages of the community and its literary means of expression, even though Menassah Ben Israel established a Hebrew printing press in 1627. Thus in America the group had only to transfer from Spanish culture to English culture. This was rapidly achieved.

In another paragraph he concludes:[5]

In short, American Jews of the second half of the eighteenth century seemed to have had much in common with the non-Jews

---

[2] Marshall Sklare, *Conservative Judaism* (Gencoe: The Free Press, 1955), p. 21.

[3] *Ibid.*, p. 26; also refer to Rischin's and Glazer's quotations in chapter one above.

[4] Bernard D. Weinryb, "Jewish Immigration and Accommodation to America," in Marshall Sklare, *The Jews* (Glencoe: The Free Press, 1958), p. 5.

[5] *Ibid.*

with whom they frequently congregated and with whom they did business.

Thus, while they were associating freely with gentile Americans, they were not nearly so well inclined toward fraternizing with the Ashkenazic Jews who started arriving in the 18th century. Henrietta Szold observes that:[6]

> The small Sephardic communities, in defense of their own individuality, could not, and, by reason of their own hidalgo pride would not, continue to absorb the new elements (the German immigrants).

Weinryb ultimately finds that "the pattern which evolved among the Sephardim was that of a group assimilated in terms of *language* (italics added) and external way of life, being little versed in Jewish learning."[7] We have seen that in New Orleans and in New York the Sephardim seized every opportunity to shift their cultural patterns from Spanish to English.

The next important influx of Jews came from Germany. The German immigration presented an interesting phenomenon of social mobility and acculturation. The early immigrants came mainly from Prussia and western Poland. They were poor, traditional, and Yiddish-speaking. They lived within their own subcultural group, apart from the non-Jewish environment. They were not accepted by the Sephardim and suffered social exclusion.[8]

By the middle of the 19th century this group experienced dramatic social changes. The German immigration became more massive. Higher economic and social status developed and encouraged a philosophy of Americanization. Now they were forming a Jewish elite, attempting to rid themselves of their less attractive traditional identity. They embraced Reform as a solution and "being free of most of the attributes of Jewish group identification, this group of

---

[6] "Elements of the Jewish Population in the United States," in Charles S. Bernheimer, *The Russian Jews in the United States* (Philadelphia: 1915), p. 11.

[7] Weinryb, p. 10.

[8] *Ibid.*, p. 11.

German Jews . . . was easily able to change over from German to English."[9] This completed the process whereby the Yiddish-speaking German Jews, who at first deferred to German, eventually embraced American English as their language and culture.

This phenomenon is clearly illustrated by the three examples cited above regarding the transformations in three leading American synagogues: Detroit's Congregation Beth-El, Cincinnati's K. K. Beneh Yeshurun, and New York's famous Temple Emanu-El.

In both the Sephardic and German instances, we saw examples where the minority language, or mother-tongue, was abandoned in favor of the dominant language and culture.

The final and the largest migration came from the Eastern European countries that were largely under Russian influence. Speaking of the Eastern European community, Professor Wirth found that:

> The American Ghetto (Jewish community), on the other hand, is, as a rule, split up into various sections, containing various national groups of Jews and reflecting the influence of heterogeneous waves of immigration, as well as successive generations of the same group.[10]

> The social distances between Roumanian Jews and Hungarian Jews, between Lithuanians and Poles, between Poles and Russians, and between Russians and Galicians are sometimes so great as to make corporate action within the Ghetto almost impossible.[11]

These newest American Jews represented a broad spectrum of groupings: Different countries and provinces of origin, conflicting temperaments, and conflicting social attitudes. There were various shadings of orthodoxy; there were atheists, anarchists, socialists, and assimilationists. Yet they effected the clearest identity and left the strongest impact as a unified community. They were united by their large numbers and common social problems and needs. However, the greatest instrument or cultural tool in their unity was the Yiddish language, as the rich Yiddish cultural institutions that were

---

[9] *Ibid.,* p. 14.
[10] Wirth, p. 204.
[11] *Ibid.,* p. 224.

forged by the language evince. It may be appropriate to repeat the quotation from Robert Ezra Park's famous study of the American immigrant press:

> No other foreign language press has succeeded in reflecting so much of the intimate life of the people which it represents, or reacted so powerfully upon the opinion, thought, and aspirations of the public for which it exists. This is particularly true of the Yiddish daily newspapers of New York City.[12]

Through the vehicle of the press, the language and culture were brought into every Jewish home and became part of every Jew's life. In support of this, we again call attention to the remark of the authoritative journalist and critic, Samuel Niger: "The Yiddish press and the social movement it represented gave the intelligentsia a people, and the people an intellectual leadership. . . . Creative individuals found an audience, and the spiritually thirsty masses found an opportunity to quench their thirst."[13] Letter-writing by the readers to their favorite Yiddish newspaper took on a special social character. In addition to the typical "Dear Abby" material, there was a clear, transparent, almost naked, reflection of the social problems, the needs, and the desires of the Yiddish-speaking masses.[14]

We have seen, too, that the Yiddish mother-tongue was an integral factor in the development of the fraternal and landsmanshaft movement. Here, powerful expressions of nostalgia, which tied the immigrants to the old culture by planting the name of the old shtetl and its culture and language in a new soil, helped them adapt their lives and needs to the new environment.[15]

The Jewish labor movement stands out consistently in the background of our analyses and descriptions of Yiddish institutional life. Here the language was a basic tool in the hands of the leaders. Moreover, it was never an artificial device. The language of the

---

[12] Robert Ezra Park, *The Immigrant Press and its Control* (New York: 1922), p. 89.
[13] Samuel Niger, "Yiddish Culture," in *Jewish People: Past and Present,* 4:289.
[14] See Appendix B to Chapter 7, the *Forverts' Bintl Brief.*
[15] See Appendix A to Chapter 8, *Constitutions of the Landsmanshaften.*

people and their native culture were naturally and logically integrated into their social movements. The sweatshop and the trade union were Yiddish phenomena in a Yiddish ghetto world.

The Eastern European Jews lived in a world of Jewish values and attitudes. There was an ethnic unity expressed through the medium of a national language and culture. From all this evolved the communal homegeneity that impressed itself lastingly upon the American culture.

We have also noted that the historical, economic, and social factors that have effected a restratification of the American population generally have, even more, reshaped the Jewish community. The end of immigration, the native character of the Jewish population, and the new middle-class status have combined to produce an apparently altered American Jew.

But is this "new Jew" so completely divorced from the "old"? We think not. An examination of the membership, and even to a large extent the leadership, of the Conservative and Reform movements will reveal that they consist almost entirely of first and second generation descendants of the East-European immigrants.[16] One study of the development of an American Jewish upper-class community reveals that a Ukrainian-born Jewish businessman "was the most powerful member of Philadelphia's Jewish community and one of the most influential men in the whole city."[17] There is also an endless list of Americanized Eastern European Jews (too long, too redundant, and too obvious to include here) and their descendants who have taken leadership in business and industry, in the fields of community relations, social work, and the arts and sciences.

An interesting phenomenon is the rekindling of Yiddish cultural awareness in the breasts of second-generation American Jews who have been imbued with the national culture in their childhood but have partially lost it somewhere in growing up. Under the auspices of Wayne State University, Sarah Zweig Betsky has published an anthology of 46 Yiddish poems, transliterated and translated into

---

[16] Digby Baltzell, "The Development of the Jewish Upper Class in Philadelphia," in Sklare, *The Jews*, p. 283; see also Sklare, *Conservative Judaism*.
[17] Baltzell, p. 284.

English.[18] Seventeen 20th-century Yiddish poets are represented, twelve of whom are still alive and vigorously creating. Although Mrs. Betsky shares the current doubts about the "long continuance of Yiddish" and sees it lying "in an unmarked grave, along with seven million mouths that gave it voice," she herself is evidently largely a product of this Yiddish culture, and is driven by a deep power to give it contemporary expression. It is noteworthy that in her preface the poetess reveals her indebtedness to several forces that made it possible for her to produce her work. There are her parents, "whose vanished beauty only the tenderness of Yiddish can describe." There is the Yiddish press as exemplified by the *Jewish Daily Forward*. And the *Arbeiter Ring* Yiddish language schools, "which have helped several generations of American-born Jews share in the culture which might otherwise been denied them," are acknowledged. Then she thanks the Congregation Shaarey-Zedek of Detroit, and a Jewish artist for permission to use his Torah pointers as illustrations in the book. At the very outset she thanked Wayne University for making her work possible. A glance will show us that here we have an example of the modern intellectual American Jew, a product of: 1) a Yiddish parental heritage, 2) Yiddish education and cultural environment, 3) influence of modern religious institutions, and 4) modern university higher-education and scholarship.

Bernard Weinryb writes a perceptive summation:[19]

The Eastern European Jew and his American descendants have, with some exceptions, preserved many emotional loyalties to their tradition and heritage, vestiges of group identification, and a feeling of sympathy and kinship with brethren abroad and with those in Israel. As the Americanized Eastern European Jew and his children have become the leaders of Jewish organizations these trends make themselves felt in varying degrees in contemporary Jewish community life. . . . He is little versed in Jewish learning and lax in religious observance, but clings to vestiges of his heritage, activates Jewish values and survival, has an emotional attachment to the group, and experiences the feeling of Klal Yisroel.

---

[18] *Onions, and Cucumbers and Plums* (Detroit: Wayne State University Press, 1958).
[19] Weinryb, p. 21.

We may thus conclude that the Yiddish culture of the Eastern European Jewish community has had a valid existence and has not vanished into nothingness. It has instead been altered in appearance because of changed social and cultural needs. It still lives in the body of the contemporary Jewish community where its influence is being continuously felt and manifested.

What is the future of the Yiddish language per se to be?

We have traced the birth and the development of the language, showing that it was not a contrived "jargon" but rather a regulated language of literary merit. Maurice Samuel has written that "Yiddish is a language like others, with certain inalienable values and an inalienable spirit."[20] And we have seen that the language developed in response to a social need for the Jews of medieval times to develop a means "outside the feudal order," of communication, education, and recreation in their society. As all languages do, it evolved from stage to stage, following the historical and social process of the people. It had a particularly vital importance to the people serving, as it did, a persecuted and wandering folk.

Commenting historically on the survival of Jewish languages, Salo Baron has written:[21]

> The renaissance of Yiddish letters was . . . amazing. The language previously disparaged . . . developed a new literature, artistic and scientific, which could stand comparison with many a literature of the western world.

In the dessert of pessimism there are oases of hope. Judah Pilch writes:[22]

> It seems to us . . . that just as in the case of the Jews themselves, who survived . . . Yiddish letters will live on notwithstanding the operation of all laws of logic that indicate . . . natural decline.

[20] Maurice Samuel, *Prince of the Ghetto* (New York: Alfred A. Knopf, 1948), p. 275.
[21] Salo W. Baron, *A Social and Religious History of the Jews* (New York: Columbia University Press, 1937), 2:334.
[22] *Jewish Life in our Times* (New York: Behrman's Publishing Company, 1943), p. 51.

A. A. Roback is an interesting and interested commentator on Yiddish institutions. In his study of Yiddish literature he writes:[23]

> Yiddish readers and theatre public are declining in America. . . . However, there is no dearth of writers: and fifty years hence, yes, even a century from now, Jewish writers, poets, and playwrights will probably still inject their hormones into the American bloodstream."

He develops an interesting thought process:

> Paradoxically enough, the national death instinct is stronger in prosperity, that is to say, when the individual is entirely dominated by the life instinct, and conversely, the national life instinct predominates at the time of a crisis, when the individual life instinct is at an ebb.[24]

In other words, when the Jews are threatened they will rally to preserve their national and cultural values. They will turn to religion, Roback says, but even more to culture and to social patterns, folkways, folk-lore, art, literature, and most of all to the vital medium, the popular language. He continues:

> What is most important, after all, is the intrinsic vitality of the group, its power of resistance, while the amount of exposure, the extent of the destructive force, must be regarded as subsidiary to the national élan, which apparently can adjust itself so as to preserve its own cultural values.[25]

As to the foreseeable future: certainly the heart of the Yiddish language and literature is not dead today. The very fact that there are many translations and adaptations of the Yiddish literature (such as Maurice Samuel's translations of Peretz and Sholem Asch, theatrical adaptations like "*The World of Sholem Aleichem*," and translations of modern poets like Mrs. Betsky's) attests to the existence and vitality of the original form.

---

[23] *The Story of Yiddish Literature* (New York: Yiddish Scientific Institute, YIVO, 1940), p. 314.
[24] *Ibid.*, pp. 320–21.
[25] *Ibid.*

Edward Sapir believed that: "Language is a cultural or social product and must be understood as such."[26] He thought of language as "a culture preserving instrument." He wrote that: "The importance of language as a whole for the definition, expression, and transmission of culture is undoubted."[27]

The future of Yiddish must depend upon social factors. History has played some tricks on our ability at prognostication. For example, the virtual destruction of Yiddish and Jewish creativeness in the Soviet Union, where Yiddish culture was making some of its greatest strides, ran counter to the expectations of most informed observers. On the other hand, the renascence of interest in Yiddish in America comes as a surprise to many.

The rich contribution of the Yiddish language has been well stamped upon our culture. The future service of the language to the Jews in America and its destiny as a cultural tool, in the final analysis, lie in the hands of the people themselves, who must shape their societies and cultural destinies to suit their special social needs.

---

[26] David G. Mandelbaum, ed., *Edward Sapir: Culture, Language and Personality* (Berkeley and Los Angeles: University of California Press, 1958), p. vi.
[27] *Ibid.*, pp. 18 and 34.

Contents of Appendixes

Appendix

to

Chapter 5

TABLE 1

Jewish Immigration into the U.S. (1881 to 1898)
(Adapted from S. Joseph, *Jewish Immigration to the U.S.* [New York: Columbia University, 1914], p. 173.)

Year	Number of Immigrants
1881	5,692
1882	13,202
1883	8,731
1884	11,445
1885	16,862
1886	21,173
1887	33,044
1888	28,881
1889	25,352
1890	28,639
1891	51,398
1892	76,373
1893	35,322
1894	29,179
1895	26,191
1896	32,848
1897	20,372
1898	23,654

TABLE 2

Jewish Immigration into the United States (1899 to 1930)
(Adapted from Mark Wishnitzer, *To Dwell in Safety* [Philadelphia:
Jewish Publication Society of America, 1949], p. 289.)

Year	No. of Immigrants	Year	No. of Immigrants
1899	37,415	1915	26,497
1900	60,764	1916	15,108
1901	58,098	1917	17,342
1902	57,688	1918	3,672
1903	76,203	1919	3,055
1904	106,236	1920	14,292
1905	129,910	1921	119,036
1906	153,748	1922	53,524
1907	149,182	1923	49,989
1908	103,387	1924	10,292
1909	57,551	1925	10,267
1910	84,260	1926	11,483
1911	91,223	1927	11,639
1912	80,595	1928	11,639
1913	101,330	1929	12,479
1914	138,051	1930	11,526

TABLE 3

Jewish Immigration into the United States (1881–1910)
Showing Country of Nativity
(Adapted from Joseph, p. 162.)

Country of Nativity	Total	Absolute Numbers			Percentages		
		1881–1890	1891–1900	1901–1910	1881–1890	1891–1900	1901–1910
Russia	1,119,059	135,003	279,811	704,245	69.9	71.1	72.1
Austria-Hungary	281,150	44,619	83,720	152,811	23.1	21.3	15.7
Romania	67,057	6,967	12,789	47,301	3.6	3.2	4.8
United Kingdom	42,589			42,589			4.4
Germany	20,454	5,354	8,827	6,273	2.8	2.3	.7
British North America	9,701			9,701			1.0
Turkey	5,081			5,081			.5
France	2,273			2,273			.2
All Others	15,436	1,078	8,369	5,989	.6	2.1	.6
Total	1,562,800	193,021	393,516	976,263	100.0	100.0	100.0

TABLE 4

Destination of Jewish Immigrants, 1899 to 1910,
By Division
(Adapted from Joseph, p. 195.)

Division	Jewish Immigrants	Percent
North Atlantic States	923,549	86.0
North Central States	110,998	10.3
South Atlantic States	25,149	2.3
South Central States	8,324	.8
Western States	6,384	.6
Total	1,074,404	100.0

TABLE 5

Destination of Jewish Immigrants, 1899 to 1910,
By Principal States
(Adapted from Joseph, p. 195.)

State	Jewish Immigrants	Percent of total
New York	690,296	64.2
Pennsylvania	108,534	10.1
Massachusetts	66,023	6.1
Illinois	50,931	4.7
New Jersey	31,279	3.2
Ohio	20,531	1.9
Maryland	18,700	1.7
Connecticut	16,254	1.5
Missouri	12,476	1.2
Minnesota	7,029	.7
Wisconsin	6,369	.6
Michigan	5,970	.6
Rhode Island	5,023	.5
All others	31,989	3.0
Total	1,074,404	100.0

TABLE 6

Jewish Immigrants Reporting Occupations, 1899 to 1910
(Adapted from Joseph, pp. 187–188.)

Group	Number	Percent
Professional	7,455	1.3
Skilled laborers	395,823	67.1
Laborers	69,444	11.8
Servants	65,532	11.1
Merchants and dealers	31,491	5.3
Farm laborers	11,460	1.9
Farmers	1,008	.2
Miscellaneous	8,051	1.3
Total	590,267	100.0

TABLE 7

Jewish Immigrants Engaged in
Professional Occupations
(Adapted from Joseph, pp. 187–88.)

Occupation	Number
Actors	232
Architects	108
Clergymen	350
Editors	84
Electricians	359
Engineers	484
Lawyers	34
Literary and scientific persons	385
Musicians	1,624
Officials (gov.)	18
Physicians	290
Sculptors and artists	357
Teachers	2,192
Others	938
Total	7,455

TABLE 8

Jewish Immigrants Reporting Skilled
Occupations, 1899 to 1910
(Adapted from Joseph, pp. 187–88.)

Occupation	Number	Percent of total skilled
Tailors	145,272	36.6
Carpenters, joiners, etc.	40,901	10.3
Dressmakers and seamstresses	39,482	10.0
Shoemakers	23,519	5.9
Clerks and accountants	17,066	4.3
Painters and glaziers	16,387	4.1
Butchers	11,413	2.9
Bakers	10,925	2.8
Locksmiths	9,385	2.4
Blacksmiths	8,517	2.2
Total	322,867	81.5

TABLE 9

Number of Jews in Largest Cities of United States
(Adapted from Jacob Lestchinsky, "Economic and Social Development of American Jewry," in *Jewish People: Past and Present*, New York, 4:58.)

City	Number of Jews	
	1900	1925
New York	500,000	1,600,000
Los Angeles	2,000	40,000
Chicago	60,000	270,000
Philadelphia	75,000	250,000
Boston	40,000	70,000
Detroit	10,000	45,000
Baltimore	25,000	55,000
Cleveland	20,000	70,000
Newark	15,000	50,000
Pittsburgh	10,000	50,000
San Francisco	15,000	25,000
St. Louis	25,000	45,000

TABLE 10

Jewish population of New York City, as estimated by the New York Kehilla and as reported in the *Jewish Communal Register* of 1917–18

Manhattan	696,000
Bronx	211,000
Brooklyn	568,000
Queens	23,000
Richmond	5,000
Total	1,503,000

TABLE 11

Growth of Jewish Population in United States
(1820–1953)
(Adapted from Lestschinsky, p. 56.)

Year	No. Jews	% of Total U.S. Pop.	% of World Jew Pop.
1820	5,000	0.05	0.16
1850	50,000	0.21	1.06
1880	275,000	0.55	3.44
1900	1,100,000	1.45	10.00
1925	3,800,000	3.25	27.14
1945	4,700,000	3.35	44.80
1953	5,100,000	3.25	44.00

Appendixes

to

Chapter 7

Appendix A

This section consists of translations of headlines selected from the major publications. The samples were taken from 48 different issues of the Yiddish newspapers during the years of 1906 and 1909.

FRONT PAGE NEWS TOPICS SELECTED ON THE BASIS OF FEATURED HEADLINES

Forverts

February 1, 1906

1. George Gapon and Krushevan are candidates for election to the Russian parliament (Duma)—Registration for the elections are taking place.

February 4, 1906

1. The Jews of Homel are in great danger—"Haman" has arisen against the unfortunate city.
2. Revolutionaries inform the Turkish Sultan that his end is near.

February 7, 1906

1. Ludmilla Wolkenstein shot in Vladivostok—600 are felled by Nicholas' murderers—amongst them are the famous revolutionary and her husband.
2. Russian soldiers refuse to shoot at the masses and officers man the machine guns themselves.

February 11, 1906

1. Zubatov, the spy and the black-character Meshchersky are again taking up their devilish work.
2. Admiral Tchuknin shot by a woman.
3. General strike of knee-pants workers. All New York shops are closed today.

February 14, 1906

1. It is true that Nicholas has taken the money and money-orders (sent for relief to Russian Jews). But he will be forced to relinquish it.
2. No pogrom in Kalarash; a dispatch to the *London Times* denies yesterday's report.

February 21, 1906

1. Minsker Cossacks force Jews to submit to the sign-of-the-cross.

February 28, 1906

1. The handsome Italian, the "kind" cadet and the still "kinder" policeman—a panorama of the "Tenderloin" in court.
2. A real Parliament? A report that Nicholas has become pious, and the Duma will be a genuine Parliament—the higher chamber will be half elected.

Warheit

February 1, 1906

1. Another hangman executed; factories dynamited and bombed throughout Russia.
2. Damage in Homel amounts to $2,000,000; a student is martyred.

February 4, 1906

1. Revolutionaries suffer hunger-torture. The Vilna Governor orders murder. No mercy in Vilna!

February 7, 1906

1. Our relief fund pocketed by the Russian police.
2. 13 revolutionaries shot; government distrusts its defenders.
3. Jews again driven out of Moscow; bombs in Odessa!
4. America becoming distrustful of Russian commerce.
5. Gould's son-in-law will duel Rothschild. The "graff" is broke— penniless.

February 14, 1906

1. A secret congress of Jews; gathering will pledge unity in the battle against the enemy.

February 21, 1906

1. The Hero of Sevastopol stands before his "judges." Captain Schmidt and 37 sailors and 2 students face military tribunal.
2. Cossacks are fighting under the red banner.

February 25, 1906

1. Nicholas permits execution of 1,400 revolutionaries. The hangman of Moscow resigns out of fear.
2. Rumanian Queen preaches anti-semitism in America. Elizabetha publishes article attacking Rumanian Jews.

February 28, 1906

1. When he needs a loan he becomes "liberal." Czar promises Duma rights, abolition of miltary courts; will free prisoners, halt execution of revolutionaries.
2. The *Tageblatt* is being sold at auction through court-appointed receiver.

Yiddishes Tageblatt

February 1, 1906

1. ARSONIST. Five man-made fires in East Side tenements. Five buildings destroyed in several hours at East Broadway and Division Street. Many lives endangered; was it the work of an anti-Semite?

February 4, 1906

1. Police Chief of Homel is leader of Pogroms. Cossacks and soldiers under his orders rob and burn Jewish property.
2. East Side Jews turned away. Many Jews are asked to "go home" when they visit the building of the United Hebrew Charities

where they wish to testify about the manner in which relief funds are being distributed; they are turned back by the "big shots" in the "back rooms."

February 7, 1906

1. Have the Russian police confiscated our fund? The *London Times* reports that the police have taken our relief funds; our representatives do not believe it to be true.
2. There is no self-defense for the Jews of Homel.
3. A hooligan murders old Jew on Scamel St. It is a mystery!

February 11, 1906

1. The tyrant of Sevastopol is shot by woman. She is killed. Revolutionaries kill hooligans.

February 14, 1906

1. Jewish "Napoleon" captured—Rubenstein arrested in Riga. After months of diligent work the police arrested the man who planned and led the Baltic revolt. He was known as the Baltic "Napoleon" because of his military skill.

February 18, 1906

1. Durnova plans new pogroms, is caught red-handed.
2. Details of the murder of Reb Benyomen Rabinovich.

February 21, 1906

1. 40 thousand workers are starving in St. Petersburg.
2. A report of the fund. At a large meeting of the relief fund a description was given of how the funds were blocked in Russia. Schiff's son is treasurer.

February 25, 1906

1. Jewish Congress in Russia. Statistics revealed at St. Petersburg show that thousands of freedom-fighters were slaughtered.
2. Polish arrests, and 600 million ruble damage. Tyrant of Warsaw killed.

February 28, 1906

1. Nicholas breaks his chains; the Duma a genuine Parliament. Mass executions prohibited.

Morgn Zhurnal (Morning Journal)

February 1, 1906

1. Russian Premier openly opposes parliamentary government.

February 4, 1906

1. Russian Premier tells Jews that they may expect very little from the Duma.
2. Homel's pogrom was similar to Kishinev; soldiers and police aided the hooligans in beating the Jews.
3. The order to stop chaos comes too late; jailed revolutionaries are starving to death.

February 7, 1906

1. A Jew is murdered on Scamel St. in New York.
2. Poles guilty of multiple crimes.

February 11, 1906

1. Kessler's murderer is found.
2. Johnson is innocent; the convicted Negro divulges the murderer of Miss Allenson.
3. New uprising of the sailors of the Baltic Fleet.

February 14, 1906

1. Artillery and hand grenades used against Jews; new attacks against Jews in many Russian cities; Cossacks attack Jews in Bessarabia.
2. Homel in state of siege.
3. Bundists take 6,000 rubles from the Rabbi of Trisk.
4. The castle at Schlisselburg becomes a museum.

February 21, 1906

1. Wilhelm wants war. France appeals to the world at large. The conference over Morocco is reaching critical point.
2. The manner in which our money is distributed. Report at the Relief Committee. Report is given on what has been observed in the Czar's "Medina" (country).
3. Homel received 40,000 rubels.

February 25, 1906

1. Historical Sabbath. Dry goods stores in the Jewish quarter are closed.
   Scores of retail stores that are normally open were closed yesterday throughout the East Side of New York. Campaign planned to close all stores on the Sabbath.
2. Jewish Congress condemns the "Bund."
3. The bloody result of the Czar's month of "freedom":
   1,400 revolutionaries executed, 10,000 arrested, 78 publications closed, 58 editors jailed.

February 28, 1906

1. Jews mobilize army of self-defense. The Jewish *Samo Oborona* is organizing Jews under the age of 30 into a gigantic army to fight against new impending pogroms. The weapons may not be used for revolutionary purposes. Nicholas becomes liberal again.
2. Big Murder Mystery (local).

Freie Arbeiter Shtimme (Weekly)

February 3, 1906

1. Our Russian comrades.
2. An example of striker's freedom.
3. Visiting the banquet of the actor's union.
4. Campaigning for Jesus on the barricades.

February 10, 1906

1. The impending miners' strike.

2. Dr. Merrison's speech about "Territorialism"; the debate between him and Dr. Zhitlowski.
3. News from Russia—prospects of the Revolution.

February 17, 1906

1. Alice Roosevelt
2. The revolution lives! (in Russia)
3. Will the miners strike?

February 24, 1906

1. They demand blood! (references to American capitalists)
2. Nicholas has the money.

March 3, 1906

1. JOHANN MOST—the celebration of his 60th birthday.
2. The conspiracy!
3. Tuesday at the Grand Theatre: benefit for the *Freie Arbeiter Shtimme*.

Forverts

November 1, 1909

1. Thoughtful people, do not forget to assert yourself! (Vote Socialist!)
2. How your vote should be registered tomorrow. (Vote Socialist!)
3. Do not permit them to steal Socialist votes!
   (Below these headlines there is a prominent picture of William Carlin, Socialist candidate for Assembly. This is also supported with an editorial urging Socialist votes.)

November 4, 1909

1. The horrible confession of a Jewish youth. Alvin Cohen, seventeen, confesses murder of three-year-old Alex Cohen.
2. Serious post-election considerations (analysis of election losses and the role of Hearst).
3. The verdict against Gompers (story about labor injunction against A. F. of L. by capitalist court).

November 7, 1909

1. ACCIDENT AT PENN STATION!

November 10, 1909

1. News from the "Madam Steinheil case" from Paris.
2. Executive Committee of Federation recommends appeals (references to A. F. of L. Convention).

November 16, 1909

1. Court of Appeals rejects Gompers' appeal; appeal to highest court of the land is last alternative.
2. Labor leaders oppose two-week general strike.
3. Story about three hundred trapped miners.

November 22, 1909

1. The spectacular rescue of those who were buried alive (the rescue of the coal miners).
2. To Louis Miller! (a letter involving the feud between the *Forverts* and the *Warheit,* and its editor, L. Miller).
3. Another Socialist victory in Germany!

November 25, 1909

1. The entire ladies' waist trade in New York is stopped! All eastside halls filled with strikers; many manufacturers are meeting union demands; unusual enthusiasm amongst the strikers!

November 28, 1909

1. More on the Philadelphia murder trial.
2. Police are already becoming "active" in the ladies' waist strike.
3. Upper East Side Jewish Woman swindled of $15,000 in effort to get divorce.

Tageblatt

November 1, 1909

1. Citizens' wife must be admitted regardless of eye disease (a ruling of U.S. judge on immigration case).

2. Mine explosion in Pennsylvania.
3. Election campaign ends today; Hearst's mass meeting in Madison Square Garden.
4. Story regarding hold-up
5. Fast speed of ship saves thousands!

November 4, 1909

1. A two-column spread on "Madam Steinheil case" in Paris.

November 7, 1909

1. Bloody battle to save a Jewish girl from apostasy; war between Jews and Christians in Radam develops into bloody slaughter and pogrom.

November 10, 1909

1. Rabbi I. M. Asher dies; our great loss (this Rabbi was well known Harlem orthodox leader).

Appendix B

THE BINTL BRIEF

This section contains 10 letters drawn as early samples from the Bintl Brief Column of the *Forverts*. The letters are preceded by a study of Wolfe's "Analytic Index."

(In a separate sociological study, this writer hopes to analyze a number of "Bintl Briefs," selected from different historical periods, seeking to find in them, through the eyes of the letter-writers, a reflection of social change and social restratification of the American Jews over a period of six decades.)

In Wolfe's study of the Bintl Brief (involving a sample of 400 letters), he developed an "analytic Index" based on content. He found the following 24 topics to be the most popular, the most frequently repeated:

1. America, attitude toward —·—
2. Bintel Brief, attitude toward —·—
3. Child-parent conflict — Parent-child relationship
4. Children, attitude of parents toward — Parent-child relationship
5. Desertion — Family problems
6. Divorce — Family problems
7. Domestic discord — Family problems
8. Family interference — Family problems
9. Friends and relatives sought ———
10. Husband, attitude of wife toward — Family problems
11. Immigrant demoralization — Immigrant
12. Immigrant, economic adjustment of — Immigrant
13. Immigrant, miserable environment of — Immigrant
14. Landsman, role of — Immigrant
15. Love, attitudes toward — Sex and love
16. Marital infidelity — Family problems
17. Marriage, attitude toward — Family problems
18. Parents, attitude of children toward — Parent-child relationship
19. Separation — Family problems
20. Sexes, relations of — Sex and love
21. Socialists ———
22. Suicide ———
23. Wife, attitude of husband toward — Family problems
24. Woman, participation in economic life — Sex and love

Our analysis of the above topics reveals that one-half (12) deal directly with family problems; nine of which concern "man-and-wife," and three "parent-child" relationships. Three captions involve: sex, love, and the role of the woman; four concern the immigrant and landsleit. The other five topics include single entries. Please note that, where it applies, we have indicated the broader category in the column at the right. On the left we have retained Wolfe's alphabetical order (24 topics).

Letter No. 1

March 5, 1906

Dear Mr. Editor:

I am going to do a certain thing and if you will be friendly enough and answer me, what to do, I shall do as you will advise. But I beg of you to answer me soon if possible, *because I will not do anything until I read your answer.*

I came to America, leaving a boy in Europe, with whom I was in love for two years. When I had to leave, we agreed, that he should come soon after at his own expense. But now a year has already passed, since I came here, and now he asks me, that I send him a ticket for the boat and money. Now in the meantime *a very fine and rich boy fell in love with me.* And so, I ask of you, dear Mr. Editor, what I should do; *send for the one in Russia or marry the one here.* That is why I want a speedy answer from you, because the boy *here does not want to wait, and he knows that my answer to him depends upon your advice.*

Letter No. 2

February 21, 1906

Dear Editor:

Permit me to turn to you with the following request.

I am a young woman, who came to this country 3 years ago. Here a boy fell in love with me and I likewise.

But as I have three older sisters and they are all unmarried, they hinder me and make all sorts of scenes, and my whole family does the same.

The reason that they give for their anger and rows is, that I, as a younger sister have no right to go out with a boy and expecially to marry him. The only thing I can do is to leave home and my whole family.

But, before I decide upon such a step I want to ask the opinion of the worthy readers of your paper, *whom I will positively obey, no matter how they advise me.*

I hope that you will not deny my request, and you will be so kind and not print my name.

Letter No. 3

February 6, 1906

Dear Mr. Editor:

Permit me to ask you how to act in the following situation. I have been here but a short time, and fell in love with a girl, who is American born. She, like all American girls, loves to dance, to attend balls and above all to have a good time, and I as a *Socialist, who have just come from such a revolutionary country, do not care for that.* When it comes to love, I love with my innocent heart. If I should ask her, whether she loves me too, she would no doubt be unable to refuse me and would say that she loves. But I know in my own heart that if I too attended dances, balls, she would certainly love me. *I cannot influence her with my socialist ideas.*

Can you perhaps explain to me how one can get those follies out of her head.

Your Constant Reader.

Letter No. 4

February 5, 1906

Dear Mr. Editor:

With this letter a poor mother with a bitter heart turns to you. And as I know that your paper does not refuse space for the letters of the unfortunate, the worried, and the embittered, I am certain that my words too will be printed in your worthy paper.

My trouble consists of this: I have a son, who is otherwise quite a good child, devoted to his family, but . . . he is too much of a socialist. I am by no means opposed to that; let him be whatever he wants to be, especially when socialism teaches him to be a good man and a devoted child. But socialism hinders my son from becoming a husband and a father of children. My son has a bride, a very dear child, but he is so devoted to the movement that it is not possible to persuade him to get married. Since the revolution in Russia began, he is so caught up in it that it is simply impossible even to talk to him about marriage. My heart is broken. I cannot bear the pain of the bride. Perhaps you will advise me, dear Editor, how to influence my son, that socialism is socialism and getting married too is a human affair.

The Troubled Mother

Letter No. 5

March 6, 1906

Dear Mr. Editor:

I am a greenhorn. I have only been five weeks in the country. I am a jewelry maker. I left a blind father and a stepmother in Russia. Before my departure my father begged me not to forget him. I promised that I would send him the first money I should earn. I walked around two weeks and looked for work. But at the end of the third week I succeeded in getting a job. I worked a week and received eight dollars for the week. I am working the third week now. I paid for my board and bought certain necessities, such as a hat, shoes, and some small items, and I have a few dollars, too. Now, Mr. Editor, I want to ask you to give me some advice, as to what to do. Should I send my father a few dollars for Passover, or should I keep them for myself? Because the work at our place is at an end, and I may have to be without work. So that I do not know what to do. I hope that you will give me some advice, and I shall obey you just as you tell me.

Y. Mednikoff

Letter No. 6

February 20, 1906

Dear Editor:

Working for a very long time with a Gentile woman in the shop, I came to know her very intimately, and we began to go out together very often. In the end, we fell in love with each other. Naturally, we decided that I should not be a Gentile nor she a Jewess. But in the course of a year I realized that we were not compatible. Whenever an acquaintance, a friend, comes home, I note a great dissatisfaction on her face. When she sees me reading a Jewish paper, her face changes color. She does not tell me anything, but I see that the woman is wasting away like a candle. I feel that she is very unhappy with me although I am certain she loves me. On top of that, she is to become a mother soon. Her tie to me becomes stronger. Only a few weeks ago Christ awoke within her. Every Sunday she rises at dawn, hurries to church and comes back with eyes swollen from crying. Whenever I go out with her and it happens that we pass a church, tremors seize her.

Give me, dear Mr. Editor some advice as to what I should do. To convert to Christianity is out of the question. She will not stop going to church. What can be done, that there may not be so much trouble in our home?

Hyman Frumkin

Letter No. 7

March 15, 1906

Dear Mr. Editor:

The story I want to tell you is this. I have two little girls, one 10 years and the other 13. Both go to school. A few months ago a friend of mine told me, that he saw one of my girls walking around arm-in-arm with a little boy, who probably goes to the same school with her. I happen to be a busy man, I have a stationery store and am always occupied, I cannot even get away for a minute. Of course my wife is busy with a new one, and she too cannot leave the house. So with tears in my eyes I begged my friend, to stop working for a few days at my expense and watch my two girls. My friend did not refuse me this favor, and he spied on my two girls on the other sidewalk, as soon as the children left school. And he saw something horrible. As soon as my daughters walked out of school, they walked up to the corner of the street and stood waiting. . . . About fifteen minutes later two boys from the same school met them. My friend followed them, and he saw how the boys took candy, chocolates and peanuts from their pockets and treated my daughters. The girls would take the presents and for this would drag around for many hours through tens of streets. It would not have grieved me, because they walked around, but my friend saw such wicked behavior on the part of the boys, who are very much like the 'gang' of the great bandits. At each street corner they would go into a hallway. My daughters would laugh out loud, and my friend heard both times how they agreed to meet in the evening at a certain spot in Hester Street Park. My friend watched them in the park too, and his face burned for shame at what he saw the little bandits do and at the indifference of the two girls. Walking home from the park, they several times walked into other hallways. What they did there, this my friend did not see, because I told him, not to show himself to my daughters since they know him.

I cannot keep them in the house: And so I can find no way out. I am afraid to turn to the police, lest they be given over to the Gerry Society and even there, I think, they do not turn into nuns.

What is to be done, dear Editor?

The Unhappy Father

Letter No. 8

February 4, 1906

Dear Mr. Editor:

I am yet a very young woman, and I do not want to praise myself, but anyone who sees me admits that I am very pretty, tall, healthy and strong, and full of desire to live. But notwithstanding my good qualities I remained on account of various circumstances lonely, without friends. But by chance I met a man who is not only a very kind person but quite an educated man as well, whom I came to love greatly for his precious qualities, so I married him.

But after living with him a short time, I realized that he is my direct opposite. I am tall, and he is very small, short. I am healthy, strong, and he is *nebach* slim and slight like a splinter: I am pretty and attractive and he is a horror: hollow cheeks, twisted teeth and so on and so on. Just as he is enchanting spiritually so is he disgusting physically.

Living with him a short time, I learned to hate him. When he was not home, I loved and respected him; as soon as he would enter the house I could not look at him. And as I could no longer go on living a dual life, I separated from him.

And here a worse tragedy began with me. My two sisters butted in and do not let me live, and torment me and torture me for the great crime that I committed against this man.

I therefore turn to you dear Editor, you shall tell me the truth, if I truly deserved to be condemned for separating from the man as I am condemned by my sisters or whether it is possible to justify me somehow.

Do not print my name and my city and this is really because I do not want to cause any grief or humiliation to that man, whom I love and honor as a human being but not as a husband or a life companion.

Anonymous

Letter No. 9

March 27, 1906

Dear Mr. Editor:

My wife is one of those types who loves when passing someone to rub her shoulder, so that one may feel that she is present. She is a great preacher of women's rights. Women, she says, stand on a much higher plane than men, and the woman who cannot control her husband is an animal. Wherever she puts her foot, there you find accidents. She is very nervous. She has a big mouth, cries easily, and hates to listen to anyone. Such is my wife. I myself am a peace-loving, quiet man. I conduct a small business, a two-by-four grocery store. My wife is the business lady in the family. This is how she talks to me: 'What can I do when I have a dummy for a husband, such a *schlemiel*.' And so, she is the head of the business, and I am the arm. Work for me, says she, she has plenty, a steady job for day and night. If there is no work for me in the store, says she, then do the housework. For me, home is a prison. I am out in the open just once a year: on Yom Kippur when the store is closed and my old woman is in the synagogue. During the entire year, when there is any time, she is the first to go out. And when she goes out she sees to it that I have so much work that I cannot go out even. There is always quarreling in the house. If I order goods, it's all wrong. If I charge high prices, I drive away customers. If I sell cheap, I waste her money. If I am sick, I am lazy. If I want to read the paper she argues, 'Why should a businessman read a paper? You have to help conduct Russian politics? Aren't you ashamed of yourself, just like a little boy. . . .'

In short, I smuggle in a paper. Just listen how it is done: In the morning, when my wife is still sleeping, the first thing I do is to twist and wrinkle the paper in such a way that it should appear in case of danger like yesterday's paper. Then I unroll it slowly that no sound be heard, I hastily glance at the headlines, and I check the most interesting ones where they are found. All this I do with the greatest caution, not losing for a moment the thought that she might hear. Then I bury it somewhere and breathe freely.

How can one stand for so much? I have children whom I love, and their fate frightens me. A divorce can be of little use to me. I see no way out.

Do not publish my name; also pardon me for writing so much. This is not even a tenth of my heavy heart.

The Woman's Husband

Letter No. 10

March 13, 1906

Dear Editor of the *Forward*:

My married life consists of the following: We are living in a room and bedroom on the top floor on Allen Street. We cannot pay more than eleven dollars a month. I have two children so they are pale, without a drop of blood. More than once the doctor told me I should move, because the children haven't enough air. Lately, however, I realized that many of my acquaintances, who are not better off than we, live nevertheless in nice, comfortable rooms and in a better neighborhood. They have each several boarders, and in this way the rent does not come to much. I began to reason with my husband that we ought to do the same, so he does not want to listen. He does not want to have any boarders, because he fears, that on account of them there would be quarreling between us. He is simply afraid that I would become jealous, if we were to take in a female boarder, and that he would become jealous if a male boarder is taken in. 'Who can tell what may happen!' he says. I laughed at it, but he is like steel and iron and does not want to hear of it. He is in the shop the whole day and when he comes home, he eats and goes somewhere or goes to bed. But I want to work hard, wait on boarders so that I may have comfortable rooms for my children, and for myself too.

Mr. Editor, which of us is right?

Rose Eisenberg

Appendix C

YIDDISH NEWSPAPERS AND PERIODICALS APPEARING IN THE UNITED STATES AS OF THE YEAR 1900

(Adapted primarily from the *American Jewish Year Book*, Vol. 1)

Abendblatt. New York City. Daily. Organ of SLP. Est. 1894.

Ashmadai, Der. New York City. Weekly. Eds. M. Rosenfeld and A. M. Sharkansky. Est. 189–?

Blumengorten, Der. Pittsburgh. Weekly. Ed. J. Liebling. Est. 189–?

Chicagoyer Yiddisher Tageblatt. Daily. Ed. L. Zolataroff. Est. 189–?

Farmer Zeitung. Est. 1885.

Folksfreind un Yiddisher Post. Pittsburgh. Ed. Joseph S. Glick.

Folksvechter, Der. Philadelphia. Weekly. Ed. John Paley. Est. 189–?

Fraye Gezellshaft, Di. New York. Monthly. (October, 1895–June, 1897) Eds. M. Leontiev and M. Katz.

Freie Arbeter Shtimme. New York. Weekly. Est. July, 1890.

Gegenvarts, Di. Philadelphia. Weekly. Ed. David Apotheker. Est. 1895–?

Groise Baitch, Di. New York. Ed. David Apotheker and Joseph Petrikovski. Est. 188–?

Hoizfreind. New York. Eds. J. Jaffa and J. Petrikovski. (September 19, 1889–January 17, 1890.

Israelit, Der. Baltimore. Weekly. Ed. William Schur. March, 1891–1893.

Israelitishe Presse. Chicago. Weekly. Eds. N. B. Ettelson and S. L. Marcus. Est. 1879–?

Licht, Dos. Philadelphia. Weekly. Ed. N. Mosessohn. Est. 1891.

Litvakl, Der. New York. Weekly. Ed. J. Jaffa. Est. 1889.

Menshnfreind, Der. New York. Weekly. Ed. N. M. Shaikewitz. Est. 1889–1891.

Mershuveth Zion. New York. Weekly. Ed. Abner Tannenbaum. Est. 1898.

Minikes Yom-Tov Bletter. New York. Ed. Ch. Jacob Minikes. Est. 1899–?

Morgenstern, Der. New York. Weekly. Eds. Dr. Braslavsky, J. Jaffa and Abner Tannenbaum. Est. 1889–90.

Natur Un Lebn. New York. Monthly. Ed. Jacob Terr. Est. August, 1897–February, 1898.

Naye Zeit, Di. New York. Monthly. Pub. SLP. May 1898–?

Nayste Post, Di. New York. Weekly. Eds. David Apotheker and Morris Wechsler. Est. 1888.

New Yorker Abend Post. New York. Daily. Ed. G. Selikovitsch. Est. February 3, 1899–?

New Yorker Yiddishe Folkszeitung. New York. Weekly. Eds. Moses Mintz and Dr. Braslavsky. Est. 1886–1887.

New Yorker Yiddishe Illustrirte Zeitung. New York. Semi-Monthly. Ed. Abraham Goldfaden. Est. October 22, 1887–July 12, 1888.

New Yorker Israelit. New York. Weekly. Ed. Mordecai Jalomstein. Est. 1875.

New Yorker Yiddishe Zeitung. New York. Weekly. Pub. K. H. Sarasohn. Est. 1872.

New Yorker Yiddishe Zeitung. New York. Weekly. Ed. Morris Wechsler. Est. 1885–1889.

Ontzaiger, Der. Brooklyn, New York. Weekly. Pub. V. E. Pomeranz. Est. 1897–?

Philadelphia Stodtzeitung. Philadelphia. Weekly. Eds. Hyman Brodsky and Ch. Malitz.

Philadelphier Post. Philadelphia. Weekly. Ed. Osias Wagman. Est. 1898.

Shulamith. New York. Weekly. Ed. Joseph Aaron Bluestone. Est. 1890.

Tegliche Presse. New York. Daily. Ed. G. Selikovitsch. 1898.

Teglicher Herold, Der. New York. Daily. Ed. M. Mintz. Est. 1894–1905.

Telefon. New York. Monthly. Pub. I. K. Buchner. Est. 1898.

Telegraf, Der. New York. Weekly. Ed. Osias Wagman. Est. 1890–1899.

Tzeit, Di. New York. Monthly. Ed. Menuchem Mendel Dolitzky. Est. 1897–1898.

Tzionist, Der. New York. Monthly. Ed. Isaac Mirsky. Est. 1898.

Tzukunft, Der. New York. Monthly. Pub. SLP. Est. 1892–1897.

Vahrheit, Di. New York. Weekly. Pub. "Pioneers of Liberty." Est. 1889.

Vechter, Der. New York. Weekly. Ed. J. Jaffa. Est. 1893.

Vegveizer In Der Amerikaner Bizness Velt, Der. New York. Weekly. Issued by N. M. Schaikewitz. Est. 1892.

Veibershe Zeitung, Di. New York. Weekly. Ed. Morris Wechsler. Est. 1888.

Velt, Di. New York. Weekly. Ed. Rayevsky. Est. 1887.

Yiddisher Farmer. New York. Monthly. Ed. Herman Rosenthal. Est. 1892–1893.

Yiddishe Folkszeitung, Di. New York. Weekly. Pubs. M. Toplowsky and G. Landau. Est. 1878.

Yiddishe Gazaetten. New York. Weekly. 7ds. M. Jalomstein, J. Paley, I. J. Zevin, L. Zolotkoff, and G. Bublick. Est. 1874.

Yiddishe Gazetten Fun Der Vest. Chicago. Weekly. Ed. George Selikovitsch. Est. 1894–1896 ?.

Yiddisher Herold, Der. New York. Weekly. Ed. G. Selikovitsch. Est. 1890.

Yiddisher Kuriyer, Der. Chicago. Weekly. Eds. L. Zolotkoff and S. M. Mwlamed. Est. December 2, 1887–1910.

Yiddishe Nayes, Di. New York. Weekly. Ed. Jacob Cohen. Est. 1871.

Yiddisher Odler, Der. Boston. Weekly. Ed. George Selikovitsch. Est. 1893.

Yiddishe Post, Di. New York. Weekly. Ed. Henry Gersoni. Est. 1872.

Yiddishe Presse, Di. Philadelphia. Ed. John Paley. Est. 1892–1894.

Yiddisher Progress, Der. Balt. Ed. Alexander Harkavy. Est. 1899.

Yiddisher Puck, Der. New York. Weekly. Eds. N. M. Shaikewitz and M. Seiffert. Est. 1894.

Yiddisher Recorder, Der. New York. Weekly. Est. 1893–1895.

Yiddishes Tageblatt. New York. Daily. Est. 1885. (Absorbed by Morgn Zhurnal April 30, 1928.)

Yiddisher Vechter, Der. New York. Weekly. Mgr. S. S. Schnur.

Yiddishe Velt, Der. New York. Weekly. Ed. Leon Zolotkoff. Est. 1892–1893.

Zun, Di. New York. Weekly. Eds. Morris Rosenfeld, Joel Aronson, Jacob Terr. Est. June–July, 1892.

Appendix D

YIDDISH NEWSPAPERS AND PERIODICALS APPEARING IN THE UNITED STATES AS OF THE YEAR 1924

(Adapted from the *American Jewish Year Book*, Vol. 26)

Der Amerikaner (The American). New York. Weekly. Est. 1904.

The Boston Jewish American. Massachusetts. Weekly. Est. 1908.

The Brooklyn Brownsville Post. Brooklyn, New York. Weekly. Est. 1909.

California Jewish Star. California. Daily. Est. 1923.

The Chicago Jewish Daily Forward. Chicago. Daily. Est. 1919.

The Daily Jewish Call. Chicago. Daily. Est. 1900 as "Der Taeglicher Yiddisher Kol."

The Daily Jewish Courier (Der Taeglicher Juedischer Courier). Chicago. Daily. Est. 1887.

The Day. New York. Daily. Amalgamation of "The Day" (Der Tog), Est. 1914, and "The Warheit" (The Truth), Est. 1905.

Far'n Folk. New York. Bi-monthly. Est. 1923.

Fraye Yugend. New York. Monthly. Est. 1923.

Die Feder. New York. Monthly. Est. 1919.

Die Freie Arbeiter Stimme (Free Voice of Labor). New York. Weekly. Est. 1899.

Freiheit. New York. Daily. Est. 1922.

Der Grosser Kundes (The Big Stick). New York. Weekly. Est. 1909.

In Sich. New York. Monthly. Est. 1922.

The Indiana Jewish Chronicle. Indianapolis. Weekly. Est. 1921.

The Jewish Daily News (Yiddishes Tageblatt). New York. Daily. Est. 1885.

The Jewish Gazette (Die Yiddishe Gazetten). New York. Weekly. Est. 1874. Weekly edition of "The Jewish Daily News."

Jewish Leader. 3 Tremont Row, Boston, Massachusetts. Weekly. Est. 1923.

The Jewish Morning Journal (Der Morgen Journal). New York. Monthly. Est. 1923.

The Jewish Press. Milwaukee. Weekly. Est. 1919.

The Jewish Record (Der Yiddisher Record). Chicago. Weekly. Est. 1909.

The Jewish Record. St. Louis. Weekly. Est. 1913.

The Jewish Volksfreund. Pittsburgh. Weekly. Est. 1889; Reorganized 1921.

The Jewish World. San Francisco. Daily. Est. 1921.

The Jewish World. Cleveland. Daily. Est. 1908.

The Jewish World. Philadelphia. Daily. Est. 1914.

Kinder Journal. New York. Monthly. Est. 1920.

Light of Israel (Yiddische Licht). New York. Weekly. Est. 1923.

Der Milwauker Wochenblatt (The Milwaukee Weekly). Milwaukee. Weekly. Est. 1914.

Saturday Post. Minneapolis. Weekly. Est. 1921.

Shriften (Writings). New York. Quarterly. Est. 1912.

Thealit. New York. Monthly. Est. 1923.

Vorwaerts (Jewish Daily Forward). New York. Daily. Est. 1897.
Dos Wort. New York. Monthly. Est. 1921.
Yiddish Wochenblatt. Fort Worth. Weekly. Est. 1921.
Dos Yiddishe Folk. New York. Weekly. Est. 1909.
Yiddisher Arbeiter. New York. Weekly. Est. 1923.
Die Zukunft (The Future). New York. Monthly. Est. 1895.

Appendix E

LIST OF NEW YORK CITY DAILIES PUBLISHED
BETWEEN 1885 AND 1923

(Source: *American Jewish Year Book*, Vol. 26)

Yiddishes Tageblatt. Est. 1885. Pub. K. H. Sarasohn. Present Ed.
   G. Bublick.
Der Yiddisher Herold. Est. 1890. Ed. G. Selikowich (26 numbers
   only).
Der Teglicher Herold. Est. 1891–1904. Ed. Michael Mintz; English
   Department, 1903–1904, Ed. Louis Lipsky.
Abend Blatt. Est. 1894–1902. Organ of the Socialist Labor Party.
Forverts. Est. 1897. Labor, Socialist. Editor Abraham Cahan.
Die Tegliche Presse. Est. 1898. Ed. G. Selikowitch (existed several
   months only).
Die Yiddishe Abend Post. Est. 1889–1905. Eds. J. Saphirstein and
   A. Rosenbaum.
Die Tegliche Volks-Zeitung. Est. 1899. Organ of the United Hebrew
   Trades.
Der Kol Von Der Ghetto. Est. 1901. Political.
Die Yiddishe Welt. Est. 1902–1904. Eds. Joseph Jacobs, Jacob de
   Haas, I. L. Bril and others, with an English page.
Der Morgen Journal. Est. 1901. Eds. Jacob Saphirstein and Peter
   Wiernick.
Der Amerikaner. Est. 1905–1906. Ed. Jacob Pfeffer. Pub. W. R.
   Hearst.

Morgen Blatt. Est. 1905. Ed. Morris Rosenfeld (only several months).

Die Warheit. Est. 1905. Ed. L. E. Miller, until 1914, then I. Gonickman.

Die Abend Zeitung. Est. 1906. Ed. S. Yanovsky (only three months).

Der Tog. Est. 1914. Ed. Herman Bernstein until 1916, then William Edlin.

Der Fihrer. Est. 1915. Ed. L. E. Miller (only several months).

Haint. Est. 1919. Ed. Herman Bernstein (only several months).

Die Zeit. Est. December, 1920–May, 1922. Ed. D. Pinski. Organ of Poale Zion Party.

Freiheit. Est. April 2, 1922. Eds. M. Olgin and Benjamin Gitlow. Organ of Workers' Party.

Appendix F

YIDDISH DAILY NEWSPAPERS PUBLISHED IN NEW YORK CITY IN 1923

(Source: *American Jewish Year Book*, Vol. 26)

Yiddishes Tageblatt or the Jewish Daily News. 185-7 East Broadway. Has special English page. Est. 1885 by K. H. Sarasohn. Ed. Gedalia Bublick. English page—I. L. Bril. Republican in politics—Orthodox, Zionist. Circulation, 1923—49,875.

Forverts or Jewish Daily Forward. 175 East Broadway. Est. 1897. Pub. Forward Association. Ed. Abraham Cahan. Labor Organ. Socialist in politics. Circulation, 1923—153,639.

Der Yiddisher Morgen Journal or the Jewish Morning Journal. 77 Bowery. Est. 1901 by Jacob Saphirstein. Ed. Peter Wiernick. Managing Ed. J. Fischman. Only Yiddish morning paper. Republican in politics—Orthodox, Zionist. Circulation, 1923—76,660.

Der Tog or The Day. 185 East Broadway. Est. 1914 by Herman Bernstein, merged in 1919 with the Jewish Daily *Warheit.*

Ed. William Edlin. English Section—Maurice Samuel. Non-Partisan in politics. Liberal, Zionist. Circulation, 1923—69,720.

Freiheit. 47 Chrystie Street. Est. April 2, 1922 by Freiheit Pub. Ass'n. Pres. and Ed. M. Olgin. Organ of Workers' Party of America. "Left-wing," labor-radical. Circulation, 1923—49,875.

Appendix G

CIRCULATION OF THE YIDDISH DAILY PRESS IN NEW YORK CITY FOR TWELVE YEARS (1912 to 1923, inclusive)

(Source: *American Jewish Year Book*, Vol. 26)

1912—360,123
1913—375,666
1914—487,591
1915—525,690
1916—537,982
1917—411,492
1918—383,583
1919—362,746
1920—360,918
1921—392,828
1922—352,436
1923—383,638

Appendixes

to

Chapter 8

Appendix A

Constitutions of the Landsmanshaften

The following is a list of significant extracts from thirteen society constitutions. The first two are Lodges of orders, the others are unaffiliated, or independent, societies.

The material has been culled from a study of the file of landsmanshaft constitutions at YIVO, in New York. Emphasis is added.

1. From the By-Laws of *Royal Lodge, No. 198 Brith Shalom,* Chartered 1913, New York, 1933, English.

   (Language)
   The business and proceedings of the Lodge shall be transacted in the English language, but any member shall have the *right to express himself or herself in Yiddish,* except that required ballots on elections shall be in *both languages.*

   (Eligibility)
   Any man between the ages of 18 and 45 years and who is of the Hebrew faith, is mentally and physically sound and is of good moral character and who has been a resident of this country six months is eligible to become a member of the Lodge; and his legal wife, provided she be of the Hebrew faith, who is mentally and physically sound and of good moral character, shall also be eligible for membership.

2. Excerpts from the Constitution of the *Supreme Camp of the Order Sons of Zion,* New York, no date, English and *Yiddish* editions.

(Language) Art. 1, Sec. 3

The records of all proceedings of the Supreme Camp [the governing body of the Order] shall be kept and conducted in the English language; communications to the subordinate camps shall be in the language employed by the camp local branch to which such communications may be addressed.

(Purpose) Art 1, Sec. 4

a) To establish a Death Benefit Fund . . .

b) To establish and maintain a disability benefit fund . . .

c) To aid by all means within its power the Zionist Congress in its efforts to secure for the Jewish people a legally assured home in Palestine, and to promote the knowledge of the Hebrew language and culture, but no moneys contributed by the members on account of insurance shall in any way be used for either of these purposes.

3. Constitution of the *First Shpoler Benevolent Aid Society,* New York (organized 1901, revised 1928), Yiddish and English

(Language) Art. 1, Sec. 3

All *transactions* of this Organization shall be conducted and *recorded in Jewish* (Yiddish). Members may be permitted to speak in English but the President or any member he may designate, shall translate for the members into Jewish (Yiddish).

(Exclusiveness) Art. 4, Sec. 8

The Inner Guard shall permit no one to enter the meeting room without the password unless he has special permission of the President.

(Duties of *Sick Aid Committee*) (Excerpt)

The Sick Aid Committee consists of 7 members which the *Hospitaler* shall appoint. When a brother gets sick, he shall notify it to the Hospitaler. The Hospitaler shall send a card to the patient which shall be signed by each committee member visiting the sick brother. At the end of the week, the Hospitaler shall visit the patient, get the card with the signatures of the committee, the doctor's report and hand it in at the next meeting. The Sick Aid Committee must bring in a report of the sickness at the next meeting. When a brother is sick, and confined in the hospital, the Hospitaler shall visit him there.

(Duties of the *Funeral Committee*) (Excerpt)

The Funeral Committee shall consist of the President, Vice-

President, Treasurer, Recording Secretary, Finance Secretary, and Trustees. They must be in the funeral procession up to the cemetery and wait there till after the completion of the burial. They have the right to send representatives in their place.

(Membership)
Any person who wishes to join this Society, must be of the Jewish religion; also his wife and children. He must have good character and be in good physical and mental condition. He must be able to support his family. He must be at least six months in this country.

(Art. 8, Sec. 19)   In case of death of a member or his wife, the body shall be treated according to the Jewish rites.

(Art. 11)   If a member was requested to attend a funeral and failed to appear there, *he shall be fined one dollar.*

4. Constitution and By-Laws of the *Progressive Slutzker Young Men's Benevolent Association* (organized 1904), New York, 1933, English and Yiddish

(Object) Preamble
The object of this organization is to help its members in case of illness or distress, also their dependents in case of their decease, as provided in its Constitution and By-Laws.
It is also the object of this organization to help all progressive movements for the good of workers as well as for the good of society in general.
The Society, *therefore, will support the workers' movement* and will fight against the enemies of that movement. It will not accept in its ranks any one known to be opposed to the workers' movement in any of its branches. It will not initiate as *members persons who are or who have been strikebreakers or scabs during strikes of workers,* or persons who assisted employers in obtaining strikebreakers. It will neither initiate as members such persons who do not belong to the union of their trade.

5. Constitution of the *First Sick Benefit Association of the Bronx,* 1938, Yiddish and English

(Purpose) Art. 1, Sec. 2
The purposes are to help the needy, the sick, the bereaved, and to provide the last resting place.

(Language) Art. 1, Sec. 5

All business and records of the organization shall be in *the Yiddish language,* except that the financial records may be in English.

(Eligibility) Art. 7, Sec. 1

Applicants for membership in the organization shall be at least 21 years of age and not more than 45. He must be of Jewish faith. He must be of good moral character and in good health. He must be able to support his family. He must be a resident of the United States at least six months, and he must be able to sign his name.

(Oath)

In the name of the First Sick and Benefit Association of the Bronx I pledge in the presence of all the members assembled here to faithfully observe and uphold the Constitution, By-Laws and Rules of this Society and pledge not to disclose to non-members the affairs of this organization. So help me God. Amen.

6. Constitution *Independent Sherpser Young Men's Benevolent Association* (organized 1906) 1935, English and Yiddish

(Presents) Art. 8B

1. When a member *is about to be married and officially* invites the Society not later than the meeting before the wedding, he shall receive a present *of $10 and a committee* shall be sent to his wedding.

2. When a member's child is married, either he or she shall receive a present of $10. . . . At other joyous occasions of members to which the Society is officially invited and decides to send a committee, a present of $5 shall be given.

7. Constitution, *Meicheter Bruderlicher Unterstitzung Verein* (organized 1905), Yiddish and English

Language of organization: *Yiddish*

(Duties of Members) Art. 9 (Excerpts) Sec. 2

Every member must be tolerant of the opinion of other members, even if that opinion conflicts with his. No member shall commit an injustice against another member either by word or deed, in order to uphold the spirit of fraternalism in the ranks of the organization.

(Member's Declaration) (Oath) Art. 16

I declare that I will observe the principles and interests of the Meicheter Brotherly Aid Society. I recognize the need of *mutual aid in times of need and illness.* I recognize the need of friendship, fraternalism and comradeship in the *abnormal life we lead in this big city* because of *the injustice that exists in present day society.* I therefore declare that I will exert myself to the utmost so that the work of the Society may be successful, and that I will cooperate and support any activity of the Society, in order to aid and abet those who are in need of aid.

8. Constitution and By-Laws, *Lodzer Young Men's Benevolent Society of New York* (Organized 1902), 1925, English

(Purpose) Art. 1, Sec. 2

It shall be the endeavor of this Society, through association and gathering, to promote and perpetuate a feeling of Brotherly Love, to encourage mutual aid, to provide medical aid and relief when necessary, and to contribute to worthy Jewish causes.

(Eligibility) Art. 2, Sec. 2

Candidates must be not less than 18 years of age, and not older than 35 years of age; in good physical condition; of the Jewish faith; have a respectable occupation; be a resident of greater New York.

Candidates must have been in this country at least six months; have a good reputation; be able to read and write; be in accord with the laws of this Society. If married; a candidate's wife must be Jewish.

9. Constitution of the *Prusiver Charitable and Benevolent Association, Inc.* (Founded 1888) New York. 1921, English and Yiddish

(Purpose) Art. 1, Sec. 3

The object of the Association is: To render aid in case of sickness or need and funeral benefits.

(Eligibility) Art. 2, Sec. 1

. . . a candidate must be of male sex and possess the following qualifications:

a) He must be of Jewish faith.

b) He must be not less than 20 nor more than 40 years of age.

c) He must have been a resident of the United States at least six months.

d) He must be of good moral character.

10. Constitution and By-Laws, *Stashover Beneficial Association of Philadelphia* (organized 1895), English and Yiddish

(Language)
All business of the Association shall be conducted in the *Jewish language, orally or written,* but any member has the right to use the English language if he can express himself better that way.

Correspondence can be conducted either in the Jewish (Yiddish) or English language.

11. Constitution, *First Turover Aid Society* (Benevolent Association of the People of Turov), (organized 1903), New York, Constitution accepted 1935, Yiddish and English

(Purpose and Language)
This society exists for the purpose of aiding the sick and needy brothers, also to pay funeral and cemetery expenses, and endowment payments.
The language of the books of this society shall be in Yiddish.

12. Constitution, *Bessarabian Young Men's Beneficial and Educational Club* (founded 1903), 1932, Yiddish and English

(Language) Art. 1, Sec. 3
All business of the Club shall be conducted in the *Yiddish language* except that the books of accounts and finances, as well as the reports pertaining thereto shall be in the English language. It is, however, expressly provided that members are accorded the privilege of addressing themselves at all meetings in the English language.

13. Excerpt from the Constitution of the *Waterbury Hebrew Ladies' Aid Association* (founded 1902), 1937, Yiddish and English

All business of the Association shall be transacted in Jewish, whenever possible. *The minutes shall be kept in Jewish* (Yiddish), if possible.

The *purpose* of the Association is to aid all *needy Jews*; i.e., no matter what the predicament of a family or an individual may be, they will be assisted by the Ladies' Aid.

The Waterbury Hebrew Ladies' Aid Association should help through the media of food, coal, medical attention, clothing and monetary assistance, if necessary.

The following contents of constitutions have been selected from a group of traditional societies and "Farains," many of which were synagogue-oriented. All are published only in Yiddish. The selections were made to illustrate the universal character of the mutual-aid features and the emphasis on the use of Yiddish.

It is impossible to translate the character of the Yiddish used in these constitutions. I made a futile effort to keep some of the flavor. For example, the reader will notice the variety of references to *Yiddish:* Jargon, Jargonic, Judaeo-German, pure Yiddish, and so on. As a matter of fact, most of the Yiddish is anything but pure, grammatically. What does emerge as pure is the universal desire to keep the mother-tongue alive.

1. From the Constitution of the Smarganer Benefit Society, New York. Founded 1903, Yiddish

   All deliberations and correspondence of this society shall be conducted in the jargon (Yiddish).

2. From the Constitution of the First Levertover Progressive Verein, New York. Founded 1911, Yiddish

   Art. 1, Sec. 2
   The business of this farain shall be conducted in the Yiddish language, though each member is permitted to use the English language if he so wishes.

3. From the Constitution of the United Minsker Benevolent Association, New York. Founded 1903, Yiddish

   (Purpose) Art. 1, Sec. 2
   The purpose of this farain is to supply voluntary mutual aid

in cases of illness, *Shiva* (period of mourning), need, and cases of death.

(Language) Art. 1, Sec. 3
The books and all deliberations of this farain shall be conducted in the Yiddish language, though one may speak any other language he chooses.

4. From the Constitution of the Liber Brider Untershtitsung Farain, New York. Founded 1906, Yiddish

(Art. 1, Sec. 3)
The books of this farain, as well as all deliberations must be conducted exclusively in the Yiddish language and script. The same applies to all motions, amendments, etc. Everything must be expressed in Yiddish.

5. From the Constitution of Bereziner Untershtitzung Farain, New York. Founded 1902, Yiddish

(Art. 1, Sec. 3)
All books and business of the Farain must be kept in clean Yiddish "jargon-language."

6. From the Constitution of the Lechevitcher Progressive Beneficial Association, Philadelphia. Founded 1907, Yiddish

(Language) Art. 6
The business of this Farain shall be conducted in the Yiddish language, but it is permitted to use other languages at the proceedings of the meetings.

7. From the Constitution of Wolkovisker Young Men's Benevolent Association, New York. Founded 1896, Yiddish

(Purpose)
The purpose of this Farain is to aid the needy members; offer sick benefit, and provisions for needs arising from cases of death.

(Language)
The proceedings and the books of this Farain shall be conducted in the Yiddish language; however, if one wished not to

use the Yiddish language he may speak English, and the chairman is obligated to translate into Yiddish.

8. From the Constitution of Greater New York Untershtitzung Farain. Founded 1897, Yiddish

   (Language) Art. 1, Sec. 2
   Jargon, or Judaeo-German is the official language of the Farain, and all minutes and correspondence as well as the proceedings of the meetings shall be conducted in this language—it is, however, permitted to use another language during the debates at the meetings.

9. From the Constitution of the Hebrew Progressive Association (New Brunswick and Perth Amboy, New Jersey). Founded 1902, Yiddish

   (Purpose) Art. 1, Sec. 2
   Our purpose is to provide mutual aid in cases of need, illness and death.

   (Language) Art. 1, Sec. 3
   All business, correspondence and bookkeeping of this Farain shall be conducted in Yiddish-Jargon.

10. From the Constitution of the Independent Bukarester Sick Aid Association, New York. Founded 1901, Yiddish

    (Art. 1, Sec. 2)
    The financial books shall be conducted in the English language, but the book of minutes and proceedings shall be kept in the Yiddish language.

11. From the Constitution of the First Zbaraver K.U.V. Founded 1896, Yiddish

    (Art. 1, Sec. 2)
    The proceedings and books of this Farain must be conducted in the Judaeo-German language and script.

12. From the Constitution of the Friendly Sister Association, New York. Founded 1900, Yiddish

(Art. 1, Sec. 4)
The meetings and minutes must be conducted in pure Yiddish language.

13. From the Constitution of the Satanover Benevolent Society, New York. Constitution adopted 1911, Yiddish

(Art. 1, Sec. 2)
All records and proceedings of this society shall be kept in the Judaeo-German (Jargon) language. The membership lists and receipt records may be kept in English.

14. From the Constitution of Dinaburger Brothers Benevolent Association, New York. Founded 1909, Yiddish

(Art. 2, Sec. 2)
The proceedings of the Farain shall be conducted in the "Jargonic" language or in English. Each member is permitted to speak another language.

15. From the Constitution of the Portchester Independent Hebrew Lodge, Port Chester, New York. Founded 1906, Yiddish

(Art. 1, Sec. 2)
Our purpose is mutual aid in time of need when a member is sick, or when there is a case of death.

(Sec. 3)
All business and correspondence and records of this lodge shall be conducted in the Yiddish language.

Appendix B

Statistics on Founding and Membership of Landsmanshaften in New York

The following tables have been adapted from the Yiddish Writers' Project work, *Di Yiddishe Landsmanshaften fun New York,* published in New York, 1938. Please note that all the data applies only to landsmanshaften within New York City. (There are no available figures on a national scale.)

The information contained in the tables is drawn from replies to a questionnaire that was used by the writers in their literary study in 1938. It is based on information from 1,905 organizations out of a total of 2,045 who replied; 423 groups failed to answer. Altogether, the project was able to ascertain the existence of 2,468 landsmanshaft bodies in New York City.

TABLE 1

General Distribution of Organizations

Type of Organization	No. of Units	Membership in 1938	No. American Born
Mutual Aid Societies	714	114,260	17,685
Mutual Aid Societies Associated with Congregations	41	9,374	1,970
Landsmanshaft Chevras ("Anshes")	249	33,162	3,268
Ladies Benevolent Societies	71	6,101	589
Ladies Aid Societies (Auxiliaries)	287	22,431	2,598
Ladies Auxiliaries Associated with Lodges	2	190	55
Branches of the Workmen's Circle	164	25,976	1,477
Women's Clubs of the Workmen's Circle	63	3,676	207
Youth Clubs of the Workmen's Circle	6	220	178
Branches of the International Workers Order	53	11,341	1,013
Women's Clubs of the International Workers Order	11	383	19
Youth Clubs of the International Workers Order	2	37	33

TABLE 1—*Continued*

Type of Organization	No. of Units	Membership in 1938	No. American Born
Branches of Jewish National Workers Alliance	14	1,209	118
Women's Clubs of Jewish National Workers Alliance	2	58	2
Lodges of Independent Order Brith Abraham	16	2,992	321
Miscellaneous Landsmanshaft Lodges (Order Affiliated)	5	923	269
"Name" Lodges of Independent Order Brith Abraham	2	325	100
Family Circles	76	7,734	3,821
"Name" Societies	45	7,482	1,772
Miscellaneous Landsmanshaft Organizations	18	9,193	2,919
TOTAL	1,841	257,067	38,414
"Relief" Federations	39		
Patron Groups	25		
FINAL TOTAL	1,905		

TABLE 2

Landsmanshaft *Chevras* or *Anshes*

(Showing year of founding and membership distribution)

Year Founded	No. Founded	No. of Members When Founded	No. of Members in 1938	No. of American Born Members in 1938
1858				
1859				

TABLE 2—*Continued*

Year Founded	No. Founded	No. of Members When Founded	No. of Members in 1938	No. of American Born Members in 1938
1860				
1861				
1862	1	10	200	60
1863				
1864	1	7	90	10
1865				
1866				
1867				
1868				
1869				
1870	1	10	140	84
1871				
1872	1	7	45	30
1873	1	12	120	24
1874				
1875				
1876				
1877	2	32	360	65
1878				
1879				
1880	3	50	605	43
1881				
1882				
1883	2	42	365	82
1884	6	97	1,170	235
1885	3	60	610	152
1886	4	64	1,025	58
1887	7	112	1,130	169
1888	11	362	1,412	216
1889	6	89	1,017	89
1890	10	191	1,095	118
1891	6	95	710	46

TABLE 2—*Continued*

Year Founded	No. Founded	No. of Members When Founded	No. of Members in 1938	No. of American Born Members in 1938
1892	6	143	744	58
1893	7	141	785	108
1894	6	97	730	41
1895	5	111	647	70
1896	1	40	100	5
1897	8	152	1,345	145
1898	13	245	2,046	140
1899	6	200	1,315	154
1900	11	188	1,413	182
1901	4	65	250	13
1902	7	152	942	34
1903	10	145	1,480	143
1904	5	95	604	59
1905	7	105	958	71
1906	4	67	315	30
1907	6	73	835	83
1908	7	92	880	37
1909	4	106	450	32
1910	2	60	133	2
1911	5	92	580	82
1912	4	52	435	20
1913	7	208	735	32
1914	3	40	275	6
1915	1	10	75	
1916	3	54	285	33
1917	5	130	336	52
1918	6	78	345	10
1919	1	150	2,000	20
1920	4	121	405	9
1921	4	124	252	18
1922	3	41	194	27
1923	5	78	240	7

TABLE 2—*Continued*

Year Founded	No. Founded	No. of Members When Founded	No. of Members in 1938	No. of American Born Members in 1938
1924	5	149	254	22
1925	1	17	100	10
1926	2	30	75	
1928	5	361	450	32
1931				
1932	1	10	60	
1933				
1934				
1935				
1936				
1937				
TOTALS	249	5,262	33,162	3,268

TABLE 3

Mutual Aid Societies

(Showing year of founding and membership distribution)

Year Founded	No. Founded	No. of Members When Founded	No. of Members in 1938	No. of American Born Members in 1938
1858				
1859	1	7	490	not given
1860				
1861				
1862				
1863				

TABLE 3—*Continued*

Year Founded	No. Founded	No. of Members When Founded	No. of Members in 1938	No. of American Born Members in 1938
1864				
1865				
1866				
1867				
1868				
1869				
1870	1	25	180	9
1871				
1872				
1873				
1874				
1875				
1876				
1877				
1878				
1879				
1880				
1881				
1882				
1883	1	20	110	16
1884	1	7	314	62
1885				
1886	3	33	1,013	307
1887	3	50	675	154
1888	6	86	1,715	450
1889	7	121	1,610	387
1890	5	80	1,144	238
1891	6	126	1,451	463
1892	10	248	2,525	563
1893	8	114	2,675	447
1894	3	30	760	121
1895	8	115	2,402	512

TABLE 3—*Continued*

Year Founded	No. Founded	No. of Members When Founded	No. of Members in 1938	No. of American Born Members in 1938
1896	11	234	2,802	457
1897	12	225	2,254	299
1898	12	210	2,708	590
1899	14	206	3,224	548
1900	37	696	8,665	1,596
1901	20	458	4,933	665
1902	28	929	6,226	1,454
1903	39	602	6,806	1,194
1904	38	656	8,970	1,069
1905	34	542	5,737	832
1906	27	471	3,882	585
1907	31	573	4,473	532
1908	25	454	3,020	455
1909	23	384	2,781	282
1910	20	500	2,712	339
1911	17	655	2,236	215
1912	15	204	1,986	221
1913	29	462	3,074	325
1914	29	534	3,212	478
1915	21	345	2,042	230
1916	20	479	1,904	138
1917	14	440	1,546	146
1918	9	275	1,036	161
1919	10	146	851	125
1920	23	561	2,306	258
1921	12	278	860	108
1922	10	107	1,004	69
1923	12	165	1,068	97
1924	11	178	1,125	98
1925	5	97	460	8
1926	7	155	343	29
1927	4	46	345	45

TABLE 3—*Continued*

Year Founded	No. Founded	No. of Members When Founded	No. of Members in 1938	No. of American Born Members in 1938
1928	5	125	445	17
1929	3	54	370	32
1930	3	27	234	8
1931	2	40	135	6
1932	2	30	150	14
1933	1	6	50	5
1934	4	217	270	36
1935	8	233	716	112
1936	3	83	160	7
1937	1	15	75	71
TOTALS	714	14,159	114,260	17,685

TABLE 4

Mutual Aid Societies Associated with Congregations
(Showing year of founding and membership distribution)

Year Founded	No. Founded	No. of Members When Founded	No. of Members in 1938	No. of American Born Members in 1938
1879				
1880				
1881				
1882				
1883				
1884				
1885				
1886				

TABLE 4—*Continued*

Year Founded	No. Founded	No. of Members When Founded	No. of Members in 1938	No. of American Born Members in 1938
1887	1	10	300	100
1888				
1889	1	12	225	67
1890				
1891				
1892	1	7	125	25
1893				
1894	1	10	135	20
1895	4	45	665	135
1896	1	10	300	30
1897	5	65	1,305	192
1898	1	20	115	38
1899	3	60	630	70
1900	4	85	625	47
1901	3	55	1,010	235
1902				
1903	2	45	560	34
1904				
1905	2	47	580	206
1906	2	85	315	169
1907	1	7	75	60
1908				
1909	1	12	75	10
1910	2	38	283	20
1911	2	35	210	41
1912	2	112	1,570	453
1913	1	20	45	
1914				
1915				
1916	1	100	186	18
TOTALS	41	880	9,374	1,970

TABLE 5

Ladies Aid Societies (Auxiliaries)
(Showing year of founding and membership distribution)

Year Founded	No. Founded	No. of Members When Founded	No. of Members in 1938	No. of American Born Members in 1938
1898	1	10	50	
1900				
1901				
1902	1	15	350	52
1903				
1904	1	50	100	3
1905				
1906				
1907				
1908	1	18	150	7
1909	1	40	210	55
1910				
1911	1	12	70	
1912	1	8	300	
1913	2	30	225	19
1914				
1915	1	8	65	12
1916	1	25	100	
1917				
1918	8	119	635	51
1919	4	47	520	22
1920	5	107	320	18
1921	3	75	185	3
1922	4	36	320	12
1923	9	171	2,025	322
1924	9	354	580	24
1925	7	496	700	24
1926	9	109	749	26
1927	14	215	1,130	141

TABLE 5—*Continued*

Year Founded	No. Founded	No. of Members When Founded	No. of Members in 1938	No. of American Born Members in 1938
1928	21	497	1,278	82
1929	10	163	660	81
1930	10	75	530	48
1931	13	189	902	62
1932	22	431	1,438	217
1933	16	273	990	88
1934	26	733	2,161	316
1935	24	487	1,710	238
1936	25	513	1,630	368
1937	26	538	1,832	274
1938	11	182	516	33
TOTALS	287	6,026	22,431	2,598

TABLE 6

Ladies Benevolent Societies

(Showing year of founding and membership distribution)

Year Founded	No. Founded	No. of Members When Founded	No. of Members in 1938	No. of American Born Members in 1938
1895	1	7	200	30
1897	3	37	132	
1898	1	6	75	6
1900	4	65	470	68
1901	1	10	45	
1902	2	22	185	

TABLE 6—*Continued*

Year Founded	No. Founded	No. of Members When Founded	No. of Members in 1938	No. of American Born Members in 1938
1903	4	143	355	49
1904	4	112	370	38
1905	1	80	50	2
1906	2	106	207	38
1907	5	405	27	
1908	2	55	106	
1909	2	30	200	
1910	4	61	470	
1911				
1912	1	15	245	49
1913	1	6	56	
1914	3	33	255	19
1915	2	26	130	13
1916	4	50	176	8
1919	1	7	70	
1920	1	8	50	
1921	4	91	453	38
1922	3	45	285	30
1923				
1924	2	17	75	2
1925	3	47	281	37
1926	1	10	30	2
1927	2	28	140	5
1928	2	112	85	25
1929				
1930	2	20	180	63
1931				
1932				
1933	2	14	200	
1934				
1935	1	120	120	4
TOTALS	71	1,788	6,101	589

TABLE 7

Family Circles

(Showing year of founding and membership distribution)

Year Founded	No. Founded	No. of Members When Founded	No. of Members in 1938	No. of American Born Members in 1938
1887	1	10	225	60
1898	1	7	150	15
1899				
1900				
1901				
1902				
1903				
1904				
1905				
1906				
1907	1	60	105	25
1908				
1909				
1910	2	14	180	119
1911				
1912	1	35	150	105
1913	3	46	740	370
1914				
1915				
1916	1	10	48	3
1919	3	38	140	64
1920	3	53	506	372
1921	1	4	100	30
1922				
1923	2	362	436	100
1924	1	20	85	51
1925				
1926	1	8	240	120
1927	4	35	390	230
1928	5	138	507	176

TABLE 7—*Continued*

Year Founded	No. Founded	No. of Members When Founded	No. of Members in 1938	No. of American Born Members in 1938
1929	1	7	40	40
1930	1	18	60	30
1931	3	74	311	169
1932	4	67	245	40
1933	7	200	695	345
1934	11	597	1,105	691
1935	2	60	100	41
1936	10	472	896	467
1937	4	118	193	109
1938	3	59	87	49
TOTALS	76	2,512	7,734	3,821

Bibliography

English Sources

ACWA Documentary History: 1914 to 1952. New York, 1952.

Adler, Cyrus. *I Have Considered the Days.* Philadelphia: Jewish Publication Society of America, 1941.

————. *The Voice of America on Kishineff.* Philadelphia: Jewish Publication Society of America, 1904.

Ain, Abraham. "Swislocz: Portrait of a Jewish Community in Eastern Europe." In *Yivo Annual of Jewish Social Science* 4. New York: Yiddish Scientific Institute, 1949.

American Committee for Ameliorating the Condition of the Russian Refugees (Laws and Regulations). New York, 1891.

Angoff, Charles. *Something about My Father.* New York. Thomas Yoseloff, 1956.

Antin, Benjamin. *The Gentlemen from the 22nd* (Autobiography). New York: Boni & Liveright, 1927.

Antin, Mary. *From Plotzk to Boston.* Boston: W. B. Clarke & Co., 1899.

————. *The Promised Land.* Boston: Houghton, Mifflin Co., 1912.

Ausubel, Nathan. *A Pictorial History of the Jewish People.* New York: Crown Publishers, 1954.

————, ed. *A Treasury of Jewish Folklore.* New York: Crown Publishers, 1948.

Ayer, N. W. & Sons. *American Newspaper Directory.* Philadephia.

Baltzell, E. Digby. "The Development of a Jewish Upper-Class in Philadelphia: 1782–1940." In *The Jews: Social Patterns of an American Group,* edited by Marshall Sklare. Glencoe, Ill.: The Free Press, 1958.

Baron, Salo W. *Bibliography of Jewish Social Studies.* New York, 1941.

————. *Cultural Problems of American Jewry.* New York, 1939.

————. *The Effect of the War on Jewish Community Life.* New York, 1942.

————. *The Jewish Community.* 3 vols. Philadelphia: Jewish Publication Society of America, 1942.

————. *The Russian Jew Under Tsars and Soviets.* New York: The Macmillan Co., 1964.

————. *A Social and Religious History of the Jews.* New York: Columbia University Press, 1937.

Barron, Milton L., ed. *American Minorities.* New York: Alfred A. Knopf, 1957.

————, ed. *Minorities in a Changing World.* New York: Alfred A. Knopf, 1967.

Baskerville, Beatrice C. *The Polish Jew: His Social and Economic Value.* New York: The Macmillan Co., 1906.

Berkson, I. B. *Theories of Americanization.* New York: Teachers College, Columbia University, 1920.

Berman, Jeremiah J. "Jewish Education in New York City." In *Yivo Annual of Jewish Social Science.* New York: Yiddish Scientific Institute, 1954.

Bernheimer, Charles S. *The Russian Jew in the United States.* Philadelphia, 1905.

Betsky, Sarah Zweig. *Onions and Cucumbers and Plums* (46 Yiddish Poems in English. Detroit: Wayne State University Press, 1958.

Birmingham, Stephen. *Our Crowd.* New York: Harper & Row, 1967.

Birnbaum, Salomo. "Literature, Yiddish" (A & B, I, II). In the *Universal Jewish Encyclopedia.* New York, 1942, pp. 125–129.

Blau, Joseph L., and Baron, Salo W. *The Jews of the United States, 1790–1840: A Documentary History.* New York: Columbia University Press; Philadelphia: Jewish Publication Society of America, 1963.

Blaustein, Miriam. *Memoirs of David Blaustein, Educator and Communal Worker.* New York: McBride, Nast & Co., 1913.

Bloom, Bernard H. "Yiddish Speaking Socialists in America, 1892–1905." *American Jewish Archives,* 12, no. 1 (April 1960).

Bloomgarden, Solomon. "Yiddish Literature." *Jewish Outlook,* 6 March 1908.

B'nai B'rith, International Order of (District Grand Lodge No. 2). *Report of Committee on Roumanian Immigration and Condition of Immigrant Jews.* Cincinnati, 1901.

Bogen, Boris D. *Born a Jew.* New York: Macmillan Co., 1930.

————. *Jewish Philanthropy: An Exposition of Principles and Methods of Jewish Social Science in the United States.* New York: The Macmillan Company, 1917.

Brickner, Barnett R. "The History of Jewish Education in Cincinnati." *Jewish Education,* 8 (1936).

Broches, S. "A Chapter in the History of the Jews of Boston." *Yivo Annual of Jewish Social Science,* 9 (1954).

————. "The History of the Yiddish Press in the State of Massachusetts, 1882–1938." *Annual of the American Branch of Yivo* (1939).

Budish, J. M., and Soule, George. *The New Unionism in the Clothing Industry.* New York: Harcourt, Brace & Howe, 1920.

Burgin, Herz. *History of the Jewish Labor Movement.* New York: United Hebrew Trades, 1915.

Cahan, Abraham. "Russian Jews in America." *Atlantic Monthly,* July 1898.

Carsel, Wilfred. *History of the Chicago Ladies Garment Workers' Unions.* Chicago: Normandie House, 1940.

Chipkin, Israel S. "Twenty-five Years of Jewish Education in the United States." *American Jewish Year Book* 38 (1936).

Clurman, Harold. "Ida Kaminska and the Warsaw Yiddish Theatre." *Midstream* 14, no. 1 (January 1968).

Cohen, Israel. "The Zionist Movement." In *Zionist Organization of America.* New York, 1946.

Cohen, Julius Henry. *They Builded Better than They Knew.* New York: J. Messner, Inc., 1946.

Cohen, Morris Raphael. *A Dreamer's Journey.* Boston: Beacon Press, 1949.

Cohen, Morris Raphael. *The Reflections of a Wandering Jew*. Boston, 1950.

Cohen, Samuel H. *Transplanted* (Autobiography). New York, 1937.

Commons, J. R. *Races and Immigrants*. New York: Macmillan & Co., 1907.

Congregation Beth-El Historical Committee. "A History of Congregation Beth El, Detroit, Michigan, from Its Organization to Its Semi-Centennial, 1850–1900." Detroit, 1900.

Cooperman, Hasye. "Yiddish Literature in the United States." In *The American Jew: A Reappraisal,* edited by Oscar I. Janowsky. Philadelphia: The Jewish Publication Society of America, 1964.

Cowen, Philip. *Memoirs of an American Jew*. New York: The International Press, 1932.

Danish, Max D., and Stein, Leon. *ILGWU News-History, 1900–1950*. New York, 1950.

Davidson, Gabriel. *Our Jewish Farmers and the Story of the Jewish Agriculture Society*. New York: L. B. Fischer, 1943.

Davis, Moshe. "Jewish Religious Life and Institutions in America." In Louis Finkelstein, *The Jews: Their History, Culture and Religion* 1. Philadelphia, 1949.

Dawidowicz, Lucy S., ed. *The Golden Tradition*. New York: Holt, Rinehart and Winston, 1967.

————. "Louis Marshall's Yiddish Newspaper, *The Jewish World,* A Study in Contrasts." *Jewish Social Studies* 25 (1963).

Documentary History of the Amalgamated Clothing Workers. New York, 1954.

Dubnow, S. M. *History of the Jews in Russia and Poland from the Earliest Times until the Present Day* (Translated from Russian). Philadelphia: Jewish Publication Society of America, 1916–1920, 3 vols.

Dubofsky, Melvyn. "Organized Labor and the Immigrant in New York City, 1900–1918." *Labor History* 11 (1961).

Duker, Abraham Gordon. *Jewish Community Relations: An Analysis of the MacIver Report*. New York: Jewish Reconstructionist Foundation, 1952.

————. "Socio-Psychological Trends in the American Jewish Community since 1900." *Yivo Annual of Jewish Social Science* 9 (1954).

Dushkin, A. M. "Jewish Education in New York City." In *Bureau of Jewish Education*. New York, 1918.

Ediden, Ben M. *Jewish Community Life in America*. New York: Hebrew Publishing Co., 1947.

Ellinger, M. "Report to the Hebrew Emigrant Aid Society of the United States." *Immigration Journal* (New York) (1882).

Engleman, Uriah Zvi. "The Fate of Yiddish in America." *Menorah Journal* 15 (July 1928).

———. "Jewish Statistics in the United States Census of Religious Bodies (1850–1936)." *Jewish Social Studies* 9 (1947).

Epstein, Melech. *Jewish Labor in the U.S.A.* 2 vols. New York, 1950, 1953.

———. "The Yiddish School Movement." *Contemporary Jewish Research,* no. 6 (June 1943).

Epstein, Melech. *Profiles of Eleven*. Detroit: Wayne State University Press, 1965.

Fast, Howard. *The Jews, Story of a People*. New York: The Dial Press, 1968.

Felsenthal, Bernard. *Judisches Schulwessen in America*. Chicago, 1866.

Fishman, Joshua A., et al. *Language Loyalty in the United States*. The Hague: Mouton & Co., 1966.

———. "Yiddish in America: Socio-Linguistic Description and Analysis." *International Journal of American Linguistics* 31, no. 2 (April 1965).

———. "Yiddish in America: A Socio-Psychological Portrait." (Unpublished as of 1965.)

Foner, Philip. *The Fur and Leather Workers Union: A Story of Dramatic Struggles and Achievements*. Newark: Nordan Press, 1950.

Friedman, Lee M. *Early American Jews*. Cambridge, Massachusetts: Harvard University Press, 1934.

Friedman, Philip. "Political and Social Movements and Organizations." In *The Jewish People: Past and Present* 4. New York, 1955.

Friedman, Theodore, and Gordis, Robert, eds. *Jewish Life in America.* New York: Horizon Press, 1955.

Frumkin, Jacob; Aronson, Gregor; and Goldweiser, Alexis, eds. *Russian Jewry (1890–1917).* New York: Thomas Yoseloff, 1966.

Gamoran, Emanuel. *Changing Conceptions in Jewish Education.* New York: Macmillan Co., 1924.

Gans, Herbert J. "The Origin and Growth of a Jewish Community in the Suburbs: A Study of the Jews of Forest Park." In *The Jews: Social Patterns of an American Group,* edited by Marshall Sklare.

Ginzberg, Eli. *Agenda for American Jews.* New York: King's Crown Press, 1949.

Ginzberg, Louis. *The Jewish Primary School.* Philadelphia, 1907.

Gittler, Joseph B., ed. *Understanding Minority Groups.* New York: John Wiley & Sons, Inc., Science Editions, 1964.

Glanz, Rudolf. "The History of the Jewish Community in New York." *Yivo Annual of Jewish Social Science* 4 (1949).

————. "The Immigration of German Jews up to 1880." *Yivo Annual of Jewish Social Science* 2–3 (1947–48).

————. "Jewish Social Conditions as Seen by the Muckrakers." *Yivo Annual of Jewish Social Science* 9 (1954).

————. "Source Materials on the History of Jewish Immigration to the United States, 1800–1880." *Yivo Annual of Jewish Social Science* 1 (1951).

Glazer, Nathan. "The American Jew and the Attainment of Middle-Class Rank: Some Trends and Explanations." In *The Jews: Social Patterns of an American Group,* edited by Marshall Sklare.

————.*American Judaism.* Chicago: The University of Chicago Press, 1957.

————, and Moynihan, Daniel P. *Beyond the Melting Pot.* Cambridge, Massachusetts: Harvard University Press, 1963.

Goldberg, A. H. "A Conference of the Yiddish Language." *The American Hebrew,* 14 August 1908.

Goldberg, David, and Sharp, Harry. "Some Aspects of Detroit Area Jewish and Non-Jewish Adults." In *The Jews: Social Patterns of an American Group,* edited by Marshall Sklare.

Goldberg, Nathan. "Occupational Patterns of American Jews." *Jewish Review,* April and October–December 1945, and January 1946.

Goldman, Emma. *Living My Life.* New York: A. A. Knopf, 1931.

Gompers, Samuel. *Seventy Years of Life and Labor.* 2 vols. New York: E. P. Dutton & Co., 1925.

Goodman, Abram V. *American Overture: Jewish Rights in Colonial Times.* Philadelphia: Jewish Publication Society, 1947.

Gordin, Jacob. "Yiddish Stage Has Deteriorated." *Jewish Comment,* 28 February 1908.

Graeber, Isacque, and Britt, Steuart A. *Jews in a Gentile World.* New York: The Macmillan Company, 1942.

Grayzel, Solomon. *A History of the Jews.* Philadelphia: Jewish Publication Society, 1948.

Green, Charles H. *The Headwear Workers: A Century of Trade Unionism.* New York, 1944.

Greenberg, Louis. *The Jews in Russia.* 2 vols., 1944 and 1951. New Haven: Yale University Press.

Greenfield, Judith. "The Role of the Jews in the Development of the Clothing Industry in the United States." *Yivo Annual of Jewish Social Science* 2–3 (1947–48).

Greenstone, J. H. "Jewish Education in the United States." *American Jewish Year Book* 16 (1914).

———. *Statistical Data of Jewish Religious Schools in Baltimore and Pittsburgh.* Philadelphia, 1909.

Grinstein, Hyman B. *The Rise of the Jewish Community of New York: 1654–1860.* Philadelphia: Jewish Publication Society, 1945.

Halpern, Ben. "America Is Different." In *The Jews: Social Patterns of an American Group,* edited by Marshall Sklare.

Handlin, Oscar. *The Uprooted.* Boston, 1951.

———. *Boston's Immigrants.* Cambridge, Massachusetts, 1941.

———, ed. *Conference on Jewish Experience in America.* New York, 1948.

————, and Handlin, Mary F. "A Century of Jewish Immigration to the United States." *American Jewish Year Book* 1 (1948–49).

Hapgood, Hutchins. *The Spirit of the Ghetto.* New York: Funk and Wagnalls, 1902; Cambridge, Massachusetts: Harvard University Press, 1967.

Hardman, J. B. S. "Jewish Workers in the American Labor Movement." *Yivo Annual of Jewish Social Science* 7 (1952).

Hardy, Jack. *The Clothing Workers.* New York: International Publishers, 1935.

Harris, Herbert. *American Labor.* New Haven: Yale University Press, 1939.

Harris, Maurice R. "New York Jewish History: A Quarter-Century Survey." *American Hebrew,* 8 November 1907.

Har Sinai Congregation. *History of Har Sinai Congregation, Baltimore.* (Published on 75th anniversary.) Baltimore, 1918.

Hasanovitz, Elizabeth. *One of Them.* Boston: Houghton-Mifflin, 1918.

Havemann, Ernest, and West, Patricia. *They Went to College.* New York, 1952.

Hebrew Emigrant Aid Society. *Report of Mr. Julius Schwarz on the Colony of Russian Refugees at Cotopox, Colorado.* New York, 1882.

————. *Colonization of Russian Refugees in the West.* New York, 1882.

Heller, James G. *As Yesterday When It Is Past.* (A History of the Isaac M. Wise Temple—K. K. B'nai Jeshuran of Cincinnati.) Cincinnati, 1942.

Herberg, Will. "The Jewish Labor Movement in the United States." *American Jewish Year Book* 53 (1952).

————. *Protestant, Catholic, Jew.* New York: Doubleday, 1955.

Herskovits, Melville J. "Who Are the Jews?" In *The Jews: Their History, Culture and Religion,* edited by Louis Finkelstein. Philadelphia, 1949.

Hertz, Judith. "East Side Jewish Plays and Playwrights." *The New Era* 4 (December 1903).

Heschel, Abraham Joshua. "The Eastern European Era in Jewish History." *Yivo Annual of Jewish Social Science* 1 (1946).

Hillquit, Morris. *Loose Leaves from a Busy Life: Turn of the Century Memoirs.* New York: The Macmillan Co., 1934.

Honor, Leo L. "Jewish Education in the United States." In *Jewish People: Past and Present* 2. New York, 1948.

Horwich, Bernard. *My First Eighty Years.* Chicago: Argus Books, 1939.

Howe, Irving, and Greenberg, Eliezer, eds. *A Treasury of Yiddish Stories.* New York: Viking Press, 1954.

Hourwich, I. A. *Immigration and Labor.* New York: G. Putnam & Sons, 1912.

Hurwitz, M. *The Workmen's Circle.* New York: The Workmen's Circle, 1936.

Hyman, H. Joseph. "Hebrew Education, Baltimore." *Jewish Education* 6 (1934).

Jacob, Heinrich E. *The World of Emma Lazarus.* New York: Schoken Books, 1949.

Jacobs, Joseph. "On the Racial Character of Modern Jews." *Journal of the Royal Anthropological Institute* 15 (London) (1885).

Jaffe, A. J., and Stewart, C. D. *Manpower Resources and Utilization.* New York, 1951.

James, Edward. *The Immigrant Jew in America.* New York: B. F. Buck & Co., 1906.

Janowsky, Oscar I., ed. *The American Jew: A Reappraisal.* Philadelphia: The Jewish Publication Society of America, 1964.

———. *The Jews and Minority Rights.* New York: Columbia University Press, 1933.

———. *The Jewish Welfare Board Survey.* New York, 1948.

Jewish Agriculturists Aid Society of America (Chicago). *Report of the Society's Work and Achievements.* Chicago, 1901.

Jewish Communal Register, 1917–1918. New York, 1918.

Jewish Encyclopedia. 12 vols. New York: Funk & Wagnalls, 1906.

Joseph, Samuel. *History of the Baron de Hirsch Fund: The Americanization of the Jewish Immigrant.* Philadelphia: Jewish Publication Society, 1935.

————. *Jewish Immigration to the United States from 1881–1910.* New York: Columbia University, 1914.

Josephson, Matthew. *Sidney Hillman: Statesman of American Labor.* Garden City: Doubleday & Co., 1952.

Kallen, Horace M. "Democracy Versus the Melting Pot." *The Nation,* 18 and 25 February 1915.

Kallen, Horace M. *Judaism at Bay.* New York, 1932.

Kaminsky, J. *Forty Years Workmen's Circle.* New York, 1940.

Karp, Abraham J. "New York Chooses a Chief Rabbi." *Publications of the American Jewish Historical Society* 44 (1955).

Karpf, Maurice J. *Jewish Community Organization in the United States.* (An outline of types of organizations, activities and problems.) New York: Bloch Publishing Co., 1938.

Kautsky. *Are the Jews a Race?* (Translated from the German.) New York: International Publishers, 1926.

Kazdan, C. S. "The Yiddish Secular School Movement Between the Two World Wars." In *Jewish People: Past and Present* 2. New York, 1948.

Kertzer, Morris N. *Today's American Jew.* New York: McGraw-Hill, 1967.

Kish, Guido. *In Search of Freedom: A History of American Jews from Czechoslovakia.* London: E. Goldston & Son, 1949.

Kissman, Joseph. "The Immigration of Rumanian Jews up to 1914." *Yivo Annual of Jewish Social Service* 2–3 (1947–48).

Klein, Aaron. "A History of Jewish Education in Buffalo." *Jewish Education* 14 (1942).

Kohler, Max J. *The German Jewish Immigration to the United States.* New York, 1905.

Kohs, Samuel C. "The Jewish Community." In *The Jews: Their History, Culture, and Religion,* edited by Louis Finkelstein.

Komarowsky, Mirra. "The Voluntary Associations of Urban Dwellers." *American Sociological Review* 11 (1946).

Kopold, Sylvia, and Selekman, Ben. "The Epic of the Needle Trades." *Menorah Journal* 15 (October 1928).

Korey, Harold. "The Story of Jewish Education in Chicago Prior to 1923." *Jewish Education* 6 (1934).

Korn, Bertram W. *American Jewry and the Civil War*. Philadelphia: Jewish Publication Society, 1951.

Krug, Mark M. "The Yiddish Schools in Chicago." *Yivo Annual of Jewish Social Service* 9 (1954).

Learsi, Rufus. *The Jews in America*. New York: The World Publishing Co., 1954.

Leavitt, Moses A. *The JDC Story, 1914–1952*. New York, 1953.

Lebeson, Anita L. *Jewish Pioneers in America*. New York: Brentano: 1931.

Lebeson, Anita L. *Pilgrim People*. New York: Harper & Bros., 1950.

Leftwich, Joseph, trans. and ed. *The Golden Peacock*. New York and London: Thomas Yoseloff, 1961.

Lehrer, Leibush. "The Jewish Secular School." *Jewish Education* 8 (1836), pp. 33–42.

Lennard, Henry L. "Jewish Youth Appraising Jews and Jewishness." *Yivo Annual of Jewish Social Science* 2–3 (1947–48), pp. 262–281.

Lestchinsky, Jacob. *Crisis, Catastrophe and Survival: A Jewish Balance Sheet, 1914–1948*. New York: Institute of Jewish Affairs of the World Jewish Congress, 1948.

———. "Economic and Social Development of American Jewry." In *The Jewish People: Past and Present* 4. New York, 1955.

———. "Jewish Migrations, 1840–1946." In *The Jews: Their History, Culture, and Religion,* edited by Louis Finkelstein. The Jewish Publication Society of America, 1949.

Levin, Louis. "The Year 5667." *American Jewish Year Book* (1907).

Levine, Louis. *The Women's Garment Workers*. New York: B. W. Huebsch, 1924.

Lifson, David S. *The Yiddish Theater in America*. New York: Thomas Yoseloff, 1965.

Lillienblum, Moses Loeb. "Is Yiddish the National Language of the Jews?" *American Hebrew,* 13 December 1907.

Linfield, H. S. *The Communal Organization of the Jews in the United States, 1927*. New York, 1930.

Linfield, H. S. "A Survey of the Year 5683." *American Jewish Year Book* 25 (1923–24).

Lipsky, Louis. "The Future of Yiddish Theatre." *Maccabean,* April 1909.

Lowenstein, Solomon. "Jewish Communal Organization in America." In *Proceedings of the National Conference of Jewish Social Service,* 1923.

Lurie, H. L. "Jewish Communal Life in the United States." In *The Jewish People: Past and Present* 4. New York, 1955.

———. *A Heritage Affirmed: The Jewish Federation Movement in America.* Philadelphia: Jewish Publication Society, 1961.

MacIver, Robert M. *Report on the Jewish Communities Relations Agencies.* Section 1. New York, 1951.

Mahler, Raphael. "The Economic Background of Jewish Emigration from Galicia to the United States." *Yivo Annual of Jewish Social Science* 7 (1952).

———. "The Social and Political Aspects of the Haskalah in Galicia." *Yivo Annual of Jewish Social Science* 1 (1946).

Malin, Irving. *Jews and Americans.* Southern Illinois University Press, 1965.

Mandel, Irving Aaron. "An Account of German Jews' Reaction to Eastern European Immigration." *American Jewish Archives,* 1950.

Mandelbaum, David G. "Change and Continuity in Jewish Life." In *The Jews: Social Patterns of an American Group,* edited by Marshall Sklare.

———, ed. *Edward Sapir: Culture, Language and Personality.* Berkeley and Los Angeles: University of California Press, 1958.

Mann, Arthur, ed. "Solomon Schindler: German Rebel." In *Growth and Achievement: Temple Israel, 1854–1954.* Cambridge, Massachusetts, 1954.

Marcus, Jacob Rader. "Background for the History of American Jewry." In *The American Jew: A Reappraisal,* edited by Oscar I. Janowsky. Philadelphia: Jewish Publication Society, 1964.

———. *A Brief Introduction to the Bibliography of Jewish History.* Cincinnati: Hebrew Union College, 1935.

————. *Early American Jewry.* 2 vols. Philadelphia: Jewish Publication Society, 1951–53.

Margoshes, S. "Jewish Press in New York City." *The Communal Register,* 1917.

Mark, Yudel. "The Language of J. L. Peretz." *Yivo Annual of Jewish Social Science* 4 (1949).

————. "Yiddish Literature." In *The Jews: Their History, Culture and Religion.* New York: Harper & Bros., 1949.

Mayer, Carl. "Religious and Political Aspects of Anti-Judaism." In *Jews in a Gentile World,* edited by Graeber, Isaque and Britt. New York: The Macmillan Company, 1942.

Medem, Vladimir. "The Youth of a Bundist." In *The Golden Tradition,* edited by Lucy S. Dawidowicz. New York: Holt, Rinehart & Winston, 1967.

Meites, H. L. *History of the Jews of Chicago.* Chicago: Jewish Historical Society of Illinois, 1924.

Mendelsohn, Ezra. "The Jewish Socialist Movement and the 2nd International, 1889–1914: The Struggle for Recognition." *Jewish Social Studies* 26 (1964).

Menes, Abraham. "The Am Oylom Movement." *Yivo Annual of Jewish Social Science* 4 (1949).

————. "The Jewish Labor Movement." In *The Jewish People: Past and Present* 4. New York, 1955.

Minkoff, N. B. "Old Yiddish Literature." *Jewish People: Past and Present* 4. New York, 1952.

Mitchell, William E. "Descent Groups Among New York City Jews." *Jewish Journal of Sociology* 8 (1961).

Morris, Robert, and Freud, Michael, eds. *Trends and Issues in Jewish Social Welfare in the United States, 1899–1952.* Philadelphia: Jewish Publication Society, 1966.

Mizrachi in America. New York, 1936.

National Council of Jewish Women. *First Fifty Years: History of the National Council of Jewish Women (1893–1943).* New York, 1953.

Niger, Samuel. "Yiddish Culture." In *Jewish People: Past and Present* 4. New York, 1955.

————. "Yiddish Literature in the Past 200 Years." In *Jewish People: Past and Present* 3. New York, 1952.

Noble, Shlomo. "The Image of the American Jew." *Yivo Annual of Jewish Social Science* 9 (1954).

————. "Sacred and Secular in the Language of the Yiddish Bible Translation." *Yivo Annual of Jewish Social Science* 1 (1946).

Obst, Stella D. *The Story of Adath Israel*. Boston, 1917.

Oelsner, Toni. "The Jewish Ghetto of the Past." *Yivo Annual of Jewish Social Science* 1 (1946).

One Hundred Contemporary Jewish Painters and Sculptors. New York, 1947.

O'Neal, James. *A History of the Amalgamated Ladies' Garment Cutters Union Local 10*. New York, 1927.

Opatoshu, Joseph. "Fifty Years of Yiddish Literature in the United States." *Yivo Annual of Jewish Social Science* 9 (1954).

Panitz, Esther. "In Defense of the Jewish Immigrant (1891–1924)." *American Jewish Historical Quarterly* 55, nos. 1–4 (September 1965).

Park, Robert Ezra. *The Immigrant Press and Its Control*. New York, 1922.

Philipson, David. *My Life as an American Jew*. Cincinnati: J. G. Kidd & Son, 1941.

Pilch, Judah. *Jewish Life in Our Times*. New York: Behrman's, Publisher, 1943.

Pine, Max. *Fiftieth Anniversary of the United Hebrew Trades*. New York, 1938.

Poll, Solomon. *The Chasidic Community of Williamsburg*. New York: The Free Press, 1962.

Poll, Solomon. "The Role of Yiddish in American Ultra-Orthodox and Hasidic Communities." *Yivo Annual of Jewish Social Science* (1965).

Pollack, Gustav. *Michael Heilprin and His Sons*. (Memoirs.) New York: Dodd, Mead & Co., 1912.

Pool, David deSola. *Portraits Etched in Stone*. New York: Columbia University Press, 1952.

Progressive News, no. 3 (1937). (Published by Progressive Monasterczyska Young Brothers, Inc., New York.)

Rabinowitz, Benjamin. *The Young Men's Hebrew Associations, 1854–1913.* New York: National Jewish Welfare Board, 1948.

Rappaport, Joseph. "The American Yiddish Press and the European Conflict in 1914." *Jewish Social Studies* 19 (1957), pp. 113–128.

Reich, Nathan. "The Economic Structure of Modern Jewry." In *The Jews: Their History, Culture and Religion,* edited by Louis Finkelstein.

Reznikoff, Charles. *The Jews of Charleston: A History of an American Jewish Community.* Philadelphia: Jewish Publication Society of America, 1950.

Rich, J. C. "The Jewish Labor Movement in the United States." In *The Jewish People: Past and Present* 2. New York, 1948, pp. 399–429.

―――. "Sixty Years of the Forward." *The New Leader* (Special Supplement), 3 June 1957.

Riesman, David. *The Lonely Crowd.* New Haven: Yale University Press, 1950.

Riis, Jacob. *The Children of the Poor.* New York: Scribner, 1892.

―――. *How the Other Half Lives.* New York: Scribner, 1890.

Rischin, Moses. "The Jewish Labor Movement in America." *Labor History* 4 (1963), pp. 227–247.

―――. *The Promised City: New York's Jews, 1870–1914.* Cambridge, Massachusetts: Harvard University Press, 1962.

Roback, A. A. "The Epic of Yiddish Periodicals." *Chicago Jewish Forum.* Chicago, 1959.

―――. *The Story of Yiddish Literature.* New York: Yiddish Scientific Institute (YIVO), 1940.

Robinson, Donald B. *Spotlight on a Union.* (A history of the United Hatters, Cap, and Millinery Workers International Union.) New York: Dial Press, 1948.

Robinson, Leonard G. *Agricultural Activities of Jews in America.* New York, 1912.

Robison, Sophia M., and Starr, Joshua. *Jewish Population Studies.* New York, 1943.

Rogoff, Harry. *An East Side Epic: The Life and Work of Meyer London.* New York, 1930.

Rosen, Ben. *Survey of Jewish Education in New York City.* New York, 1928.

Rosenberg, Stuart E. *The Jewish Community in Rochester, 1843–1925.* New York: Columbia University Press, 1954.

Rosenstock, Morton. *Louis Marshall, Defender of Jewish Rights.* Detroit: Wayne State University Press, 1965.

Rosenthal, Eric. "Acculturation Without Assimilation." *American Journal of Sociology* 66, no. 3 (November 1960).

Rosten, Leo. *The Joys of Yiddish.* New York: McGraw-Hill, 1968.

Roth, Cecil. *Jewish Life in the Middle Ages.* London: Edward Goldston, 1932.

———. *The History of the Marranos.* Philadelphia: Jewish Publication Society, 1932.

———, ed. *The Standard Jewish Encyclopedia.* Garden City, New York, 1959.

Rubin, Ruth, ed. *A Treasury of Jewish Folk Songs.* New York: Schocken Books, 1950.

Ruppin, Arthur. *The Jews of Today.* New York: H. Holt & Co., 1914.

Sachar, Abram Leon. *A History of the Jews.* New York: Alfred A. Knopf, 1953.

Sachs, Howard F. "Development of the Jewish Community of Kansas City, 1864–1908." *Missouri Historical Review* 60, no. 3 (April 1966).

Sapir, Edward. *Language.* New York: Harcourt, Brace & Company (Harvest), 1949.

Samuel, Maurice. *The Gentleman and the Jew.* New York: Alfred A. Knopf, 1950.

———. *The World of Sholem Aleichem.* New York: Alfred A. Knopf, 1943.

———. *Prince of the Ghetto.* New York: Alfred A. Knopf, 1948.

Schachner, Nathan. *The Price of Liberty: A History of the American Jewish Committee.* New York: American Jewish Committee, 1948.

Schappes, Morris U., ed. *A Documentary History of the Jews in the United States, 1654–1875.* New York: The Citadel Press, 1950.

————. *The Jews in the United States.* New York: Tercentenary Book Committee, 1958.

Scharfstein, Zevi. *History of Jewish Education in Modern Times.* New York, 1947.

Schildkraut, Joseph. *My Father and I.* New York: Viking Press, 1959.

Schlossberg, Joseph, ed. *Documentary History of the Amalgamated Clothing Workers of America.* New York, 1914–16.

Seidman, Aaron B. "The First Performance of Yiddish Theatre in America." *Jewish Social Studies* 10 (1948), pp. 67–70.

Seidman, Joel. *The Needle Trades.* New York: Farrar & Rinehart, 1942.

Seligman, Ben B., and Antonovsky, Anton. "Some Aspects of Jewish Demography." In *The Jews: Social Patterns of an American Group,* edited by Marshall Sklare.

Seman, Philip L. "Jewish Community Life: A Study in Social Adaptation." *Observer* 13, June 1924.

Shapiro, Judah J. "Jewish Culture." In *The American Jew: A Reappraisal,* edited by Oscar Janowsky. Philadelphia: The Jewish Publication Society of America, 1964.

Shatzky, Jacob. "Some Letters to and from Jacob Gordin." *Yivo Annual of Jewish Social Science* 9 (1954), pp. 126–136.

————, ed. Studies in *the History of the Yiddish Press in America.* New York, 1934.

Shepard, Richard F. "A New Dictionary Says It in Yiddish." *The New York Times,* 30 December 1966.

Shosteck, Robert. *Five Thousand Women College Graduates Report.* New York: B'nai B'rith Vocational Service Bureau, 1953.

Shriver, W. P. *Immigrant Forces.* New York, 1913.

Shunami, Shlomo. *Bibliography of Jewish Bibliographies.* Jerusalem, 1936.

Silver, Louis. "The Jews in Albany, N.Y., 1965–1914." *Yivo Annual of Jewish Social Science* 9 (1954), pp. 212–246.

Simkhovitch, Mary K. *Here Is God's Plenty.* New York: Harper, 1949.

Simmel, Georg. "The Stranger." In *The Sociology of Georg Simmel,* translated and edited by Kurt H. Wolff. Glencoe: The Free Press, 1950.

Sklare, Marshall. "Aspects of Religious Worship in the Contemporary Conservative Synagogue." In *The Jews: Social Patterns of an American Group*. Glencoe: The Free Press, 1958. Edited by Marshall Sklare.

——. *Conservative Judaism*. Glencoe, Ill.: The Free Press, 1955.

——, and Vosk, Marc. *The Riverton Study*. New York: American Jewish Committee, 1957.

Soltes, M. *The Yiddish Press, an Americanizing Agency*. Philadelphia: Jewish Publication Society, 1925.

Steffens, Lincoln. *The Autobiography of Lincoln Steffens*. New York: Harcourt, Brace & Co., 1931.

Stolberg, Benjamin. *Tailors Progress*. New York: Doubleday, Doran & Co., 1944.

Strong, E. D. *Amalgamated Clothing Workers of America*. Grinnell, Iowa, 1940.

Strunsky, Hyman. "Theatre that Abraham Goldfaden Created." *Jewish Comment*, 17 January 1908.

Sulzberger, David. *Fifty Years of the Hebrew Education Society of Philadelphia*. Philadelphia, 1899.

Szold, Henrietta. "Elements of the Jewish Population in the United States." In *The Russian Jew in the United States*, edited by Charles S. Bernheimer. Philadelphia, 1915.

Teller, Judd L. *Strangers and Natives*. New York: Delacorte Press, 1968.

Tyler, Gus. "The Legacy of the Jewish Labor Movement." *Midstream* 11, no. 1 (March 1965).

Union of American Hebrew Congregations. *Official Correspondence Relating to Immigration of Russian Exiles*. Washington, 1891.

Universal Jewish Encyclopedia. 10 vols. New York, 1939–43.

Untermeyer, Louis. "The Jewish Spirit in Modern American Poetry." *The Menorah Journal* 7 (1921).

United States Bureau of the Census. *Statistical Abstract of the United States, 1965*. 86th ed. Washington, D.C., 1965.

Vladeck, B. Charney. Personal Papers and Correspondence. New York University Tamiment Library, New York.

Wald, Lillian. *The House on Henry Street.* New York, 1930.

Warner, W. Lloyd, and Srole, Leo. *The Social Systems of American Ethnic Groups.* New Haven: Yale University Press, 1945.

Weber, Max. *Ancient Judaism,* translated by Hens H. Gerth and Don Martindale. Glencoe: The Free Press, 1952.

Weinreich, Uriel. *College Yiddish.* New York: Yivo Institute for Jewish Research, 1949.

————. *Modern English-Yiddish Dictionary.* New York: McGraw-Hill, 1968.

————, ed. *The Field of Yiddish Studies in Yiddish Language, Folklore and Literature.* New York, 1954.

Weinryb, Bernard D. "The Adaptation of Jewish Labor Groups to American Life." *Jewish Social Studies* 8 (1946).

————. "Bund." *Universal Jewish Encyclopedia* 2, pp. 587–590.

————. "Jewish Immigration and Accommodation to America." In *The Jews: Social Patterns of an American Group,* edited by Marshall Sklare.

Weisberg, Harold. "Ideologies of American Jews." In *The Jews: A Reappraisal,* edited by Oscar Janowsky. Philadelphia: Jewish Publication Society of America, 1964.

Wiener, Leo. *The History of Yiddish Literature of the 19th Century.* New York, 1899.

Wiernik, Peter. *History of the Jews in America.* New York, 1912.

Wirth, Louis. *The Ghetto.* Chicago: The University of Chicago Press (Phoenix), 1956.

Wischnitzer, Mark. "The Impact of American Jewry on Jewish Life Abroad: Philanthropic and Political Aspects." In *Jewish People: Past and Present* 4. New York, 1955, pp. 243–263.

————. *To Dwell in Safety: The Story of Jewish Immigration since 1800.* Philadelphia: Jewish Publication Society of America, 1949.

Wolfe, George. "A Study of Immigrant Attitudes and Problems Based on an Analysis of 400 Letters Printed in the 'Bintel Brief' of the *Jewish Daily Forward.*" Unpublished Master's thesis, Columbia University, New York, 1929.

Yaffe, James. *The American Jews.* New York: Random House, 1968.

Yefroikin, S. "Yiddish Secular Schools in the United States." In *Jewish People: Past and Present* 2. New York, 1948, pp. 144–150.

Yiddish Scientific Institute. *The Classification of Jewish Immigrants and Its Implications.* New York, 1945.

"The Yiddish Stage." *Jewish Comment,* 21 May 1909.

"The Yiddish Stage." *Reform Advocate,* 20 and 27 February 1909.

Zangwill, Israel. *The Melting Pot: Drama in Four Acts.* New York: The Macmillan Co., 1921.

Zborowski, Mark, and Herzog, Elizabeth. *Life Is with People.* New York: International Universities Press, 1952.

Zinberg, Israel. "A Defense of Yiddish in Old Yiddish Literature." *Yivo Annual of Jewish Social Science* 1 (1946).

Zion, Sidney. "Chasidic Jews Celebrate 3 Days of Simchas Torah." *The New York Times,* 30 October 1967.

Yiddish Sources

Adler, Celia. *Celia Adler Dertzeilt* (Memoirs: The Celia Adler Story). 2 vols. New York: Celia Adler Foundation, 1959.

Arbeter Ring Boiyer un Tuyer (Founders and Workers of the Workmen's Circle). Edited by I. Yeshurin. New York, 1962.

Axelrod, Pavel B. "Pogrommen un di Revolutzionere Bavegung mit 34 Yor Tsurik." *Zukunft* 29 (1924).

Bailin, I. B. *Perzenlichkeiten in der Geshichte fun Yidn in Amerike* 2. New York, 1965.

Blechman, M. "Landsmanshaften and the Central Relief Organizations." In *Di Yiddishe Landsmanshaften fun New York,* edited by I. E. Rontch. New York: Jewish Writers Union, 1938.

Borochov, D. B. *Poale Zion Shriften.* New York, 1920.

Brainin, Reuben. *Fun Mayn Lebnsbuch.* New York: Ykuf, 1946.

Buchwald, N. *Teater.* New York: Komitet Teater, 1943.

Budish, J. M. *Di Geshichte fun Cloth-Hat, Cap un Millinery Arbeter.* New York, 1926.

Bund Almanach. Warsaw, 1922.

"Bund" in der Revolutzie, 1905–1906. Warsaw, 1930.

Burgin, Herz. *Di Geshichte fun der Yiddisher Arbeter Bavagung in Amerike, Russland, un England.* New York, 1915.

Cahan, Abraham. *Bleter fun Mayn Lebn.* New York, 1926.

Chaikin, J. *Yiddishe Bletter in Amerike.* New York, 1946.

Charney, Samuel. *In Kamf far a Neier Derzieung* (Di Arbeter Ring Shulen). New York: Arbeter Ring Educational Committee, 1940.

Cohen, Joseph. *Di Yiddish-Anarchistishe Bavegung in Amerike.* Philadelphia, 1945.

Edlin, William. *Velt Berimte Operetten.* New York, 1907.

Erik, Max. *Die Geshichte Fun Der Yiddisher Literatur.* Warsaw, 1928.

Feinstone, M., and Lang, H,. eds. *Gewerkshaften Zammelbuch Tzu Fuftzik Yor Lebn di Fareinikte Yiddishe Gewerkshaften.* New York, 1938.

Frank, H. "Yiddish in Amerike." *Zukunft* 42 (February 1937).

Friedman, Philip. "Di Landsmanshaft Literatur in de Faraynikte Shtatn far di letzte Tzen Yohr." *Jewish Book Annual* 9 (1951–52).

Gelbaum, H. *Die Mishpoche Shteinberg.* Warsaw: Verlag H. Bszoza, 1939.

————. *Mordche Ettinger.* New York: Verlag Grohar un Stodolski, 1926.

Gladstone, J., Niger, S., and Rogoff, H., eds. *75 Yor Yiddishe Presse in di Fareinigte Shtatn, 1870–1945.* New York, 1945.

Goldberg, I. *Unzer Dramaturgie.* New York: Ykuf, 1961.

————. *Di Orden Shulen.* New York: IWO Almanach, 1940.

Goldberg, N. "Di Idishe Presse in Di Faraynikte Shtatn." *YIVO Bleter* 22 (November–December 1941).

Gorin, B. *Di Geshichte fun Yiddishn Teater.* 2 vols. New York: Max N. Meisel, 1923.

Green, Ber. "Di Yiddishe Literatur in Amerike." *In Ykuf Alanach,* edited by Nachman Meisel. New York, 1967.

Harkavy, Alexander. *Di Yiddishe-Daitshe Sprach.* New York, 1866.

──────. *Yiddisher Verterbuch* (Yiddish-English Dictionary). New York, 1898.

Hertz, J. S. *Fuftzig Yor Arbeter Ring in Yiddish Lebn.* New York, 1950.

──·───. *Di Yiddishe Sotsialistishe Bavegung in Amerike.* New York, 1954.

Hoffman, B. *Fuftzig Johr Cloakmacher Yunion.* New York, 1926.

Idishe Familien un Familien Kreizn fun New York. New York: Yiddish Writers Group, Federal Writers Project, 1939.

Idisher Natsionaler Arbeter Farband, 1910–1946 (Zammlbuch). New York, 1946.

Joffe, Judah A. "Yiddish in Amerike." *YIVO Bletter* (1936).

Katz, Moishe. *A Dor Vos Hot Farlorn di Moire.* New York, 1956.

Kobrin, Leon. *Fun Daitshmerish Tzu Yiddish in Amerike.* New York, 1944.

──────. *Meine Fuftzik Yor in Amerike.* New York, 1966.

Lehrer, Leibush. *Di Moderne Yiddishe Shul.* New York: Max N. Maisel, 1927.

──────. "Yiddish in der Yiddisher Shul." *Yiddisher Kemfer* 2 (1961), pp. 3–5.

Lestschinsky, Jacob. *Dos Yiddishe Folk in Tzifern.* Berlin, 1922.

Liessen, Abraham. *Zichriones un Bilder.* New York, 1954.

Mahler, Raphael. *Di Geshichte fun Yiddishn Folk.* 2 vols. New York: Ykuf, 1957.

Malachi, A. R. "Yiddishes Vochnblatt." In *Zammlbuch Lekoved dem 250-tn Yoyvl far der Yiddisher Presse,* edited by J. Shatsky. New York, 1937.

Margoshes, Joseph. *Erinerungen fun Mayn Lebn.* New York, 1936.

Mark, Yudel. "Englishe Elementn in der Yiddisher Sprach." In *Yohrbuch fun Amopteil* (Yivo). New York, 1938.

──────. *Shimen Dubnov.* New York, 1962.

Marmor, Kalman. *David Edelstadt.* New York, 1950.

──────. *Der Onhoib fun der Yiddisher Literatur in Amerike, 1870–1890.* New York, 1944.

──────. *Morris Winchevsky, Sayn Lebn, Shaffn un Virkung.* New York, 1927.

————. "Vissnshaftliche Forshungen in Yiddish." In *Ykuf-Al-manach*. New York, 1967.

————. *Yakov Gordin*. New York: Ykuf, 1953.

————. *Yoisef Bovshover*. New York: Kalman Marmor Yubilai Komitet, 1952.

Masliansky, Z. H. *Zichroines*. New York, 1924.

Medem, Vladimir. *Fun Main Lebn*. 2 vols. New York, 1923.

Meisel, Nachman. *Ber Borochov*. New York: Ykuf, 1963.

————, ed. *Ykuf-Almanach*. New York, 1967.

Menes, Abraham. "J. L. Peretz un di Yiddishe Arbeter Bavegung." *Zukunft* (March 1962).

Mestel, Jacob. *Unzer Teater*. New York: Folks-Bibliotek, Ykuf, 1943.

Minkoff, N. B. *Elye Bocher, and his Bove-Buch*. New York: Vaxer Publishing, 1950.

Mukdoini, A. "Jewish Drama of the Immigrants." In *Yivo Amoptayl*. New York, 1938.

————. *Yitschok Leibush Peretz un dos Yiddishe Teater*. New York: Ykuf, 1949.

Niger, S. "Di Yiddishe Literatur in Amerike." *Zukunft* (May–June 1942).

Osherowitch, M. *Di Geshichte fun Forverts, 1897–1947*. New York, 1947.

Perlmutter, Sholem. *Yiddishe Dramaturgen un Teater Kompoziters*. New York, 1953.

Reisin, Z. *Lexikon fun der Yiddisher Literatur, Presse, un Filologie*. Vilna, 1928–29.

Rontch, I. E. "Der Itztiker Matzev fun di Landsmanshaften." In *The Yiddishe Landsmanshaften fun New York*. New York, 1938.

Rosenberg, Abraham. *Erinerungen fun di Klokmacher un Zaiere Yunions*. New York, 1920.

————. "Metodn un Taktik fun der Yiddisher Arbeter Bavegung." *Zukunft* (November 1910).

Sachs, A. S. *Geshichte fun Arbeter Ring*. New York, 1925.

Saltzman, R. *Tzu der Geshichte fun der Fraternaler Bavegung*. New York, 1936.

Scheinfeld, S. *Geshichte fun der Yiddisher Shriftzetser Yunion.* New York, 1938.

Schlossberg, Joseph. "A Halber Yohrhundert Yiddishe Arbeter Bavegung." *Zukunft* (July 1942).

Schulman, Elias. *Geshichte fun der Yiddisher Literatur in Amerike, 1870–1900.* New York, 1943.

Schwartz, Samuel. "Landsmanshaftn-Federatzies." In *Di Yiddishe Landsmanshaften fun New York.* New York, 1938.

Shapiro, Lamed. "Immigratzie un Landsmanshaft." In *Di Yiddishe Landsmanshaften fun New York.* New York, 1938.

Shatzky, J. *Archiv far der Geshichte fun Yiddishn Teater un Drame.* New York, 1930.

———. "Presse bei Yidn: Geshichte fun der Yiddisher Presse." *Allgemeine Entziklopedie* (Supplement 3). New York, 1942.

Shatsky, J., ed. *Zammlbuch tzu der Geshichte fun der Yiddisher Presse in Amerike.* New York, 1934.

Shiper, I. *Geshichte fun Yiddishn Teater un Kunst.* 3 vols. Warsaw, 1925.

———. *Yiddishe Folks-Dramatic biz 1750.* Warsaw, 1928.

Shtarkman, M. "Tzu der Geshichte fun Yiddish in Amerike." In *Yorbuch fun Amopteil* (Yivo). New York, 1939.

———. "Vichtige Momentn in der Geshichte fun der Yiddisher Presse in Amerike." In *Yorbuch fun Amopteil* (Yivo). New York, 1939.

Shule Almanach. Central Committee, Workmen's Circle. Philadelphia, 1935.

Tcherikower, Elias. *Geshichte fun der Yiddisher Arbeiter Bavegung in di Fareynekte shtatn.* New York, 1943–45.

Thomashefsky, Boris. *Mayn Lebnsgeshichte.* New York, 1937.

Der Ukrainer Yid, 1948. New York: Federation of Ukrainian Jews in America, 1948.

Unger, Menashe. *Pshische un Kozk.* Buenos Aires: Central Alliance of Polish Jews in Argentina, 1949.

Verschleiser, E. "Di Konstitutzies fun di Landsmanshaften." In *Di Yiddishe Landsmanshaften fun New York.* New York, 1938.

Weiner, M. *Etudien Vegn Mendelen.* Moscow, 1935.

Weinrebe, B. A. "Di Sotziale Role fun di Landsmanshaften." In *Di Yiddishe Landsmanshaften fun New York.* New York, 1938.

Weinreich, Max. *Bilder fun der Yiddisher Literatur-Geshichte.* Vilna, 1928.

Weinreich, Uriel. *Modern Yiddish-English Verterbuch.* New York: McGraw-Hill, and Yivo Institute for Jewish Research, 1968.

Weinstein, B. *Ferzig Yohr in der Yiddisher Arbeter Bavegung in Amerike.* New York, 1924.

———. *Di Yiddishe Yunions in Amerike.* New York, 1929.

Winchefsky, Morris. *Di Geshichte fun Kamf.* New York, 1899.

———. *Gezamlte Verk.* New York, 1927.

Yeshurin, Ephim H. *100—Yohr Moderne Yiddishe Literatur.* New York: Arbeter Ring, 1965.

The Yiddishe Landsmanshaften in New York. J. L. Peretz Writer's Union. New York, 1938.

Young, Boaz. *Mein Lebn in Teater.* New York: Ykuf, 1950.

Yuditch, P. *Untern Eisen.* New York, 1954.

"Zechtzig Yor Bund, 1897–1957." *Unzer Zeit,* nos. 11–12 (November-December 1957).

Zhitlowsky, Chaim. *Der Sotsialism un di Natsionale Frage.* New York, 1908.

Zylbercweig, Zalman, ed. *Lexicon of the Yiddish Theatre* 2. Warsaw, 1934.

———. ed. *Lexicon of the Yiddish Theatre* 3. New York, 1959.

List of Tables

269

Acknowledgments

Citations from "A Century of Jewish Immigration" by Oscar and Mary Handlin in the *American Jewish Year Book*, 1948–49, by permission of the publisher.

Citations from "Yiddish Literature" by Samuel Niger in Vol. 3, *Jewish People: Past and Present*; and "Jewish Culture" by Samuel Niger; "The Jewish Labor Movement" by Abraham Menes; and "Economic and Social Development of American Jewry" by Jacob Lestschinsky, in Volume 4, *Jewish People: Past and Present,* by permission of the publishers: Jewish Encyclopedic Handbooks, Inc. and Central Yiddish Culture Organization (CYCO).

Citations from *The Ghetto* by Louis Wirth, Phoenix Books, copyright 1956 by the University of Chicago Press, by permission of University of Chicago Press.

Extracts from "Yiddish: Past, Present and Perfect," by Lucy S. Dawidowics, reprinted from *Commentary,* by permission, copyright 1962 by the American Jewish Committee.

"Bintl Briefs" reprinted from issues of the *Forverts,* by permission of *The Jewish Daily Forward.*

Citations from *The Spirit of the Ghetto* by Hutchins Hapgood, copyright 1902 and 1909 by Funk and Wagnalls Company, published by Funk and Wagnalls, by permission of the publishers.

Citations from *Our Crowd* by Stephen Birmingham, Harper and Row, 1967, by permission of the publishers.

271

Park Sholem Aleichem is Also a Bard," from *The New York Times,* copyright 1967 by the New York Times Company. Reprinted by permission.

Excerpts from "Yiddish in America: Socio-Linguistic Description and Analysis" by Joshua A. Fishman, in *International Journal of American Linguistics* 31, No. 2, April, 1965, by permission of the Research Center for the Language Sciences, Indiana University.

All citations, excerpts and statistical material from *The Yiddishe Landsmanshaften of New York,* 1938, by permission of the Editor, I.E. Rontch.

Excerpts from *Yakov Gordin,* by Kalman Marmor, Yiddisher Kultur Farband (YKUF), 1953, by permission of the publisher.

Citations and excerpts from *The Story of Yiddish Literature,* by A. A. Roback; "Fifty Years of Yiddish Literature in the United States," by Joseph Opatoshu, in the *Yivo Annual of Jewish Social Science,* Vol. 9 (1954); and "Jewish Youth Appraising Jews and Jewishness," *Yivo Annual of Jewish Social Science,* Vol. 2–3 (1947–48), by permission of the Yivo Institute for Jewish Research.

Index

275